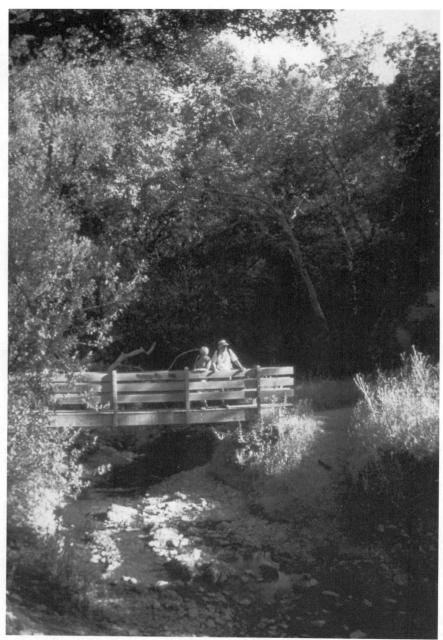

Dry Creek, Dry Creek Pioneer Regional Park

EAST BAY
TRAILS

OUTDOOR ADVENTURES
IN ALAMEDA AND
CONTRA COSTA COUNTIES

David Weintraub
Foreword by Galen Rowell

WILDERNESS PRESS
BERKELEY

Copyright © 1998 by David Weintraub
FIRST EDITION May 1998

All photos by the author
Maps by Meridian Mapping, Oakland, CA, adapted from maps created by the
    East Bay Regional Park District
Book design by Margaret Copeland—Terragraphics
Cover photos © 1998 by David Weintraub
Cover design by Larry Van Dyke

Library of Congress Card Number 97-46186
ISBN 0-89997-213-6

Manufactured in the United States of America
Published by: Wilderness Press
               2440 Bancroft Way
               Berkeley, CA 94704
               (800) 443-7227; FAX (510) 548-1355
               wpress@ix.netcom.com

               Contact us for a free catalog
               Visit our web site at www.wildernesspress.com

Cover photos: View of San Pablo Reservoir and Mt. Diablo from Wildcat
                Canyon Regional Park—Hike 53
                Mt. Diablo State Park (inset)—Hike 37

Library Of Congress Cataloging-in-Publication Data

Weintraub, David, 1949-
      East Bay trails : outdoor adventures in Alameda and Contra Costa counties /
   David Weintraub.
         p.   cm.
      Includes bibliographical references and index.
      ISBN 0-89997-213-6
      1. Hiking—California—East Bay—Guidebooks. 2. Cycling—
   California—East Bay—Guidebooks. 3. Trails—California—East Bay—
   Guidebooks. 4. East Bay (Calif.)—Guidebooks. I. Title.
   GV199.42.C22E379   1998
   917.94'60453—dc21   97-46186
                                                               CIP

Table Of Contents

Acknowledgments

Many people contributed to the making of this book, some by sharing information and expertise, others by sharing miles on the trail. Steve Fiala, trails specialist for the East Bay Regional Park District, looked over my original list of parks, gave me specific recommendations about which trails to include, and answered countless questions. His name, dropped appropriately, also gave me instant credibility with many other EBRPD staff, including Bert Johnson at the Botanic Garden, Alan Kaplan at Tilden Regional Park, Juan Carlos Solis at Black Diamond Mines, Paul Ferreira and Anthony Fisher at Coyote Hills Regional Park, and Maryanne Canaparo at EBRPD headquarters, who have been unfailingly helpful. Thanks as well to Bob Flasher and Pat Solo, East Bay Municipal Utility District ranger/naturalists for information about EBMUD lands. John Steiner, outdoor recreation planner at Don Edwards San Francisco Bay National Wildlife Refuge, provided information about the refuge, and Alvin Dockter, refuge volunteer, taught me about local plants and flowers. Mike Koslosky, Hayward Area Recreation and Park District naturalist, gave me valuable information about the San Francisco Bay shoreline.

Friends of mine were lured into the East Bay hills with promises of lunch or pizza, then subjected to endless photographs and "just a few more miles." These people deserve my thanks: Laura Wood, Paul Ash, Silvia Fernandez, Elena Ash, Jed Manwaring, Brenda Tharp, Steve Gregory, Vicki Vann, Ken Kobre, Betsy Brill, Mary Thorsby, John Macchia, Angela Macchia, Susan Rouder, and George deTuncq. Enjoying the trails vicariously, Denise Rehse transcribed countless hours of taped notes.

Author Dorothy L. Whitnah has been a great help, reviewing my original outline and keeping me informed of East Bay goings-on I otherwise would have missed. Her book, *An Outdoor Guide to the San Francisco Bay Area*, also published by Wilderness Press, has been a source of both information and inspiration.

Tom Winnett and his daughter Caroline at Wilderness Press deserve my thanks too. When I began this book, I was nervous about the apparent size of the task, but they saw past my worries, focusing instead on my enthusiasm and my curiosity; I hope their faith has been well-founded.

Finally I thank my wife, Maggi, for her love and support.

Foreword

I escape the gray pallor of summer mornings when the cities of the East Bay lie beneath a dark blanket of fog by taking a trail run before dawn through Tilden Park up to Vollmer Peak. It's easy for me to do because my house is just a block as the crow flies from a trailhead near Lake Anza. It becomes much harder when I'm joined by a fleet neighbor who was always able to outpace me, even before he founded his well-known energy bar company. But I've grown used to catching him unexpectedly on the steepest hill, nearly 2,000 feet above the Bay, as golden god beams break through misty Monterey pines. The first rays of dawn have stopped him in his tracks at the edge of the fog to watch light and mist come together into otherworldly beams. Sometimes the Specter of the Brocken casts colored glories that hover over the landscape with our shadows inside them.

At times like this, there is no other wild place on earth that I would rather be—a certitude based on travels to the seven continents and both poles. Even John Muir, who explored Yosemite and so many other wildlands of the American West, chose to live the last half of his life in the East Bay. On a multi-day solo hike in 1877, he "beheld the most ravishingly beautiful sunset on the Bay I have ever yet enjoyed" from the Berkeley Hills.

One hundred twenty years later, however, when I mention to people during my travels that I live in the San Francisco Bay Area, they assume that I seek out exotic places to get away from my six million urban neighbors. Like John Muir, I treasure my wild experiences close to home. Few residents and fewer visitors realize that no other major metropolitan center on the continent holds such an extensive system of preserved natural areas. The extraordinary totality of wild greenbelts within 40 miles of San Francisco exceeds Yosemite National Park in size, biodiversity, and visitation. Unlike Yosemite, these more than 200 preserves, parks, and other protected wild lands have no single name or governing agency.

A while back, I began taking a local friend with whom I'd climbed extensively in Yosemite and foreign countries on weekly trail runs in the East Bay. Months later he commented, "You know, I was born here too, but I never realized how infinite the possibilities are close to home until it dawned on me that we've run hundreds of miles and never done the same route twice."

I admitted to purposely varying our routes to never be the same and suggested that his livelihood as a fine home designer was as much rooted in the extent of the wild country we were exploring as in his urban configurations. Ads for prime homes often capitalize on mentioning close trail and park access. Property values that approach the highest in the nation seem to fall off in proportion to the distance to wild open space. Thus the creative residential architecture by which my friend makes his living and for which the Bay Area is rightly famous is inextricably linked to this fine balance of urban and open space.

Local governments are discovering that preserving urban wildlands is not only an environmental but also an economic imperative. Creative plans for preservation have become models for urban centers elsewhere. For example, the East Bay Regional Park District formed the nation's first multi-county regional parks. The nation's first public wildlife refuge was created at Oakland's Lake Merritt. And the East Bay Skyline National Recreation Trail is the first of its kind not on federal lands.

Besides my favorite trails in Tilden Regional Park, I especially love the series of trails that spoke out from Skyline Gate in Redwood Regional Park. Fern-lined paths through forested canyons and broad ridge trails with views of Mount Diablo interconnect into myriad options from one-mile walks to marathons. I've run these trails, walked them with my camera, with my dog, and with my wife riding her horse. I've also mountain biked the wider fire trails with a pack full of camera gear to photograph the deer, coyotes, and foxes I often encounter around dawn or dusk. Seeing wildlife in the hills and just knowing that there are mountain lions out there makes the landscape come alive and regain something of its primeval state in my mind.

In the interior of the East Bay, Mount Diablo State Park has steadily increased in size over the last 65 years from just over two square miles to thirty square miles that encompass much of the 3,849-foot peak (thanks to the efforts of the citizens' group, Save Mount Diablo). Spring wildflower displays on the upper peak are not to be missed, whether by the paved road that goes all the way to the summit or by the trails that traverse all sides. Since the wider fire trails are open to mountain bikes, one of my favorite spring outings is to coax a friend into dropping me at the summit with bike and camera pack.

When I was growing up in Berkeley, I used to think of East Bay wild places as wilderness with training wheels—places to practice for the real thing in more remote parts of the world. Experience elsewhere has taught me that those wheels were only in my mind. Trails where I once held my father's hand are no less worthy destinations today, especially as they are being connected to form the 400-mile Bay Area Ridge Trail, a circuit of the Bay that is now more than half completed. Knowing about this grand circuit changes the way I think about my experience in positive, subtle ways. Though I should be able to take each mile and moment at face value, the Ridge Trail emblem on each sign post emanates a named, formal connection to the entire Bay Area. It gives me the feeling of being in yet another part of the American West so vast that I can never fully know it in one lifetime, despite my luck to call it home.

Galen Rowell
Berkeley
October, 1997

♦ Introduction ♦

THE EAST BAY

Imagine a landscape of oak-studded hills, grassy ridges, rocky peaks, forested valleys, and salt-marsh shoreline. Picture this landscape in a region blessed with a mild climate, where ocean breezes temper summer's heat and a winter freeze makes the evening news. Parts of this area have been protected from development and preserved for future generations, with more than 1,000 miles of trails for hiking, bicycling, walking, jogging, and horseback riding. Often this kind of outdoor recreation paradise is only found tucked away in remote corners of national parks or set aside in wilderness areas, inaccessible to many of us. But all of these things can be found in the East Bay, within easy reach of millions of people.

The East Bay, which extends from San Francisco Bay to the edge of the Central Valley, and from Carquinez Strait and Suisun Bay to the foothills of Mt. Hamilton, is made up of two counties, Alameda and Contra Costa, a 1,700-square-mile area that is home to some 2.1 million people. Most of the open space within the two-county area is administered by four public agencies which together control more than 145,000 acres, or about 230 square miles: East Bay Regional Park District (EBRPD), East Bay Municipal Utility District (EBMUD), Mt. Diablo State Park, and the Don Edwards San Francisco Bay National Wildlife Refuge. The East Bay contains one large city, Oakland, and a number of smaller ones, including Berkeley, Concord, Fremont, and Hayward. Interstate highways, along with Bay Area Rapid Transit (BART) and Alameda-Contra Costa Transit (AC Transit) link population centers in the two-county area. The region is a world-renowned center of learning, culture, and the arts, and is enriched by a diverse and growing population.

Climate and Weather

The East Bay has one of the best climates in the US for year-round outdoor recreation: it is rarely too hot or too cold to go hiking *somewhere* here. When summer's heat and humidity drive residents of other parts of the country to seek air conditioning or the beach, we can enjoy a stroll through cool, fog-shrouded groves of coast redwoods. And when the northern half of the US is locked for months on end in winter's icy grip, we can often go outdoors with nothing more than a sweater and a windbreaker, taking advantage of clear skies to climb a peak and gaze at the snow-capped Sierra.

Instead of four seasons, the Bay Area has two: dry, lasting from May through October, and wet, generally from November through April. (Residents of San Francisco have a third season, fog, during the summer months, prompting Mark Twain's famous statement that the coldest winter he ever spent was the summer he spent in San Francisco.) Time of year can have a dramatic effect on trail conditions and the character of a particular hike. Although I have mentioned in the route descriptions if a trail is apt to be muddy in wet weather, or better saved for a cool day, it is impossible to predict the day-to-day effects caused by our changeable weather.

At the start of the dry season, the hills are green and decorated with blooming trees, shrubs, and wildflowers. But without rain, the hills gradually turn from green to brown, seasonal creeks dry up, and water levels in lakes and reservoirs fall. Skies are blue, but as spring gives way to summer, ocean breezes from the west and thermal low pressure over the Central Valley propel ocean fog over the western hills and through the Golden Gate into San Francisco Bay, where it often lingers for days on end, sometimes climbing up and spilling over the Berkeley Hills.

With the coming of fall, wind patterns shift and the fog is pushed out to sea. This is a time of extreme fire danger, with plenty of dry fuel and warm, dry winds. It is also a time of intense beauty in the East Bay, when the leaves of bigleaf maple, western sycamore, poison oak, and California wild grape take on autumnal hues, and the grasses that blanket the hills are golden brown. As high pressure over the Eastern Pacific weakens, the way is clear for storms to move in from the Gulf of Alaska or the sub-tropics. When the rains finally arrive, the East Bay undergoes a magical transformation, turning from brown to green almost overnight. Creeks fill and swell, often overflowing their banks and spilling onto the trail. Even as the calendar says winter, our early blooming manzanitas announce the coming of spring with clusters of white or pink flowers.

In addition to being influenced by time of year, conditions vary depending on where you are in relation to San Francisco Bay. The wind here generally blows from west to east, bringing cool, moist air inland from the Pacific Ocean. Starting with the Oakland and Berkeley hills and going east, each successive set of hills presents a further barrier to this marine air, making nearby valleys progressively hotter and drier in summer. So while Tilden Park in the Berkeley Hills might be comfortable in July, Mt. Diablo, farther east, would be unpleasantly hot. But the waters of the Bay also have a stabilizing effect on temperature, keeping areas near its shore cool in summer and relatively warm in winter. As you move east, away from the Bay, this effect lessens and temperature extremes increase. So in January, you might find it warmer in Berkeley than in, say, Concord.

Although our climate—average conditions over the course of a year—is mild, our weather—daily atmospheric conditions—can be exciting.

Wind is perhaps the most unpredictable condition, sometimes blowing ferociously on an otherwise perfect day, at other times disappearing as you make a slight change in elevation or orientation. Strong winds can turn a pleasant hike into an ordeal, and can even be hazardous, knocking down trees and powerlines. But wind can be a bonus too, bringing relief on a hot day or clearing the air after a winter storm.

The National Oceanic and Atmospheric Administration (NOAA) broadcasts continuous weather information, including special advisories and warnings, over a network of radio stations around the country. These can be listened to on small, inexpensive receivers available at Radio Shack and outdoor stores. Anyone planning to spend time outdoors will find one of these radios useful.

Geology

The geology of the Bay Area is a complex story, written in stone, with a plot line constantly changing and an ending yet-to-be determined. The principal actors in this drama are the major fault lines, fractures in the earth's crust, that run along the east and west sides of San Francisco Bay. It is the release of tension along these fault lines that we feel as an earth-quake, a natural phenomenon both awe-inspiring and terrifying. Anyone who experienced the 1989 Loma Prieta quake felt in a mere 15 seconds some of the power of the geological forces that have been at work in the Bay Area for millions of years.

California's most famous fault, the San Andreas, runs from the Gulf of California, near the Salton Sea, northwest to Cape Mendocino and the Pacific Ocean. In the Bay Area, the fault goes through San Mateo and Marin counties, passing San Francisco just outside the Golden Gate. Two major faults associated with the San Andreas—the Hayward and Calaveras faults—cross the East Bay from southeast to northwest. The Hayward fault starts in the southern Santa Clara Valley and passes through the hills of Oakland and Berkeley. The Calaveras fault, farther east, follows a stretch of Interstate 680, passing near Pleasanton and San Ramon.

San Francisco Bay, actually the flooded mouth of the Sacramento-San Joaquin river system, lies in a basin between the San Andreas and Hayward faults. Over the past several hundred thousand years, changes in sea level caused by waxing and waning ice ages filled and drained this basin many times, the most recent being about 5,000 years ago, when water trapped in great sheets of ice that covered parts of North America was released into the oceans, raising sea level by hundreds of feet.

Rising astride the Hayward and Calaveras faults, and a network of smaller faults which criss-cross our area, are the hills of the East Bay, part of the Coast Ranges of northern California. The geology of the Coast Ranges, complex and at times mysterious, has been called "a nightmare of rocks" by the authors of *Roadside Geology of Northern California*, David D.

Alt and Donal W. Hyndman, and there are just about as many versions of how the landscape was formed as there are sources. But all sources seem to agree that the East Bay hills, built mostly from sedimentary rock and some basalt lava, were uplifted, folded, and eroded into their present shape by geological activity that began three to five million years ago and continues today.

Two parks of interest to geology buffs are Sibley Volcanic Regional Preserve, in the Oakland Hills, and Mt. Diablo State Park. Sibley Preserve contains an extinct volcano, Round Top (1763') which, along with three others nearby on private property, erupted around 10 million years ago, spewing lava, rock fragments, and ash. There is a self-guiding tour into the volcanic area, and an excellent brochure available at a small visitor center. (See the route description for "Round Top.") Mt. Diablo (3849'), the highest point in the East Bay, resembles a volcano but was actually formed when a large, rocky mass pushed up through layers of sedimentary rock and soil, sometime between one and two million years ago, twisting the layers and in places turning them upside down. You can see interesting rock formations at Rock City, on South Gate Road about 1 mile past the entrance kiosk.

Plant Communities

Most of the information about plants in this guidebook comes from a single source, Glenn Keator's comprehensive and easy-to-use book, *Plants of the East Bay Parks*, published in 1994 by Roberts Rinehart Publishers in cooperation with Mount Diablo Interpretive Association. I have summarized below some of the introductory material from Keator's book. He divides the East Bay into three habitat zones: grasslands, shrub lands, and wooded areas. I have added a fourth, marshes, to cover East Bay shoreline parks and the Don Edwards San Francisco Bay National Wildlife Refuge. Other books to help you identify plants are listed in Appendix B.

Plants carry both scientific (genus and species) and common names. But unlike birds, whose common names in the US are determined by the American Ornithologists' Union, plants have no standardized common names. Thus the same plant may be known by two different common names, while the same name may apply to two different plants. One solution is to use only the scientific name; the other is to adopt one reference book as the standard, and I have done that by using the names found in Keator's book. For marsh plants, which he does not cover, I have adopted the names found in Phyllis M. Faber's *Common Wetland Plants of Coastal California*, second edition, published in 1996 by Pickleweed Press.

If I refer to a plant more than once in a route description, the plant's name may appear the second time in shortened form if doing so will not cause confusion. Thus California bay laurel, our *only* bay tree, becomes simply bay on second reference, but California sagebrush keeps its modifier to avoid confusion with a similar plant growing in the Great Basin.

Marshes

Around the edge of San Francisco Bay you will find salt marshes—wetlands exposed to tidal flooding but protected from the high winds and waves found along ocean beaches. The Bay is the flooded mouth, or estuary, of the Sacramento-San Joaquin river system, and receives a portion of the 67 million tons of silt washed down yearly from upstream. This combines with sediment carried ashore by the tide to form fertile ground for marsh plants. Three of the most characteristic are: cordgrass, which grows in the lowest marsh zone and gets a twice-daily soaking from the tide; pickleweed, a middle zone plant which can tolerate some salt water; and saltgrass, an upper zone resident, out of reach of all but the year's highest tides.

When the first Europeans arrived here in 1769, San Francisco Bay contained more than 300 square miles of marsh; today only about 20% of the original marshland remains, the rest having been diked, drained, or filled for salt production, agriculture, housing, or industrial development. Much has been learned recently about the value of marshes and other wetlands: they are among the most fertile ecosystems on the planet, providing food and shelter for an amazing variety of animals, from tiny invertebrates to large birds such as the great blue heron. Marshes and wetlands also provide flood control by soaking up excess run-off from rivers and streams.

San Francisco Bay is one of the largest wintering grounds in the US for migratory shorebirds, with an estimated one million visiting here each year. It is also the most important stop on the Pacific Flyway, a migration route between northern breeding grounds and wintering areas in southern California, Mexico, and Central and South America. The Bay is visited by a number of threatened and endangered species, such as brown pelican, peregrine falcon, least tern, and snowy plover, and its salt marshes are home to two endangered animals, clapper rail and salt marsh harvest mouse. Efforts

Photographers on the Tidelands Trail near Newark Slough.

are underway by governmental and conservation organizations to protect the Bay's marshlands by controlling industrial and residential development in sensitive areas. Some former marshlands along the East Bay shoreline previously lost to diking have been restored by breaching dikes and allowing Bay waters to flow unhindered once more.

California poppy, the state flower.

Grasslands

Where we see green, rolling hills in East Bay parklands, the botanist sees "disturbed" areas of non-native plants and weeds which show the effects of civilization—farming, grazing, road building, and burning. Before humans intervened to alter the landscape, the grassland community in the East Bay contained mostly native bunchgrasses and a wide variety of wildflowers, and supported large grazing animals such as tule elk and pronghorn. Today those grazers are gone, replaced by cattle, and most of the grasses we see here, including wild oats, Italian rye, and fescue, are aliens from Europe and the Middle East. Also noticeable are invasive non-native thistles that often border the trail or dominate an entire hillside. In spring our grasslands are beautifully decorated with bright wildflowers, some of the most common being California buttercup, California poppy, red maids, and Henderson's shooting stars.

Shrub Lands

Shrub lands are also called chaparral, from *chaparro*, the Spanish word for scrub oak. As you hike in the East Bay, you will come upon two kinds of this fascinating plant community: soft chaparral, or coastal scrub, and hard chaparral, found inland on hot, dry slopes. Among the plants that make up soft chaparral are coyote bush and poison oak, found almost everywhere, along with California sagebrush, coffee berry, bush monkeyflower, black sage, and yerba santa. Hard chaparral is characterized by plants whose leaves are designed to minimize water loss, such as manzanita, chamise, buckbrush, and jimbrush. Other common shrubs of the East Bay include toyon, redberry buckthorn, and French broom, a non-native.

Wooded Places

The term "wooded places" refers to both dense forests and more open woodlands where the trees are spaced farther apart. In the East Bay we are lucky to have variety of wooded places, including riparian woodland, oak woodland, foothill woodland, redwood forest, and mixed-evergreen forest. One of the great joys of hiking here on a warm day is entering a deliciously cool, fragrant forest, alive with bird song.

Riparian, or streamside, woodlands often contain large, deciduous trees such as western sycamore, bigleaf maple, Fremont cottonwood, and white alder. Growing with them will be willows and perhaps California bay laurel, California buckeye, California hazelnut, and blue elderberry. Other streamside plants include snowberry, creek dogwood, vine honeysuckle, and California wild grape. Fine examples of riparian woodland can be found in Little Yosemite, on Alameda Creek in the Sunol Wilderness, and along the Mitchell Canyon Road in Mt. Diablo State Park. This type of habitat provides the best display of fall colors in the East Bay.

No tree symbolizes the East Bay better than the oak, a sturdy, long-lived tree whose leaf makes a fitting symbol for our regional parks, and whose name echoes in cities throughout California. Oak woodlands are found generally at low elevations on gentle slopes; foothill woodlands, where trees such as California buckeye and gray pine accompany oaks, occupy steeper or higher ground. If the trees have considerable room between them, making the terrain seem park-like, the area is called a savanna. Hikers with an interest in plant identification will soon learn to recognize the six common East Bay oaks—three deciduous and three evergreen or "live": valley, blue, and black, and coast live, canyon live, and interior live. Oaks are islands of life: they produce acorns that are eaten by animals and birds (and until recently, by Native Americans), and provide both shade and shelter in a sea of grass. More than 100 species of birds are associated with oak woodlands in California.

Mixed-evergreen forests contain oaks and other species, usually California bay laurel and madrone, and perhaps California buckeye and bigleaf maple as well, in a habitat that is cooler and wetter than the one occupied by oak and foothill woodlands. But the coolest, wettest conditions by far are found in redwood forests, a few pockets of which still exist in Redwood and Anthony Chabot regional parks, and in the City of Oakland's Joaquin Miller Park. (All of the East Bay's virgin redwoods are gone, most having been logged between 1840 and 1860; the trees remaining are second-growth.) Tall redwoods, with their extensive system of needle-covered branches, shade out most other species. Often western sword ferns are the only plants able to grow beneath these towering giants. Near streams in a redwood forest, where some light penetrates from above, look for evergreen huckleberry, thimbleberry, and California hazelnut.

A few notable non-native trees grow in the East Bay and help shape the character of its parklands (and produce fuel for both debate and wild-fires.) Best known is eucalyptus, represented in California by about 125 species, two of which, blue and red gum, are the most common here.

Writing in *Parkland Discoveries*, a publication of EBRPD, naturalist Alan Kaplan says eucalyptus trees were first imported from Australia in the 1850s, and were widely planted around the turn of the century as part of a "get rich quick" scheme by "would-be timber barons." Although this scheme failed—the wood takes two years to dry and season properly—the trees themselves succeeded admirably, weathering freezes, fires, and campaigns to eradicate them altogether. Eucalyptus trees, which mature quickly, literally outgrow their bark's ability to expand, thus shedding strips of bark during the year. This material, combined with fallen eucalyptus leaves and branches, creates a layer of highly combustible debris waiting to ignite.

Monterey pine, widely planted throughout the East Bay, is truly at home only in Santa Cruz and Monterey counties on California's central coast. Like eucalyptus, it is a fast growing and highly flammable tree, often reaching heights here of up to 80 feet. Monterey pine is a "closed-cone" variety of pine: its cones stay attached to the tree throughout its relatively short life span, and open to release seeds only during fires or extremely hot weather. Our other common pine, the gray pine, is a true East Bay native, found inland on hot, dry slopes. One look at its massive cones, which *do* fall to the ground when ripe, tells you this pine is of the "big-cone" variety. (Ironically, Monterey pines, exported from the US to Australia, are replacing that country's native and sometimes endangered eucalyptus forests.)

Large valley oak in Ohlone Wilderness.

Animals

Mammals

Other than squirrels, rabbits, and the occasional deer, you probably will not see many mammals on your hikes in the East Bay. Most of the mammals here, such as skunk, raccoon, gray fox, bobcat, coyote, and mountain lion, are shy and active mostly at night, after the parks close. (In the year I spent hiking in the East Bay, I saw a skunk beside the trail once, and several times heard coyotes howling, but I encountered no large mammals except for deer.) Cottontail rabbits are present in the grasslands, where they sit tight to avoid the notice of predators, bounding away at the last minute. California ground squirrels live in large colonies, and you will often see them standing by their burrows or running furtively through the grass. Black-tailed deer inhabit chaparral, as do gray fox, coyote, and bobcat. If mountain lions are present, deer are their prey of choice. Oak woodlands support deer, rabbits, and western gray squirrels, along with foxes, bobcats, and mountain lions.

Birds

More than 350 species have been recorded in the East Bay, making it one of the best places in California to look for birds. The region is doubly blessed: first, it lies on the Pacific Flyway, a major migratory route; and second, it contains a wide variety of habitats. In a single day, traveling west to east, a dedicated birder could scan a salt marsh for shorebirds in the morning, search a redwood forest for songbirds at lunch time, and spend the afternoon looking for hummingbirds and hawks on the

Gulls and shorebirds congregate on mudflats near Cogswell Marsh.

oak-and-pine covered flanks of a mountain. As an avid birder, I was thrilled by the many species I saw while hiking in the East Bay, and I mention them in the route descriptions.

Your success in finding birds depends on looking in the right place at the right time. Some birds are present year-round, while others are seasonal visitors. I cannot think of more than a few times hiking in the East Bay when I did not see a turkey vulture or a western scrub-jay, but only once did I see a lazuli bunting, a summer resident on Mt. Diablo. Avid birders often revisit the same spot throughout the year, turning up an impressive list of species. Summer brings dense vegetation that offers birds plenty of places to hide from predators and from you; instead, try your luck in late winter or early spring, when many of the tree and shrub limbs are still bare. Time of day is important—many birds sit tight during the hotter part of the day. The tide determines when shorebirds will be active and within viewing range: rising or falling is best.

Going with a group, especially one led by a knowledgeable guide who is familiar with the area, will increase your chance of seeing uncommon or even rare birds. You may even learn to identify birds by their songs and calls, a skill experts rely on when dealing with a well-hidden bird or one that is confusingly similar to another species. Schedules of East Bay bird walks are printed in newsletters published by EBRPD, Mt. Diablo State Park, and Don Edwards San Francisco Bay National Wildlife Refuge. (See below under *Where to Get More Information.*)

When bird names appear in my route descriptions, I have followed the *ABA Checklist: Birds of the Continental United States and Canada*, fifth edition, published in 1996 by the American Birding Association. This checklist follows the names used by the American Ornithologists' Union (AOU), and reflects the latest victories in the never-ending scientific war between "lumpers," who merge species, and "splitters," who separate them. Thus some familiar birds have new names: our rufous-sided towhee is now called the spotted towhee, and our scrub jay is now the western scrub-jay. And some old friends have reappeared: Bullock's oriole, for years lumped with Baltimore to form the northern oriole, has regained its status as a separate species. A common bird called, in some older field guides, brown towhee is properly California towhee; and black-shouldered kite has become white-tailed kite.

Reptiles and Amphibians

Lizards and snakes are the most common reptiles in the East Bay parklands, and it is sometimes starling to have your hiking reverie interrupted by a scurrying sound from right beside the trail. The only harmful snake in our area is the western rattlesnake (see below under *Safety*), and it is rarely encountered. The warning sound of a rattlesnake shaking its rattles is instantly recognizable, even if you have never heard it before. A harmless snake that resembles a rattlesnake is the gopher snake, California's largest snake. Whereas a rattlesnake has a triangular head, thick body, and rattles at the end of its tail, a gopher snake has a slender head, a slender, shiny body, and a pointed tail. Other common snakes in the East Bay include California kingsnake, yellow-bellied racer, and garter snake. One species, Alameda whipsnake, is currently a candidate for endangered status.

Common lizards of the East Bay parks include western fence lizard, alligator lizard, and western skink. Lizards often sit motionless on a tree trunk or rock, then dart quickly away as you approach. An animal resembling a lizard but actually an amphibian is the California newt, which spends the summer buried under the forest floor, then emerges with the first rains and migrates to breed in ponds and streams. Briones Regional Park is the site of one of the largest of these migrations, and in Tilden Regional Park, South Park Drive is actually closed during migration to protect the newts. Other amphibians you might see or hear include western toad and Pacific tree frog.

Human History

The East Bay today is an exciting and vibrant place, where many cultures and communities contribute their history and heritage, where industry and commerce thrive, and where open space has been preserved and protected for all to enjoy. Agriculture still dominates land use in the East Bay, as it did 100 years ago, but land for crops and cattle grazing is steadily being lost to residential and industrial development, much of it densely packed along freeway and highway corridors. The area is an important transportation hub, with major air, rail, and port facilities. It is a world-renowned Mecca for learning and research, a lively center of culture and the arts, and a place where the latest trends in politics, lifestyles, and fashion are conceived and then, sometimes, carried to extremes.

Since the mid-19th century, the East Bay has been a place of farms, orchards, dairies, and cattle ranches, supporting a diverse population of laborers from around the globe, including China, Japan, the Philippines, India, Mexico, Hawaii, and Portugal. During the Gold Rush and the years that followed, the East Bay helped feed the rest of California with produce from large farms centered in Alameda County. (One of these, which belonged to George Washington Patterson and his family, can be visited at EBRPD's Ardenwood Regional Preserve in Fremont.) Alameda County also became known for its wines, and in 1889 one of its winery owners, Charles Wetmore of Cresta Blanca, won a gold medal at the Paris Exposition. Hops and hay grown in the Livermore Valley gained worldwide reputations for quality.

Cattle ranching in the East Bay, which continues today on public lands under a multi-use policy, began in the 1820's after Mexico overthrew Spanish rule and made California, then called Alta (Upper) California, part of its republic. The Spanish mission system, in place in California since the 1760s, was dismantled in the 1830s, and former mission lands in the East Bay became large Mexican ranchos, supplying cowhides for leather goods and tallow for candles to manufacturing plants in the northeastern United States. The ranchos and the rich life-style they supported lasted only until 1846, when war broke out between Mexico and the US. At the war's conclusion in 1848, Mexico signed the treaty of Guadalupe Hidalgo and ceded California, which became a state two years later, to its increasingly powerful northern neighbor.

The first Europeans to explore California extensively by land were the Spanish, and in 1769 Gaspar de Portola led an expedition from Baja California to the San Francisco peninsula. Members of a scouting party from this expedition, under Jose Ortega, were the first non-Indians to gaze on San Francisco Bay, whose opening at the Golden Gate had eluded such 16th and 17th century maritime explorers as Juan Rodrigues Cabrillo, Francis Drake, Sebastian Rodrigues Cermeno, and Sebastian Vizcaino. Residents of the Bay's east shore, the Ohlone Indians, met the Spanish with a combination of hostility and fear, but contact continued over the next few years, as more of the East Bay was explored. Native Americans, who had been here for thousands of years, lived in thatched houses framed with willow wood, depended on hunting and gathering for survival, and organized themselves into various towns and nations. It is estimated that 10,000 native people lived in the Bay Area when the Spanish arrived.

In 1776 the Spanish established their first mission in the Bay Area, Mission San Francisco de Assis (now called Mission Dolores) and built the Presidio of San Francisco. More missions and settlements soon followed, including Mission Santa Clara and Mission San Jose, and the Spanish began converting the Indians to Christianity and moving them onto the missions, where their freedom was curtailed. Resistance to the mission system came from some groups of native people who refused to give up their centuries-old way of life, but their efforts were overcome by Spanish military action, along with European diseases such as measles and small pox. (A cemetery near Mission San Jose holds 4,000 Indian dead, the result of a 10-year epidemic. In 1971, descendants of the Ohlone people incorporated as the Ohlone Indian Tribe and received title to the cemetery.)

The dismantling of the Spanish mission system in the 1830s did nothing to improve conditions for the remaining native people; instead many of them became serfs and slaves on the new Mexican ranchos. When the cry of "Gold!" echoed from the Sierra foothills in 1848, what had been a trickle of immigration to California from the US and other countries turned into a flood. During the Gold Rush, newcomers used dubious means to seize many of the ranchos, and then relied on Indians serfs and slaves to work the land. When California entered the Union in 1850, the California legislature initially denied its native people citizenship.

Despite hardship, disease, and efforts to exterminate them, the East Bay's Indians clung to their cultural and spiritual values, and today Ohlone descendants work to keep alive their history, culture, religion, and language. You can learn more about this fascinating aspect of the East Bay by visiting Coyote Hills Regional Park, where there are displays, information, and interpretive programs about the Ohlone people, some presented by Ohlone descendants themselves.

East Bay Regional Park District

The agency responsible for overseeing most of the open space in the East Bay is the East Bay Regional Park District (EBRPD), governed by a publicly elected board of directors and headquartered in Oakland. With 85,000 acres of land under its jurisdiction, EBRPD administers 55 regional parklands and more than 1,000 miles of trails, including 150 miles of inter-park regional trails. This extensive network of parks and trails, which has put regional park areas within 15 to 30 minutes of each and every resident of Alameda and Contra Costa County, had its genesis in 1928, when the East Bay Municipal Utility District (EBMUD) completed its consolidation of local water systems and declared surplus approximately 10,000 acres of former watershed land.

But the true beginning of the regional park system goes back another 60 years or so, to a suggestion by Frederick Law Olmsted, famed designer of New York's Central Park, that "scenic lanes" be constructed in the Oakland and Berkeley Hills. In the years following the Civil War, however, the Bay Area was experiencing rapid growth, and Olmsted's was an idea whose time had not yet come. After the turn of the century, two prominent city planners, Charles Mulford Robinson and Werner Hegemann, each called for the creation of East Bay parklands, but they too were ignored.

It took the threat of development—EBMUD's 10,000 acres were up for grabs—to get the ball rolling. Prominent citizens like Robert Sibley, executive manager of the University of California Alumni Association, joined with outdoor groups like the Sierra Club to petition EBMUD to preserve its surplus land and open it to the public for recreation, but the District refused. In 1930, the landscape architecture firm Olmsted Brothers—run by the sons of Frederick Law Olmsted—and Ansel F. Hall of the National Park Service were hired to produce a survey of possible East Bay parks. Their 41-page report was far-sighted: it emphasized preserving easily accessible land for a variety of uses.

Supporters of parklands, now banded together in the East Bay Regional Park Association, used the Olmsted-Hall report to again petition EBMUD to open its surplus lands. When the District declined, the East Bay Regional Park Association called for the formation of a regional park district, unprecedented at the time, to include parklands in Alameda and Contra Costa counties. State Assemblyman Frank K. Mott, a former mayor of Oakland, drafted AB 1114, which was passed and signed into law in 1933, to authorizing the establishment in California of regional park districts, a new concept.

The next step, under California law, was to get approval from the voters in nine East Bay cities—Alameda, Albany, Berkeley, El Cerrito, Emeryville, Oakland, Piedmont, Richmond, and San Leandro—who would have to pay for the new parks. In response, some 14,000 people signed an initiative petition placing a measure on the November 1934 ballot to approve an East Bay Regional Park District, elect its board, and assess property owners five cents per $100, not an inconsiderable sum during the Depression, to pay for it all.

Now the plan hit a roadblock: the Contra Costa County Board of Supervisors decided against sanctioning the initiative, causing the cities of El Cerrito and Richmond to withdraw from the proposed district. The Supervisors were responding to concerns of farmers in the mostly rural county who did not see the need for additional taxes to acquire parklands when there was plenty of remaining open space at their doorsteps. The Supervisors were also concerned about taking too much land off the tax rolls, and there was sentiment in the county against creating a new tax-and-spend agency with broad powers. So voters in the remaining seven cities—all in Alameda County—would have to support the initiative on their own. (It was not until 1964 that most of Contra Costa County was annexed to the East Bay Regional Park District, and it was in 1981 that the remaining part of the county joined.)

Canada geese on the north shore of Lake Merritt, the oldest game refuge in the U.S., created in 1870.

Although it was approved by a more than two-to-one majority, the East Bay Regional Park District still had no land, and it took more than a year and a half of negotiating with EBMUD to make the first purchase. But on October 18, 1936, opening ceremonies were held to dedicate three new regional parks: Wildcat Canyon (now Tilden Regional Park), Roundtop (now Sibley Volcanic Regional Preserve), and Lake Temescal. New Deal agencies—the Civilian Conservation Corps (CCC), the Works Progress Administration (WPA), and the Public Works Administration (PWA)—contributed money and workers to the District for projects that included the construction of parts of Skyline Boulevard and the administration building at Lake Temescal.

Next came the acquisition of Redwood Regional Park in 1939, and after World War Two, Grass Valley (now Anthony Chabot Regional Park) in 1952. The 1960s brought a tremendous increase in EBRPD land acquisition under the leadership of William Penn Mott, Jr., including Briones and Coyote Hills regional parks, and Las Trampas and Sunol wildernesses. Mott, a former Oakland Superintendent of Parks, was the District's general manager from 1962 to 1967, and later went on to become director of California's Department of Parks and Recreation and then head of the US National Park Service. Mott Peak in Briones Regional Park is named in his honor.

Attention turned in the 1970s to the shores of San Francisco Bay, which were losing open space and salt-marsh habitat at an alarming rate. The District responded by acquiring land for Point Pinole, Miller/Knox, Hayward, San Leandro Bay (now Martin Luther King Jr.), and other regional shorelines. At the same time, inland parks such as Mission Peak, Morgan Territory, and Black Diamond Mines regional preserves were being developed. A system of inter-park regional trails, including the East Bay Skyline National Recreation Trail, was conceived at this time; many of the trails are in place now, with more to be developed in the years to come.

The 1980s and 1990s have seen a steady increase in the East Bay's population, along with an increased demand for accessible outdoor recreation. In 1988 voters approved Measure AA, a $225 million open-space, wildlife, shoreline, and park bond measure for land acquisition, projects, and facilities. During the eight years between 1988 and 1996, EBRPD added 20,000 acres, six new regional parklands, and 50 miles of inter-park regional trails. Future plans call for continued parkland acquisition, expansion of existing parks, and extensions of the regional trail system. Other priorities include completion of the Bay Area Ridge and San Francisco Bay trails, the expansion of camping facilities and programs for families and youth, and the development of outreach programs to bring more people into the regional parks.

(For more information about EBRPD, see Mimi Stein's official history of the agency, *A Vision Achieved*, and EBRPD's *Master Plan 1997*; the above material draws heavily on both of these sources.)

USING THIS GUIDEBOOK

The purpose of this guidebook is three-fold: first, to help you select an enjoyable trip; second, to guide you to the trailhead and along the trail; third, to provide information about some of the features you may see during the trip. My ultimate goal is to convey the excitement and wonder I felt as I explored the trails of the East Bay, and thereby encourage you to support efforts to preserve and expand our parklands.

To prepare this guidebook, I hiked every trail that is included, many of them more than once. I have tried to be as accurate and thorough as possible, but your experience of a trail will almost certainly be different from mine. Each day in nature is unique; I was on a particular trail for one or perhaps two days, and what I saw, heard, and felt will probably not be repeated, at least not exactly. I have indicated this in the text by using the word *may* instead of *will*, as in "you may see turkey vultures circling overhead," and by being specific about when things occur, such as the blooming of certain wildflowers.

If you have comments about or corrections to this book, please write: Wilderness Press, 2440 Bancroft Way, Berkeley, CA 94704. If your comments or corrections are about trail maps, trail signs, etc., please send a copy of your letter to the agency overseeing the trail or trails in question. The phone numbers, and, where appropriate, addresses of all organizations—governmental, non-profit, etc.—mentioned below can be found in Appendix C.

Selecting a Route

We all have different reasons for taking a hike. For some it is an opportunity to "get away from it all" and commune with nature. For others it is a chance to burn calories, climb high, and get great views. Whatever your reason—and it may change from day to day and year to year—there is a route in the East Bay that will be just right. Most of the "trails" here are actually dirt roads, which are generally shared by hikers, bicyclists, and equestrians; some are true single-track trails, which are almost all closed to bicycles. I have noted in the route descriptions whether a route follows a road, dirt or paved, or a single-track trail. (See specific route descriptions, and also see below for each agency's regulations governing the use of bicycles and horses.)

When selecting a route, you might ask yourself: How much time do I have? How far do I want to go? How fit am I? How challenging do I want it to be? What kind of terrain do I want to explore? What do I want to see along the way? This book answers those questions. Information about length, time, and difficulty, along with a summary of the trip and its highlights, is presented at the start of each route description. Remember to check park hours, usually posted at the entrance, and make sure you can return before the parking-area gates close.

Route length, or mileage, while important, is only part of the story. Is the terrain flat or hilly? How steep are the hills, and how continuous is the climbing? Is the route-finding easy or complex? Are there features, such as unusual plants or sweeping vistas, that might require extra time to enjoy? Will you be making rest stops? I have also given an estimate of the time each route takes, based on an average hiking pace of 1.5 to 2 miles per hour. (Bicyclists and equestrians—you will need to figure time based on your own pace.)

I have rated each route Easy, Moderate, or Difficult based on all of the above factors, plus my subjective feeling about the hike. "Easy" means the route is flat or has insignificant hills, and can usually be completed in about an hour. "Moderate" indicates a longer hike, say two to four hours, involving significant gain and/or loss of elevation. "Difficult" means an all-day outing, probably with challenging hills.

Within each route description, I also give an indication of the steepness, or grade, of various sections, using the terms gentle, moderate, and steep. For uphill travel, a gentle grade is one that can be walked without much effort by someone who is reasonably fit. A moderate grade may cause you to slow your pace somewhat, but should not interrupt the flow of the hike. A steep grade involves a slow, steady pace, much huffing and puffing, and perhaps rest stops. For downhill travel, a gentle grade means easy walking, while moderate and steep descents require an increasing amount of caution, especially over rough terrain such as loose dirt or gravel.

Time of day and time of year are two important factors to consider when selecting a route. A pleasant hike in the cool of the morning can turn into a sweltering ordeal under the noonday sun. Routes that may be beautiful in spring and fall can be unbearably hot in summer and clogged with mud in winter. In general, routes closer to San Francisco Bay are pleasant year-round, while those farther east may be too hot to enjoy during June, July, and August. The rainy season, generally November through April, swells creeks and streams beyond their banks and over many sections of trail, leaving behind a muddy mess. The difficulty of hiking over wet terrain is compounded by having to step across water-filled potholes left by the hooves of cows and horses. The East Bay Regional Park District grades the trails under its jurisdiction—mostly dirt roads—beginning in late spring when they are thoroughly dry, to repair the damage done during the rainy season.

As a matter of personal preference, most of the routes in this book are loops, i.e., they require a minimum amount of back-tracking. I selected the direction of travel based on several factors, the most important being steepness of the downhill sections. As I get older, I find hiking steeply downhill more and more challenging. It is hard on the knees and risky in terms of a fall. (When was the last time you fell going *uphill*?) On the other hand, ascending a steep incline, especially with the aid of a walking stick and using a slow, steady pace, can be done in a relaxed, almost meditative manner, provided you are in good physical condition. So if you follow the loop routes as described, you can expect to find the downhill sections less steep than the uphill ones whenever possible. If this is not to your liking, simply reverse the loop.

The rest of the routes fall into two categories: out-and-back and point-to-point. Routes which are point-to-point, such as the Ohlone Wilderness Regional Trail, segments of the East Bay Skyline National Recreation Trail, and the Ramage Peak hike, involve a car shuttle; this is noted and explained in the *Directions* section of the route description. The few out-and-back routes either have no loop possibility, or none that is worth pursuing.

Favorite Hikes

What follows is a purely subjective list of my favorite hikes in the East Bay and what I enjoyed most about each. For three places, Mt. Diablo State Park, East Bay Skyline National Recreation Trail, and Sunol Wilderness, I was unable to think of a hike that was *not* worth including, so I simply said "All."

Park/Regional Trail	Trail	Highlights
Black Diamond Mines	Nortonville Loop	History, Birds, Flowers
Dry Creek Pioneer	Tolman Peak	Views, Plants, Exercise
Huckleberry Regional Preserve	Huckleberry Path	Plants, Flowers
Las Trampas Wilderness	Corduroy Hills	Exercise, Views, Plants
MLK Jr. Regional Shoreline	Arrowhead Marsh	Birds
Mission Peak Regional Preserve	Mission Peak	Exercise, Views
Mt. Diablo State Park	All	Everything
Ohlone Wilderness Regional Trail	Sunol to Del Valle	Everything
Pleasanton Ridge Regional Park	Pleasanton Ridge	Exercise, Views, Plants
Redwood Regional Park	French Trail	Exercise, Plants
East Bay Skyline Trail	All	Everything, plus beer!
Sunol Wilderness	All	Everything
Tilden Regional Park	Wildcat Peak	Views, Birds, Plants
Upper San Leandro Reservoir	Ramage Peak	Exercise, Views

What to Wear

Boots

Although hiking is a "low-tech" sport, requiring little in the way of equipment, a pair of sturdy, well-fitting boots will increase your enjoyment and help prevent sore feet and mishaps like a fall or a twisted ankle. In the past, sturdy boots meant heavy, all-leather contraptions with a steel shanks, weighing several pounds each. Today's boots, many of them made of a combination of leather and synthetic materials, are designed more like running shoes—lightweight, flexible, yet supportive.

How to pick the right boots? Above all, a boot should fit properly; it should hold your foot snugly, but with plenty of room in the toe box. To insure a good fit, try on boots using two pairs of socks (see below). With the boots unlaced, make sure you can still wedge a couple of fingers between your heel and the back of the boot. Chosen this way, your boot size will probably be one-half to a full size larger than your street shoe size. This allows your feet to swell during a hike, which they do, and protects your toes on steep downhill trails. Then take the boots home and wear them around your house for several hours; a reputable store will allow you to return them *for any reason*, provided you do not wear the boots outdoors. Remember: boots that feel uncomfortable in the store or at home rarely feel better after several hours of hiking.

Socks

Second only to boots in importance, socks are your next line of defense against sore feet and blisters. Good socks should cushion your feet and keep them dry, and in cold weather insulate them as well. Most hikers use two pairs of socks—a thin liner sock worn next to the foot, and a thicker hiking sock over that. Use socks made only of synthetics or wool. Cotton socks retain moisture and will almost certainly give you blisters.

Other clothing

The East Bay climate is, for the most part, benign, so hiking here requires little in the way of specialized clothing. Whatever you wear should be comfortable and offer protection from the sun and hazards such as ticks and poison oak. Lightweight long pants and a long-sleeved shirt, combined with a hat, give the best protection, and are sometimes more comfortable than the traditional shorts and t-shirt combination. The biggest challenge is coping with changing conditions. By carrying several layers—a lightweight pile vest and a nylon windbreaker, for example— you can be prepared for sudden changes in the weather, such as afternoon wind and fog. Stashing a pair of lightweight gloves and an insulating headband in your windbreaker is a good idea too. Cotton clothing should be avoided if you plan to hike during the rainy season; use synthetics instead and carry a waterproof, breathable rain jacket and pants.

What to Take Along

How much to bring on a hike is one of life's perplexing questions. Should this trip be "fat and happy," with roast mutton and Dom Perignon, or "lean and mean," with nothing more than gorp and a water bottle? Certainly snacks and water—plenty of water—are required for all but the shortest trips. For longer hikes, bring at least a quart of water per person. There are few sources of safe drinking water beyond the trailhead; if you must drink surface water in an emergency, use a water purification filter or treat the water with iodine to kill *Giardia*. Sunglasses and sunscreen are essential, as are a small flashlight, knife, and basic first-aid supplies. A route description and map will keep you from getting lost, and a compass is handy too. So far, so good—your pack weighs only a few pounds.

Now for the other stuff. Extra clothes, as mentioned above, are a good idea. A trekking pole, which is nothing more than a collapsible, adjustable walking stick, is useful for maintaining a steady pace on long uphill climbs, and saving your knees on steep downhill sections. It also comes in handy for balance, as when crossing a creek on rocks or logs. (A ski pole works fine, but is apt to draw comments like "How's the snow?") You may want a camera or binoculars, which add a few more pounds, but try leaving your bird and plant identification guides in the car and taking instead a pad and pencil. If you see a bird or plant you want to but cannot identify, make a sketch with some quick notes and look it up later. This saves weight and lets you concentrate on observation. Please do not collect plant specimens.

Getting to the Trailhead

Driving directions to the trailhead are given at the start of each route description under *Directions*; the starting point is the closest major roadway. If the trailhead is equally near two major roadways, I give directions from both. I also note if you need to take different exits from an interstate or highway depending on your direction of travel—say, Interstate 580 eastbound versus westbound. Car-shuttle trips have travel directions to both trailheads.

Alameda-Contra Costa Transit (AC Transit) runs buses to some of the parks in the East Bay; these buses often connect to Bay Area Rapid Transit (BART) stations. If you plan to use public transit, it is best to check current AC Transit and BART schedules for routes, days of operation, and frequency of trains and buses. The Bay Area Travelers Information System phone number is (510) 817-1717.

Safety on the Trail

As my colleague Dorothy L. Whitnah has written, the most dangerous aspect of any hike is driving to the trailhead. While not meant to belittle concerns about safety, her comment helps to put them in perspective. Safety is relative, and hiking is a relatively safe sport as compared to, say, mountaineering. Hiking also brings health benefits, such as cardiovascular fitness, that other, "safer" forms of recreation may not. And while in certain circumstances there may be safety in numbers, I have found solo hiking and backpacking to be particularly rewarding, not only in terms of solitude and serenity, but in terms of increased self-confidence.

Injury, Illness

An injury, something as simple as a sprained ankle or a twisted knee, can reduce even the most fit and accomplished hiker to an immobile victim in a matter of seconds. And transporting an immobile victim requires a multi-person rescue effort. Fortunately, many accidents leading to injury can be prevented by a few common-sense precautions. First, know your limits: accidents can happen when your judgment is clouded by fatigue, hunger, thirst, heat, or cold. Second, use appropriate foot-wear, clothing, and equipment, including high-top boots, layered clothes, and a walking stick. Third, when walking, watch the trail; when looking at the scenery, stop walking.

One illness you may encounter on the trail is heat exhaustion, sometimes called heat prostration. It is caused by physical exertion under hot, humid conditions, and is greatly aggravated by dehydration. Symptoms include weakness, rapid pulse, nausea, headache, dizziness, and perhaps momentary loss of consciousness. Treatment includes getting the victim out of the heat, and giving fluids, especially those containing salt, to drink. If not treated in time, heat exhaustion can progress to heatstroke, a severe medical emergency.

A working knowledge of CPR and first aid can help make you feel more confident on the trail and may someday enable you to render needed assistance to someone in distress. The Mountain Medicine Institute, based in Oakland, offers several superb programs, open to the public, on first aid and wilderness medicine.

Getting Lost

Most of the trails in the East Bay area clearly marked, and anyone with a map and basic map-reading skills will probably not get lost. Still, there are times when you get confused, make a wrong turn, or head off the beaten track to explore and lose your way. If this happens, don't panic. Try to use your map and compass to establish your position by sighting on identifiable landmarks. Backtrack to the last point where you are *sure* of your position: even worse than being lost is being *more* lost, which can happen if you persist in stubbornly going ahead over unfamiliar ground.

Poison oak

Poison oak is everywhere in the East Bay. I can think of only a few hikes—those along the shore of San Francisco Bay—where I did not encounter this hearty shrub, a member of the sumac family. Known by its three shiny leaves, and in the winter by its clusters of upward-reaching branches, poison oak produces an oil that triggers an allergic reaction in many people. Even people who are immune can later develop a sensitivity to the plant. Although there are reports that a protective cream has been developed, the best prevention is to avoid touching the plant with your bare skin, and to wash everything that has come into contact with it, including pets and clothing. In late summer and fall, poison oak leaves turn red, adding beautiful swaths of color beside the trails.

Ticks

The most dangerous wild animal in the East Bay is neither mammal nor reptile, but a tiny insect, the western black-legged tick, carrier of Lyme disease. This acute inflammatory disease, serious and possibly fatal if untreated, is spread by ticks to humans from deer and mice. The ticks that carry Lyme disease are so small as to be almost invisible; their bite often but not always produces a red, ring-like rash; and the victim may come down with flu-like symptoms. Thus Lyme disease is often misdiagnosed, especially by doctors unfamiliar with it. (On Cape Cod, Massachusetts, where Lyme disease is rampant, patients

Beware of poison oak.

with a suspect rash are immediately treated with antibiotics and given a blood test to confirm or rule out the presence of the spirochete that causes the disease, which can eventually lead to cardiac and neurological disorders.)

The best prevention against tick bites is to wear protective clothing, with pant legs tucked into socks and shirt tucked into pants: also use an insect repellent containing DEET; shake out and brush all clothing, boots, packs, etc., before bringing them indoors; shower immediately after hiking; and check your body for the presence of ticks. If you find an attached tick, remove it at once with small tweezers by grasping the tick's head as close to your skin as possible and gently pulling straight out. Be careful not to squeeze the tick's body, as that might cause it to inject fluid into you. Wash the bite area and apply antiseptic; call your doctor.

Rattlesnakes

Another animal of concern in the East Bay is the western rattlesnake. Despite their fearsome reputation, rattlesnakes are shy creatures, preferring flight over fight, and they attack only when provoked, either intentionally or accidentally. Thus people may get bitten on the leg when they almost step on a snake, or on the hand when they reach up to a rock ledge when climbing. In such cases, the snake is responding in fear and may fail to open its mouth or extend its fangs. Even if the bite breaks a victim's skin, the snake may deliver only a partial dose of venom, some of which may be absorbed by clothing or boot material, if present. The best response is to seek medical attention as quickly and effortlessly as possible, to avoid spreading the venom. Prevention includes wearing high-top boots and long pants, staying on the trail, and not putting hands or feet anywhere beyond your vision.

Mountain lions

Much bad press has surrounded the mountain lion, or cougar, in recent years, based on a few tragic and well-publicized incidents. While the people who want to preserve mountain lions and those who want to kill them will never see eye to eye, one thing is certain: most of us will never encounter one outside of a zoo. Only one hiker I spoke to in the course of a year said he had seen a mountain lion, near the Horse Heaven Trail in Mission Peak Regional Preserve. If you do encounter one, experts advise standing your ground, waving your arms, and shouting.

Rabies

Rabies is a viral disease spread by warm-blooded animals such as dogs, cats, skunks, foxes, raccoons, and bats. Avoid any wild animal that acts unusually fearless, and make sure children understand this warning too.

Violent Crime

Although they may be havens from many of the pressures of modern-day urban life, our parklands are not paradise. Crime does occur, and if you are worried about being a victim it makes sense to take precautions: travel with a companion, stay keenly aware of your surroundings, use the parks during daylight hours, and let someone know where you are going and when you will return.

Park Regulations

Each agency having jurisdiction over East Bay parklands has its own set of rules and regulations, which I have either reprinted in full or summarized below. At the beginning of each route description, under *Regulations*, I have indicated which agency's rules are in force, along with any other restrictions that may apply to that particular route.

East Bay Regional Park District

Welcome to your Regional Parklands. Help protect park resources and ensure an enjoyable visit for everyone by complying with these rules and any posted regulations. The Park District's Ordinance 38, which is summarized below, lists specific rules for use and protection of Regional Parklands. Violators will be subject to citation or arrest. For further information, ask a Park Ranger, Police Officer, Volunteer Trail Patrol member, or telephone (510) 881-1833.

PARK GATES ARE OPEN to the public during hours posted at the park entrance. Unless otherwise posted, CURFEW is between the hours of 10 p.m. and 5 a.m., except for persons possessing a permit to remain on parklands.

MOTOR VEHICLES are restricted to designated parking areas and paved public roads.

BICYCLES may be ridden on designated bicycle trails, and on fire or service roads, unless otherwise posted. Bicycles are not permitted, either ridden, walked or carried, off designated trails or in areas posted "No Bicycles," or on narrow hiking or riding trails. State law requires that all bicyclists under age 18 wear an approved helmet while riding on trails and roadways. Bells are required on bicycles and should be sounded when overtaking other trail users.

DOGS must be leashed and under control at any posted area, parking lot, picnic site, lawn or developed area. No dogs or other animals are permitted at any swimming pool, beach, wetland or marsh, the Regional Parks Botanic Garden or the Tilden Nature Area. Dogs may be off-leash in open space and undeveloped areas of parklands, provided they are under control at all times. Owners must carry a leash at all times. Dangerous animals are not allowed in the parks. Your dog's waste must be removed from all developed areas or public trails. Please dispose of your dog's waste by placing it in a garbage can or undeveloped area.

SWIMMING, WADING and other water-contact activities are permitted only in designated areas. DIVING is permitted only from designated diving boards and swim platforms. SCUBA diving is prohibited in any District lake or inland waters unless authorized by the District.

PLANTS, ANIMALS, GEOLOGIC, ARCHAEOLOGIC OR HISTORIC OBJECTS are protected by law. Please do not disturb or remove any of these features.

HELP PROTECT OUR PARK WILDLIFE by not releasing or feeding ducks, cats or other animals. Do not feed wild park animals; enjoy them from a distance.

FIRES are permitted in barbecue pits or personal cooking equipment placed at least 30 feet from flammable materials. Please do not place hot coals on the ground or in a garbage can. Please dispose of burned fuel in barbecue pits or receptacles provided for that purpose.

FIREWORKS are not permitted in any Regional Park.

CAMPING is not permitted within District parklands without a permit.

A state license is required to FISH at all Regional Parks. A District fishing permit is also required when posted.

ALCOHOLIC BEVERAGES are not permitted at pools, swim beaches, on any Regional Trail, or within 50 feet of paved roads, parking lots or posted areas. Alcohol is not permitted in specific parks where alcohol has been prohibited or within 50 feet of paved roads, parking lots or posted areas. Otherwise, beer and wine are permitted at picnic areas and elsewhere on parklands.

GAMES and ACTIVITIES, including model rockets, model airplanes, hang gliding, golf and other activities with potential risk to property or park visitors are permitted only in designated areas.

ASSEMBLIES, PERFORMANCES, SPECIAL EVENTS or similar gatherings require a permit.

Please be considerate of other park visitors if you use a RADIO. A permit is required for AMPLIFICATION of voice, music or other sounds. GENERATORS may not be used without a permit.

FIREARMS or BOWS AND ARROWS are not permitted on Regional Parklands except at established ranges. Crossbows, spears, slingshots, air pistols or rifles, and other dangerous weapons are prohibited anywhere on Regional Parklands.

PARK VISITORS are responsible for knowing and following park rules.

East Bay Municipal Utility District

TRAIL USER SHALL: Sign in on trail registration form; have valid permit unless with "Trail Leader" or guest of "Adult" permit holder; exhibit or surrender permit to EBMUD upon demand; stay on trails; use trails only from sunrise to 1 hour before sunset; close all trail gates; use designated rest rooms; carry out all litter.

TRAIL USER SHALL NOT: Smoke; disturb livestock or wildlife; swim or wade or fish in reservoirs or streams; bring pets, firearms, motorized vehicles, stallions, or colts on trails; ride horses in a manner dangerous to persons or animals; allow saddle animal to stand unattended or insecurely tied; water stock from reservoirs or streams; build fires; litter; ride bicycles except on paved areas in developed Recreation Areas.

IT IS RECOMMENDED THAT TRAIL USER: Carry drinking water; hike or ride with one or more persons.

JUNIOR PERMIT HOLDERS are not allowed guests and must be accompanied by one other permittee.

ADULT PERMIT HOLDERS may take family members plus three additional guests.

TRAIL LEADER PERMIT HOLDERS are allowed to lead groups of up to 30 persons.

EBMUD Trail Use Permit is not transferable. Violation of any rule of conduct is a misdemeanor. Trails may be closed at the discretion of EBMUD.

Mt. Diablo State Park

Please do not shortcut switchbacks. Motorized vehicles of any type are prohibited on hiking and riding trails. Smoking is prohibited. Horses have the right-of-way on trails. Please do not pick wildflowers or collect any souvenirs.

DOGS—dogs are not allowed on the trails.

HORSES—the following trails are closed to horses: Fire Interpretive Trail; Summit Trail above lower summit parking lot; West Fork Sycamore Creek. A special staging area for large riding events is located at the Mitchell Canyon entrance. Most other trailheads are suitable for unloading horses, with the exception of those trailheads with only limited parking along road shoulders.

BICYCLES—all single-track trails are closed to mountain bikes. Mountain bikes may be ridden on paved roads, maintained fire roads, and authorized trails. The three trails currently open to mountain bikes are: Summit Trail from South Gate Road through Dan Cook Canyon; Mothers Trail from Angel Kerley Road to the connector trail to Burma Road; North Peak Trail from Summit Road at Devil's Elbow to Prospector's Gap. Cyclists should see park staff for other rules and regulations concerning trail use.

San Francisco Bay National Wildlife Refuge

The Refuge is open during daylight hours only. All motor vehicles are prohibited on Refuge trails. Firearms are prohibited except in designated hunting areas. Pets are permitted only on the Tidelands Trail and must be kept on a leash at all times; pets are prohibited inside the Visitor Center and elsewhere on the refuge. Parts of the Refuge are closed to visitors for safety reasons, or to protect ecologically sensitive areas or private property; please obey signs.

Trail Etiquette

Although one of the phrases associated with hiking is "the freedom of the hills," with freedom comes responsibility. By following a few simple, common-sense rules while on the trail, we can all help insure continued access to and enjoyment of our East Bay parklands. Children should be taught these rules too, and perhaps the next edition of this book can omit this entire section.

Sharing the Trail

The trails of the East Bay are not just for hikers. Horseback riders and bicyclists use them, as do joggers, dog-walkers, parents pushing strollers, and, where paved, in-line skaters. In many parks, cows use them too. Despite this varied usage, I cannot remember witnessing a single conflict between trail users during the year or more I spent researching this book.

Bicyclists can generally ride on all dirt roads that are open for hiking, and are not allowed on single-track trails, with a few exceptions. (Bicycles are not allowed on EBMUD lands.) Most trails open to hikers, including single-track trails, are also open to horses, although some are for hikers only. Hikers who see or hear horseback riders approaching should give them the right of way by stepping off the trail, remaining quiet, and waiting for them to pass. Bicyclists should slow down and call out when approaching people, and dismount when near horses.

Preserving the Environment

The common injunction to "leave only foot prints, take only photographs" is a good one to follow. Nothing you leave behind improves the environment, and it is easy to pack out your trash (and other people's too, if you see some on the trail and have room in your pack). Similarly, everything you take, such as plants or wildflowers, detracts from nature's beauty and other people's enjoyment of the parks. The practice of cutting switchbacks causes erosion and damage to the trails, and gains you little in terms of time or effort saved.

Preventing Fires

East Bay parklands are at high risk for fire, especially in the fall when grasses that carpet the hills have dried out and summer's cooling blanket of fog has retreated off shore. A major fire swept the slopes of Mt. Diablo in 1977, and in 1991 the hills of Berkeley and Oakland ignited, causing loss of life and catastrophic property damage. While lightning-caused wild fires are part of the natural cycle and play an important role in maintaining the health of certain ecosystems, fires caused by human carelessness should be prevented. Each jurisdiction has its own rules about when and where fires are permitted; if you plan to have a barbecue or camp fire, obey the rules and use extreme caution. If you must smoke, do so only when stopped and never while walking. Pack out your butts. Smoking is prohibited in Mt. Diablo State Park and on EBMUD lands.

Controlling Dogs

Each jurisdiction has its own rules about dogs. Where permitted at all, dogs must be leashed when in developed areas such as parking lots and picnic sites, and under voice command at all other times. Dogs frighten and chase wildlife; they may also frighten people who do not want to be approached by an unfamiliar animal. Carry plastic bags to clean up after your dog, and dispose of the waste in a garbage can.

Cows

Cattle graze in many of the East Bay parklands, and their presence inspires controversy. Cattle grazing on public lands in the West has been an issue of great concern to environmentalists for many years, and an article by Carol Ness in the February 16, 1997, San Francisco Examiner reported on cows as a source of Bay Area drinking water pollution. As usual, the issue is not clear-cut. On the one hand, cows, like all mammals, carry the parasite cryptosporidium, which cannot be filtered from water or treated with chlorination; it causes illness in people with compromised immune systems. On the other hand, populations of other disease-carrying animals, such as elk, feral pigs, and rodents, might increase if cows were no longer around to keep parkland grasses short, and fire danger would increase too. As you hike in parks where cattle graze, you will pass through many gates designed to keep them in or out of certain areas. Close all gates as instructed by signs; leave others in the position you found them.

Where to Get More Information

Books, Pamphlets, Etc.

Selected books, pamphlets, and other written material are listed in Appendix B.

Periodicals

Regional in Nature, published by EBRPD and sent free to members of the Regional Parks Foundation, contains news about the park district and a three-month schedule of activities, including wildflower hikes, bird walks, cultural and natural history programs, photography workshops, and classes that teach wilderness skills.

Mountain News is a newsletter published two to three times per year for members of Mount Diablo Interpretive Association, a non-profit volunteer organization which assists the California Department of Parks and Recreation in maintaining and interpreting Mt. Diablo State Park.

Mount Diablo Review, a twice-yearly newspaper with a schedule of guided hikes, nature walks, and other activities, is published by Mount Diablo Interpretive Association and Save Mount Diablo, a non-profit conservation organization, in conjunction with Mt. Diablo State Park.

Tideline is published quarterly by Don Edwards San Francisco Bay National Wildlife Refuge, with funding from San Francisco Bay Wildlife Society, whose members receive the publication for free.

Maps

East Bay Regional Park District (EBRPD) produces for each of its parks a small brochure containing a map and other information, such as history, plants, wildlife, and parkland rules. These are distributed free at park visitor centers and trailheads; a complete set can also be obtained for a small fee from the EBRPD office. A map of the Ohlone Wilderness Regional Trail, which also serves as a trail permit good for one year, is also available from EBRPD for a small fee.

East Bay Municipal Utility District (EBMUD) publishes a map of its trails, which you receive when you buy an EBMUD Trail Use Permit. Charge for the permit depends on your age, how long the permit lasts, and whether you lead group hikes. The permit is required for hiking on all EBMUD trails except those around Lafayette Reservoir and Lake Chabot, and within the San Pablo Reservoir Recreation Area.

Mount Diablo Interpretive Association (MDIA) publishes a trail map of Mt. Diablo State Park, which can be purchased when you visit the park, by mail order from MDIA, or from the Wilderness Press Map Center. The map, currently in its fourth edition (with a fifth being prepared), also has useful information about the park, along with 12 recommended hikes, five of which are included in this guide.

A copy of the Don Edwards San Francisco Bay National Wildlife Refuge map is available at the refuge visitor center.

Transit Outdoors is a public transit map and guide to San Francisco Bay Area regional parks, published by Bay Area Open Space Council and Greenbelt Alliance. The current version, dated November 1995, covers some of the parks covered in this guide. Phone (510) 817-1717 and request a copy from AC Transit.

Olmsted & Brothers Map Company publishes two trail maps for the East Bay. The Northern Section map covers Tilden, Wildcat Canyon, and Briones regional parks, and EBMUD lands around San Pablo, Briones, and Lafayette reservoirs. The Central Section map covers Redwood and Anthony Chabot regional parks, Las Trampas Wilderness; Sibley and Huckleberry regional preserves; and EBMUD lands in the Upper San Leandro reservoir watershed.

California State Automobile Association (CSAA) gives its members free maps; one of the most helpful for East Bay hikers is called *San Francisco Bay Region*. It covers Alameda and Contra Costa counties and more, taking in an area from Santa Rosa to San Jose, and from Point Reyes to Tracy.

Web Sites

Mount Diablo Interpretive Association hosts a web site, www.mdia.org, with information and publications about Mt. Diablo State Park.

Visitor Centers

EBRPD maintains visitor centers, most with interpretive displays, books, maps, and helpful staff, at the following locations: Ardenwood Regional Preserve, (510) 796-0663; Black Diamond Mines Regional Preserve, (925) 757-2620; Botanic Garden, Tilden Regional Park, (510) 841-8732; Coyote Hills Regional Park, (510) 795-9385; Crab Cove, Crown Memorial State Beach, (510) 521-6887; Del Valle Regional Park, (925) 862-2601; Garin Regional Park, open April through October, (510) 795-9385; Sunol/Ohlone Wilderness, (510) 862-2601; and Tilden Nature Area, (510) 525-2233.

Mt. Diablo State Park information is available at the North Gate and South Gate entrance kiosks, and at the ranger station at the junction of North Gate, South Gate, and Summit roads. The Mt. Diablo State Park phone number is (925) 837-2525. There is a visitor center, open Wednesday through Sunday, 10 A.M. to 4 P.M., in the mountain's summit museum, (925) 837-6119. Mount Diablo Interpretive Association, (925) 927-7222, will open an interpretive center in spring of 1998 in the Mitchell Canyon parking area.

Hayward Area Recreation and Park District runs the Hayward Shoreline Interpretive Center, (510) 881-6751, located just north of the San Mateo Bridge. The center, which has books, maps, and information, is open Tuesday through Sunday, 10 A.M. to 5 P.M.

The ranger station/visitor center in Joaquin Miller Park, (510) 482-7888, has a few small displays and printed information about Joaquin Miller and the park that was named for him, and is open 7 days a week from 9 A.M. to 5 P.M.

Don Edwards San Francisco Bay National Wildlife Refuge, (510) 792-4275, maintains an visitor center on the shoreline in Newark with interpretive displays, books, maps, and helpful staff to answer questions. The center is open Tuesday through Sunday, 10 A.M. to 5 P.M.

The Duck Pond Loop Trail is one of the attractions of Martinez Regional Shoreline.

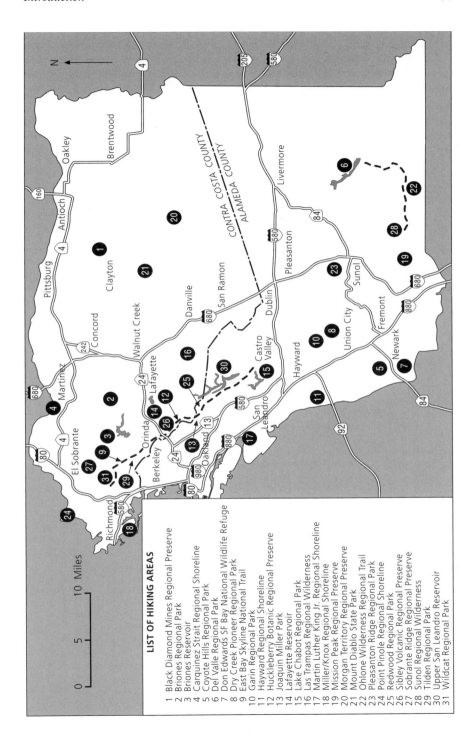

LIST OF HIKING AREAS

1 Black Diamond Mines Regional Preserve
2 Briones Regional Park
3 Briones Reservoir
4 Carquinez Strait Regional Shoreline
5 Coyote Hills Regional Park
6 Del Valle Regional Park
7 Don Edwards SF Bay National Wildlife Refuge
8 Dry Creek Pioneer Regional Park
9 East Bay Skyline National Trail
10 Garin Regional Park
11 Hayward Regional Shoreline
12 Huckleberry Botanic Regional Preserve
13 Joaquin Miller Park
14 Lafayette Reservoir
15 Lake Chabot Regional Park
16 Las Trampas Regional Wilderness
17 Martin Luther King Jr. Regional Shoreline
18 Miller/Knox Regional Shoreline
19 Mission Peak Regional Preserve
20 Morgan Territory Regional Preserve
21 Mount Diablo State Park
22 Ohlone Wilderness Regional Trail
23 Pleasanton Ridge Regional Park
24 Point Pinole Regional Shoreline
25 Redwood Regional Park
26 Sibley Volcanic Regional Preserve
27 Sobrante Ridge Regional Preserve
28 Sunol Regional Wilderness
29 Tilden Regional Park
30 Upper San Leandro Reservoir
31 Wildcat Regional Park

A word about maps in this guidebook:

The described routes are shown in dark black dashed lines. The name of every trail that the described route uses any part of appears on the maps in all capital letters. All other trails on the maps appear in gray dashed lines, and their names are in initial caps only.

The symbols for some trailhead parking and some visitor information are not in the exact location of the actual facility, but they are nearby, so keep your eye open for them. The trailhead pointer indicates both the trailhead and the direction to start the hike.

◆ Black Diamond Mines Regional Preserve ◆

This regional preserve, nestled in oak-studded foothills between Mt. Diablo and the west delta, was once the site of the largest coal-mining complex in California. From the 1860s to just after the turn of the century, the Mt. Diablo Coal Field yielded roughly four million tons of coal, or "black diamonds," to miners, mostly Welsh and Irish, wielding pick and shovel. Five mining towns were located nearby, and three of them—Nortonville, Somersville, and Stewartville—were within the current boundaries of the preserve. According to Malcolm Margolin, author of *East Bay Out*, the largest town, Nortonville, had in 1870 three general stores, three hotels, four boarding houses, six saloons, and a livery stable. Roads and railroad lines carried the coal north to river landings near present-day Antioch and Pittsburg, where it was shipped to San Francisco, Stockton, and Sacramento.

By the mid-1880s, higher quality coal from the Pacific Northwest and the increasing use of oil spelled disaster for the coal miners here, and the town sites soon were abandoned, their buildings dismantled board by board for use elsewhere. The area had a brief rebirth from the 1920s to 1949 as a source of sand for both glass-making and steel-casting: more than 1.8 million tons of sand were extracted. The East Bay Regional Park District began acquiring land here in the early 1970s and currently oversees some 3,900 acres of grassland, foothill woodland, mixed evergreen forest, chaparral, and riparian vegetation. One of the tasks faced by the District to make the preserve safe for public access was to locate potentially hazardous mine-shaft openings; the district even enlisted the help of a specially trained dog to aid its ground search teams. Most openings that were found were securely sealed, but Prospect Tunnel, just off the Stewartville Trail and marked on EBRPD's map, has about half of its 400-foot length open to the public on ranger-led tours.

In addition to Prospect Tunnel, Black Diamond's attractions include seven other mining sites, also marked on the EBRPD map, and Rose Hill Cemetery, which sits on a hill just west of the Somersville town site and the preserve's main entrance. The cemetery, containing graves of miners killed in accidents, wives who died in childbirth, and children who died in epidemics of smallpox, typhoid, diphtheria, and scarlet fever, is a fascinating place to visit.

More than 100 species of birds have been recorded in the preserve, including golden eagles, hawks, and falcons. The area is noted for its wildflowers and plants, including a few—Mt. Diablo manzanita, Mt. Diablo sunflower, and Mt. Diablo globe tulip—found only here and on Mt. Diablo. The coal miners brought with them non-native trees, which can still be seen, including black locust, Chinese tree of heaven, peppertree, almond, and eucalyptus. Located on the edge of the Central Valley, the area's 34 miles of trails are best enjoyed during fall, winter, and spring.

PARK GATES OPEN: 8 A.M. to dusk

VISITOR CENTER: (925) 757-2620

CAMPING RESERVATIONS: (510) 636-1684

Stewartville backpack camp (general public); Star Mine group camp (non-profit groups)

 1

Black Diamond Mines Regional Preserve
CHAPARRAL LOOP

Length:	2.3 miles
Time:	1 to 2 hours
Rating:	Moderate
Regulations:	EBRPD; parking fee; hikers only.
Highlights:	If you have only a few hours to spend in this wonderful preserve, consider this loop as an introduction to some of the attractions that make visiting here worthwhile: beautiful scenery, diverse plant life, and a reminder of the area's not-so-distant past as a thriving coal-mining district. This hike can easily be combined with a visit to historic Rose Hill Cemetery. (Numbers in bold face in the route description refer to sites on the EBRPD map and accompanying text.)
Facilities:	Picnic tables, water, toilet.
Trailhead:	South end of parking area.
Directions:	From Hwy. 4 in Antioch, take the Somersville Rd. exit and go south, staying in the left lane as you approach and pass Buchanan Rd. At 1.5 miles, follow Somersville Rd. as it continues straight, while the main road, now called James Donlon Blvd., bends sharply left. (There is a sign here that reads BLACK DIAMOND MINES REGIONAL PARK, and one in about a mile for BLACK DIAMOND MINES REGIONAL PRESERVE; both refer to the same place.) At 2.6 miles from Hwy. 4, you reach the entrance kiosk, park office, and emergency telephone; continue another 0.9 mile to a large parking area, right, with an overflow area, left.

From the south end of the parking area, pass a gate and continue uphill on the Nortonville Trail, a paved road, for about 200 feet to a level area and a junction, left, with the Stewartville Trail, a dirt road. Turn left and begin walking uphill on a moderate grade that soon levels off, heading southeast through open country. This part of the preserve has native trees common to inland areas of the East Bay—gray pine, blue oak, California buckeye—along with non-natives brought in by early settlers, including eucalyptus, black locust, ailanthus, or Chinese tree of heaven, and peppertree, a transplant from Peru with aromatic leaves and pink, peppercorn-like fruit. A steep, grassy ridge, lush green in winter and early spring, rises left, forming a backdrop for grazing cattle. If you turn around and look west, you can see Rose Hill Cemetery, the last resting place for some of the miners, their wives, and children, who came here in the 1860s hoping to strike it rich on coal—"black diamonds." (The cemetery, well worth a visit, is a short climb from the parking area on the Nortonville Trail.)

Once through a cattle gate, you pass the Railroad Bed Trail, left, which follows part of the old Pittsburg Railroad route, used to haul coal from the Somersville town site, near the parking area, north to Pittsburg Landing, about half-way between present-day Pittsburg and Antioch. Continue straight on the Stewartville Trail, climbing southeast to an obvious notch in the skyline. (The Stewartville Trail is part of the Black Diamond-to-Mt.

1. Chaparral Loop

Hikers heading southwest on the lower Oil Canyon Trail in Black Diamond.

Diablo Regional Trail, an 11.6-mile route from Contra Loma Regional Park to the north edge of Mt. Diablo State Park.) The open grasslands and high ridges that make up this preserve are especially favorable to raptors—birds of prey such as hawks, falcons, and eagles—as well as turkey vultures. As you climb, keep an eye out for dark shapes circling overhead. Besides common birds such as the red-tailed hawk and American kestrel, this preserve has been visited by golden eagles, huge brown birds often confused at a distance with large hawks or young bald eagles.

As you crest a ridge, you come to a junction with the Ridge Trail, right, just before you reach a barbed-wire fence with a cattle gate. Turn right and follow the Ridge Trail, a dirt road, on a gentle uphill grade through a wooded area of blue oak and California buckeye. Just before a steep section, you pass an unsigned trail, right, and then climb to a dramatic high point with a 360-degree view that takes in much of this preserve, along with landmarks such as Mt. Diablo and the Central Valley. On the way up, you will see some of the trees and shrubs that give the hot and dry areas of the East Bay their special character, such as gray pine, interior live oak, chamise, yerba santa, and narrow-leaf bush sunflower. Two plants that deserve special mention are Coulter pine, which reaches its northern limit in this preserve, and Mt. Diablo manzanita, found here and on its namesake mountain only. Coulter pine resembles gray pine but has larger cones, denser foliage, and stouter limbs. Mt. Diablo manzanita has gray, felt-like leaves that attach to the plant's limbs without stems.

Now on the crest of a ridge, you pass another unsigned trail, right, and begin a moderate descent, with several side trails heading left to viewpoints. Growing close to the ground here in small clumps is Indian warrior, recognized by its brushy red and green leaves, and magenta flowers that appear in late winter through spring. A relative of Indian paintbrush, Indian warrior is a parasite, dependent on manzanita and madrone for its survival: when you see it, the host plants are sure to be nearby. After a steep drop, the route reaches a four-way junction and the end of the Ridge Trail. To the left, a path dead-ends in a manzanita grove. Ahead and also to your right is the Chaparral Loop Trail.

Turn right and descend on the Chaparral Loop Trail, a broad dirt path that crosses exposed rock in places, through a wonderful area of manzanita, toyon, and Coulter pine. Soon you veer right at a junction, where the Lower Chaparral Trail continues straight, and continue past a fork, staying right again. A trail post, right, marks a side trail to the Powder Magazine, **3**, a man-made cave used to store explosives for mining. (A sign on the trail post, STOPE, refers to this underground excavation.) Bending left here, the route passes through a rocky area, with a view north to Somersville Road and the preserve entrance, and brings you to the Underground Mining Museum, **1**, where sand for glass-making was mined from the 1920s through 1940s. A set of narrow-gauge rail tracks disappears into a gated tunnel just uphill.

Continue downhill on the Chaparral Loop Trail, now a dirt-and-gravel road, passing a trail leading across a small wooden bridge, right. The trees lining the road here are Ailanthus, or Chinese tree of heaven, a hearty non-native known for its ability to take root under the most adverse conditions. After the tree flowers, it forms clusters of flat, winged fruit that rustle in the breeze. Soon you come to a junction: here the Chaparral Loop Trail, a dirt road, turns left, but you continue straight, passing a picnic area, left, and a road heading left to the Greathouse Portal, **2**, another gated tunnel that was the original entrance for the sand mine. As the route bends right, you pass a large area of mine tailings and soon meet the Nortonville Trail. Turn right and follow the Nortonville Trail, a partially paved road that soon becomes completely paved, uphill to the junction with the Stewartville Trail, right. Continue straight, retracing your steps to the parking area.

Black Diamond Mines Regional Preserve
NORTONVILLE LOOP

Length:	5.5 miles, excluding detours to visit Rose Hill Cemetery and three mining sites.
Time:	3 to 5 hours
Rating:	Moderate

Regulations: EBRPD; parking fee.

Highlights: This hike, in one of the East Bay's most remote, beautiful, and historic parks, takes you through part of California's largest coal-mining area, active from the 1860s through the turn of the century. On the edge of the Central Valley, the preserve is best enjoyed during cool weather, and this route is one of the driest in winter, when other trails here— and trails in other parks—may be impassable because of mud. In late winter and spring, wildflowers abound here, and it is during this time, before the trees and shrubs leaf out, that the preserve's numerous birds are easiest to spot. (Numbers in **bold face** in the route description refer to sites on the EBRPD map and accompanying text.)

Facilities: Picnic tables, water, toilet; horse staging at a parking area, left, just past the entrance kiosk.

Trailhead: South end of parking area.

Directions: See the directions for "Chaparral Loop" on p. 34.

Starting off on a paved road, the continuation of Somersville Road, you head south and gradually uphill from the parking area, following signs to CEMETERY, MINES, and NORTONVILLE, all straight ahead. This preserve is characterized by rolling hills, grassland, and blue-oak savanna; other native trees include coast live oak, gray pine, Coulter pine, and California buckeye. There are also prominent stands of non-native trees, including Ailanthus, or Chinese tree of heaven, and black locust, which flowers

2. Nortonville Loop

fragrantly in the spring. A short distance from the parking area, you pass a junction with the Stewartville Trail, left, and continue straight on the Nortonville Trail, part of the Black Diamond-to-Mt. Diablo Regional Trail, an 11.6-mile route between Contra Loma Regional Park and the north side of Mt. Diablo State Park.

Soon the pavement changes to dirt, and when you reach a fork, bear right, continuing gently uphill on the Nortonville Trail toward Rose Hill Cemetery. Along the way, you pass the Manhattan Canyon Trail, left, a single-track dirt trail. Black Diamond Mines Regional Preserve, located on the edge of the Central Valley, is very hot in summer, but lovely during the rest of the year. Whether the grassy hills here are lush green after winter rains, or gold-hued in autumn, they appear sharply etched against the typically bright blue sky. Frog croaks and bird calls may be coming from a pond, right, fringed with cattails. This preserve is home to many birds, from huge turkey vultures to tiny hummingbirds, and from aerialists like the American kestrel to ground dwellers such as the golden-crowned sparrow.

Just before the route makes a sweeping right turn, you will pass another junction with the Manhattan Canyon Trail, a faint trace leading left. Now climbing on a moderate grade, you begin to get views east, toward the Stewartville section of this preserve, a remote area worth exploring on another day. If you want to visit the Rose Hill Cemetery, turn right at a signed junction and climb a dirt path until you reach a few wooden steps and the cemetery's main entrance, graced by a planting of peppertrees.

Most of the graves in Rose Hill Cemetery are from the mid-to-late 1800s, when this was California's largest coal-mining area. Five mining towns were active nearby—Nortonville, Somersville, Stewartville, West Hartley, and Judsonville. Among those buried here are David Watts, Theophilus Watts, and Thomas D. Jones, three young Welshmen killed in an 1876 mine accident, seeking a better life far from home. Other graves hold miners' wives and children, victims of disease and the hazards of childbirth. It's hard to imagine, as you walk past the quiet grave sites and look out over the peaceful hills, that this area bustled not long ago with miners wielding pick and shovel, intent on digging nearly four million tons of coal—"black diamonds"—out of the earth.

After walking uphill and west through the cemetery, which has tall Italian cypress and other exotic plants, you take your leave via a gate and a dirt road, which soon joins the Nortonville Trail. Now the route climbs on a moderate grade toward Nortonville Pass, a notch in the western skyline. Just before reaching the pass, you go by a junction with the Black Diamond Trail, left, which you will use later on your return. Red-tailed hawks favor this area, perhaps because they can perch on nearby powerline towers, while colorful western bluebirds prefer to sit on the lines themselves. Look here also for lesser goldfinches, the males bright yellow with a black cap, black wings, and greenish backs.

Descending from the pass into a bowl-shaped valley, where Nortonville was located, you pass by mounds of earth, remnants of mining operations, then cross a creek that flows through a culvert, and soon reach a T-junction and the end of the Nortonville Trail. Here the dirt-and-gravel Nortonville Road goes right, but your route, the Black Diamond Trail, heads left. Passing through a cattle gate, you begin an uphill walk on a dirt road, heading south past a marshy area and a junction with the Coal Canyon Trail, left. Veer right and stay on the Black Diamond Trail as it climbs past a grove of black locust, then through a rocky draw to an area dominated by blue oak. On this part of the route you may also see coast live oak and interior live oak, along with California buckeye and

Greathouse Portal, near the Somersville town site, is the original opening, now gated, into a sand mine that was active from the 1920s to the 1940s.

gray pine. But the tree to watch for, growing here at the northern limit of its range, is Coulter pine, a stout, long-needled pine with huge cones.

As the route levels and joins Black Diamond Way, a paved road coming sharply from the right, you continue straight on the now-paved Black Diamond Trail, climbing on a gentle grade past a pond, left, and crossing over a culvert that carries water draining into the pond. The road makes several S-bends and reaches a clearing: look here for a metal trail post and a wide dirt path leading left a few hundred feet to Jim's Place, **4**, and the Coal Canyon Trail. Guarded by a towering Coulter pine, Jim's place is an underground dwelling of unknown origin, with a square skylight, round stovepipe hole, and shelves cut into the rock. Nearby, on the south edge of the clearing, is a marker for a placer-mining claim.

After visiting Jim's Place, continue uphill on the paved road to a heavily wooded area, stopping to admire a fine stand of manzanita, decorated in winter with white, globe-shaped flowers. A streambed, left, its banks carpeted with leaf litter, may attract woodland birds, such as dark-eyed juncos or perhaps a varied thrush, looking similar to its cousin, the

American robin. At about the 2.25-mile point, you reach a junction with the Cumberland Trail, right.

A short detour here will take you to two more mining sites. If you turn right and follow the Cumberland Trail, a dirt road, for about 120 feet, you will find a faint dirt path, marked by a trail post with the word ADIT, heading left through the grass. This will bring you, after about 100 yards, to a level entrance tunnel, or adit, **5**, used in the late 19th century to prospect for coal. (About 75 feet of the tunnel are open to the public; bring a flashlight.) Back on the Cumberland Trail, follow it northwest for about 100 yards, and just before reaching a powerline tower, look left for the entrance to an air shaft, **6**, used to ventilate a coal mine and expel harmful gases.

Now back on the paved Black Diamond Trail, you wind uphill on a moderate grade, through a beautiful blue-oak savanna, switchbacking sharply several times. The sweeping view north from this upland area takes in Pittsburg, Antioch, the west delta, the hills of Napa and Solano counties, and, on a clear day, Mt. St. Helena. Two dirt roads, one just past the other, head right, while a third, a bit farther on, continues straight and downhill to the preserve boundary. Your route follows pavement and continues to climb, soon revealing San Pablo Ridge, the hills of Oakland and Berkeley, capped by Round Top and Vollmer Peak, and on the distant horizon, Mt. Tamalpais.

The route continues southeast, following an open ridgetop above steep canyons on either side, and soon reaching a junction with a wide dirt road, left—the continuation of the Black Diamond Trail. Leaving the paved road behind, you descend east, enjoying a view that extends to the Antioch Bridge, the west delta, the Central Valley, and, if the day is clear, the snow-capped Sierra. Passing two overgrown dirt roads, left, you continue a gentle descent to a fenced pond, then begin a series of moderate ups and downs through a wooded area, passing over a creek flowing through a culvert. Across a deep valley, left, are the exposed rock cliffs of the Domengine Formation, 52-million-year-old marine sandstone that contains the coal for which this area became known.

Crossing an unnamed pass, where the view east stretches to the Central Valley, the route enters a dry, rocky area, then swings north past a pond, and reenters the trees. Just past the 4-mile point, you pass the steep Manhattan Canyon Trail, right, and a rest bench under an oak. A large area of chamise grows nearby, along with bush monkeyflower, black sage, pitcher sage, yerba santa, and manzanita. (The preserve has several types of manzanita, including the highly restricted Mt. Diablo variety, known by its stemless, clasping gray-green leaves and white flowers tinged with pink.)

At the next junction, where a connector to the Manhattan Canyon Trail heads right, you continue straight and begin a moderate climb, with powerline towers just ahead. Passing through a cattle gate and reentering oak woodland, the route makes several changes of direction before leaving the trees and descending in the open to Nortonville Pass. From here, turn right and retrace your steps to the parking area.

Black Diamond Mines Regional Preserve
STEWARTVILLE LOOP

Length: 8 miles

Time: 4 to 6 hours

Rating: Difficult

Regulations: EBRPD; parking fee; bicyclists and equestrians can follow a modified version of this loop by staying on the Stewartville and Ridge trails.

Highlights: Following the Stewartville and Ridge trails past Star Mine and the Stewartville town site is like stepping back in time, when this area echoed with the clang of pick and shovel as eager miners tried to pry coal loose from the surrounding rocks. The Old West is evident here in other ways too, as you walk through grassy valleys dotted with grazing cows or contemplate sweeping vistas from high ridgetops. Portions of the route may be extremely muddy in wet weather. (Numbers in **bold face** in the route description refer to sites on the EBRPD map and accompanying text.)

Facilities: Picnic tables, water, toilet; horse staging at a parking area, left, just past the entrance kiosk.

Trailhead: South end of parking area.

Directions: See the directions for "Chaparral Loop" on p. 34.

Follow the route description in "Chaparral Loop" on pages 35-36 to the junction with the Ridge Trail, about 0.75 mile from the parking area. From here your route, the Stewartville Trail, joined for a short distance by the Ridge Trail, continues straight through a gate in a barbed-wire fence. About 75 feet beyond the gate, you reach a **T**-junction, where the Stewartville Trail heads right and the Ridge Trail turns left. Ahead is a steep drop-off into a long valley, trending southeast, that you will explore later. Mt. Diablo's North Peak (3557') looms impressively just west of south. Here you turn left and head uphill on the moderate, then steep, Ridge Trail, a dirt road, soon arriving at another ridgetop, where your view extends to Antioch and the waterways of the west delta, spanned by the Antioch bridge and scenic Hwy. 160.

Late winter and early spring, when the blue oaks here sport mistletoe but no obscuring leaves, is a great time to look for songbirds such as western bluebirds and yellow-rumped warblers, along with jays and nuthatches. As you turn east and follow the narrow ridgetop on a generally level course, you may spot California buttercups in bloom, yellow flowers poking through the grass. Passing a junction, left, with an unnamed road, you continue straight and begin to climb; a stock pond here may be overflowing onto your route. Just past the pond you come to a junction, right, with the Corcoran Mine Trail. (One morning here in February I heard coyotes, their yips and yowls shattering the silence.) Bear left on the Ridge Trail, and as you gain elevation, your view extends east to the Central Valley, and south across a fantastic assortment of ridges and valleys, to the lands of Morgan Territory and Round Valley Regional Preserves.

The route alternates between the north and south sides of a ridge, then runs along its crest, following it moderately downhill. In addition to blue oak, this preserve also contains the East Bay's two other common

3. Stewartville Loop

deciduous oaks, black oak and valley oak, as well as two evergreen oaks, coast live oak and interior live oak. After leveling out, the route climbs gently, staying mostly in the open, then descends to a junction, just past the 2-mile point, with the Contra Loma Trail, left. Continuing straight on the Ridge Trail and making a moderate and then steep descent, you can see Contra Loma Reservoir, the heart of Contra Loma Regional Park, to your left. The Stewartville Trail, which you will rejoin soon, is the gravel road heading south from the park. The steep ridges you passed earlier begin to flatten out ahead, as you walk down the eastern edge of the East Bay hills toward the level Central Valley. Now at the end of the ridge, the road makes an almost 180-degree bend left and soon reaches the Stewartville Trail.

Ranger-led tour explores first half of 400-foot Prospect Tunnel, dug in the 1860s in search of commercial-grade coal.

Here you turn right and follow the level Stewartville Trail, a dirt-and-gravel road with sections of broken pavement, as it swings right, turning the end of the ridge you just descended. Now heading southwest, directly for Mt. Diablo's North Peak, you are in open country, with a long valley, perhaps dotted with grazing cattle, stretching back to the east. The coal in these hills lies embedded in rocks called the Domengine Formation, a 52-million-year-old layer of marine sandstone, and there are remnants of mines nearby. After walking almost a mile from the last junction, you pass a creek flowing under the road through a culvert, and come to a four-way junction, marked by a trail post, left. Here the Stewartville Trail continues straight; the trail to Prospect Tunnel, 7, which can be explored on ranger-led tours, heads right; and the Star Mine Trail goes left through a cattle gate. The creaking and groaning sounds you may hear, if not coming from you or your hiking partners, are caused by a windmill just ahead.

Turn left onto the Star Mine Trail, here a dirt-and-gravel road with paved sections, and follow it through a cattle gate, across another culvert, and past Star Mine group camp (picnic tables, toilet), where the trail begins to climb on a gentle and then moderate grade. (Bicyclists and equestrians wishing to visit the Star Mine should follow the Star Mine Trail, but will have to back-track to the four-way junction and use the Stewartville Trail to complete a loop back to the parking area.) Once past the campground, the road turns to dirt, and along its embankment you may see miner's lettuce, appropriately, and Henderson's shooting stars. Hummingbirds, western bluebirds, and dark-eyed juncos add color and song as you climb to a low point on the skyline ridge ahead. Once across the ridge, you descend to a beautiful area of open hillsides dotted with oak, buckeye, and pine. At about the 4.3-mile point, approximately 50 feet to the right of the road, you can see the gated tunnel of Star Mine, **8**, one of the last coal mines in the area to shut down. Nearby piles of dirt—mine tailings—are mute testimony to the miners' Herculean efforts.

The route turns southwest here, climbs through a rocky canyon where shrubs such as toyon and yerba santa flourish, and levels out in a pine forest. Here you bear right at a fork, staying on the Star Mine Trail. Soon you reach one of the star attractions of this route, in addition to the mines—a manzanita forest. You will notice two kinds of manzanita growing here: one of them, Mt. Diablo, is restricted to its namesake mountain and this preserve; the other, common manzanita, is found on Mt. Diablo and in Morgan Territory Regional Preserve. The difference can best be studied where the two grow side by side. Mt. Diablo manzanita has gray, felt-like leaves that clasp the branch and attach without a stem; there is an indentation in the leaf where it attaches to the branch. Common manzanita, on the other hand, has leaves that are green, shiny, and smooth, and attach to the branch with stems. Manzanitas flower in winter or early spring, bedecking themselves with masses of white or white-and-pink blossoms. Also growing here is chamise, one of the most common chaparral plants, perfectly adapted to dry, rocky soils.

The climbing is steep here, but beautiful views of angled ridges and oak woodlands reward your efforts. Mt. Diablo, the Central Valley, and the long east–west ridge you explored earlier on the Ridge Trail, are points of orientation. A nearby rest bench gives you a place to relax and enjoy the view, which includes the windmill you may have heard a while back. At about the 5-mile point, just past the rest bench, your route leaves the road, turns right, and descends on a single track, closed to bicycles and horses. Losing elevation as you switchback down a grassy hillside, past pine, oak, and buckeye, you reach a beautiful broad valley located east of the Stewartville town site. Here you pass through a wooden gate in a barbed-wire fence, and in about 75 feet reach a fork in the route. The left fork, a path through the grass, connects to the Lower Oil Canyon Trail. The right fork, your route, leads to a junction with the Stewartville Trail. Once around the corner of a ridge, you can see a windmill and a cattle pen, located in the center of a **Y**-shaped valley that opens to the north. The feeling of being in the Old West is overwhelming.

The route circles a wet area, climbs an embankment, and meets the Stewartville Trail, a dirt road. Turning left, you walk toward the windmill and the cattle pen, and, once past them, stay to the right as the road briefly splits in two. Just after the segments rejoin, you pass a junction, left, with the Lower Oil Canyon Trail. Continue straight and level, walking by grassland where cows may be grazing, following a creek on your right. Soon you come to the next junction, where the Upper Oil Canyon Trail heads left. (The Oil Canyon trails are worth exploring if you have time, or perhaps on another day.) Again continue straight, passing the Stewartville backpack camp, where a toilet is available; then walk through a grazing area, which may be flooded, to a junction marked by a trail post, right.

This is the site of Stewartville, one of five mining towns that thrived in this area between the 1860s and the turn of the century. Here you turn sharply right on the Miners Trail, a single track closed to bicycles and horses, and begin a gentle climb, soon finding another trail post, left. An

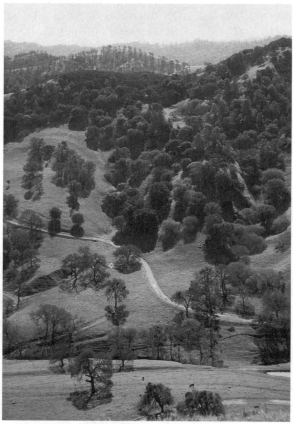

Rolling hills and oaks make up this view south from the Ridge Trail.

old dirt road runs east–west here, across your route, but you continue uphill, steeply now, on the single track, past mine tailings and the remnants of a wooden structure. Tall gray pines are joined here by black locust, perhaps planted for shade. You will also encounter on this portion of the route interior live oak, manzanita, toyon, chamise, black sage, and California sagebrush. As you climb higher, now on a narrow track cut from the hillside, you can see the Stewartville Trail, downhill and left. The drop-off is extreme, so use caution on this rocky and eroded trail.

The grade eases to moderate as the trail follows the indentations of the east–west ridge that is topped by the Ridge Trail. After crossing a possibly wet area on a small wooden bridge, you join the Stewartville Trail at the elbow of a sharp switchback, about the 7-mile point, where you bear right and continue to climb on a moderate grade. (If wet, this is the muddiest section of the hike.) After making a switchback to the right, you pass a rest bench and reach a flat area where the Stewartville and Ridge trails meet. Turn left, go through the gate, and retrace your steps to the parking area.

Hikers climbing the Oil Canyon Trail.

◆ Briones Regional Park ◆

Briones Regional Park
BRIONES CREST

Length: 6.8 miles

Time: 4 to 6 hours

Rating: Moderate

Regulations: EBRPD; fees for parking and dogs.

Highlights: This rambling loop, which includes parts of the
                   Homestead Valley, Briones Crest, Table Top, Mott Peak,
                   and Black Oak trails, offers a great introduction to the
                   southwest half of this expansive, 5,756-acre park, an area
                   of rolling hills, high ridges, and forested canyons. The
                   rewards for climbing along the Briones Crest include
                   spring wildflowers and 360-degree views.

Facilities: None at the trailhead, but picnic tables, water, and toilets
                   are located at other nearby parking areas in the park; horse
                   staging.

Trailhead: At the end of the park entrance road, just past the last
                   parking area.

Directions: From Hwy. 24 in Orinda, take the Orinda Exit and go
                   northwest 2.2 miles on Camino Pablo to Bear Creek Rd.
                   Turn right and go 4.5 miles to the park's Bear Creek Valley
                   entrance. Turn right, and after 0.3 mile reach the entrance
                   kiosk; continue 0.1 mile to the last parking area.

Part of this scenic loop follows a route named for Ivan Dickson, a dedicated member of the Berkeley Hiking Club and park enthusiast who, upon
his death in 1993 at age 95, left a surprise bequest of $500,000 to the region-
al park district. The yearly interest on this account, about $25,000, is used
for trail maintenance programs involving groups, organizations, and individuals.

   Passing a trail post with the Ivan Dickson Memorial Loop emblem, you
go through a gate and follow a paved road—the continuation of the park
entrance road—east through a brushy area, soon reaching a fork and the

end of pavement. Here Old Briones Road, once the main route between Orinda and Martinez, heads left, and the Homestead Valley Trail, your route, goes right. Bearing right and descending on a wide dirt road, you cross Bear Creek, its banks lined with coast live oak, California bay laurel, willow, madrone, and bigleaf maple.

Much of your route is in the open, climbing high atop the rolling hills that characterize this regional park, so enjoy while you can the shady canyon that holds Bear Creek, and the wide variety of trees that grow here. Birds appreciate this oasis too, and you may hear the sharp cry of a northern flicker or the call of a California quail as you climb out of the canyon, through a cattle gate, and into the open. Reaching a junction with the Crescent Ridge Trail, which goes straight, you turn right and continue on the Homestead Valley Trail, and in about 100 yards pass a junction with the Bear Creek Trail, right. A nearby swampy area is home to noisy flocks of red-winged blackbirds.

With a tributary of Bear Creek on your right, the route passes a few venerable coast live oaks, their many branches spreading from twisted trunks, and several California buckeyes, flowering beautifully in late spring. As the route begins to climb on a moderate grade, through a

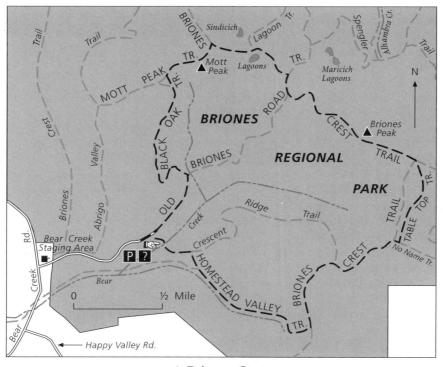

4. Briones Crest

forest of oak and bay, you may notice other spring bloomers, such as blue bush lupine and bush monkey-flower. This woodland habitat is ideal for two common towhees, California and spotted, which love to scrape through leaf litter for food. Turkey vultures and red-tailed hawks may be circling overhead, and western scrub-jays, if here, will probably announce your presence.

Breaking into the open and sweeping uphill on several sharp bends, the route passes through a gate and reaches the Briones Crest Trail. Turning left, you now follow the rolling ridgecrest through a wooded area, where dark-eyed juncos flit from tree to tree, and spring wildflowers such as California poppy, Ithuriel's spear and winecup

Bicyclists enjoy climbing the Briones Crest Trail with Mt. Diablo in the background.

clarkia emerge from the grass, dappled by sunlight. The view east is of Walnut Creek and Mt. Diablo, beautifully set off by a foreground of rolling hills.

At about the 2.25-mile point, you pass a junction, left, with the Crescent Ridge Trail. Heading straight and east, toward Mt. Diablo, the Briones Crest Trail stays in the open, on top of the world. When you reach a fork with the No Name Trail, right, bear left and descend past several cattle gates through a lush wildflower meadow sprinkled with blue-eyed grass, owl's clover, blue dicks, and Indian paintbrush. At the next junction, leave the Briones Crest Trail as it veers left; continue straight on the Ivan Dickson Memorial Loop to the Table Top and Spengler trails. Where the Spengler Trail makes a hard right, you continue straight on the Table Top Trail, past an area of chamise and California sagebrush, heading for the high ground around Briones Peak (1483').

A short, steep climb rewards you with views, west, to the Berkeley Hills, while directly ahead you can see a large cable-television facility belonging to TCI Cablevision of Contra Costa County. As you continue climbing along the crest of a ridge, more of the East Bay becomes visible to the north, including Martinez, Benicia, the Carquinez Strait, and Suisun

Bay, home to the mothball fleet of W.W.II ships. When you come to a cattle gate, you have reached the next junction. Here, the Table Top Trail bends sharply right and downhill, but you continue straight through the gate, and in a few feet rejoin the Briones Crest Trail, merging from the left.

Three birds whose names are similar—horned lark, western meadowlark, and lark sparrow—may be present nearby. Unrelated, but sharing the same habitat—open fields and grassland—each of these songbirds has distinctive markings. The lark sparrow, smallest of the three, shows a rust-and-white face pattern and a dark spot on its light gray breast. The horned lark, slightly larger, sports black tufts on its forehead, a black stripe under its eye, and a black bib under its throat. The western meadowlark, almost robin-sized, has white head stripes and a wide black bib on a yellow breast. Each bird flashes white tail feathers in flight.

After climbing to and passing through a small grove of oaks, just before the route begins to descend, you will come upon two unsigned paths, one left, the other right. The right-hand path leads up to the summit of Briones Peak, where a rest bench and terrific views await you. After a well-deserved break, return to the main route, turn right, and continue northwest over rolling terrain, mostly descending, to a T-junction with Old Briones Road. At this point, about 4.25 miles, the Briones Crest Trail, your route, turns right and follows the same downhill route as Old Briones Road, leaving it in about 0.1 mile at a junction, where you turn left.

When you walk by a fenced pond on your left, one of the two Sindicich Lagoons, you will also pass the Lagoon Trail, right, and a narrow path, left. Continue straight and uphill, looking back from time to time to admire an unobstructed view of Mt. Diablo, east, and the other, larger lagoon, north. The lagoons are the breeding grounds for thousands of California newts, which migrate here in early spring from hiding places in nearby forests. Soon you come to a junction with the Mott Peak Trail, a wide dirt road, where you turn left and climb toward a saddle just north of Mott Peak (1424'). Mott Peak was named for William Penn Mott Jr., general manager of EBRPD from 1962 to 1967, who led an expansion drive that incorporated Briones, among others, into the regional park system. Mott left EBRPD to become director of California's Department of Parks and Recreation, and was later named head of the National Park Service.

Once across the saddle, you descend to a cattle gate and continue downhill on a moderate grade, with a view west to the Oakland and Berkeley hills, anchored by Round Top and Vollmer Peak, and beyond to Mt. Tamalpais. At the next junction, leave the Mott Peak Trail, right, and continue straight on the Black Oak Trail, which is level for a short distance, then drops past a cut-off, right, to the Mott Peak Trail. A short, steep uphill section leads you to the top of a rise, where a nearby rest bench beckons. Now the route heads downhill on a gentle and then moderate grade, following the crest of a narrow ridge. At the next rest bench the route turns left and makes a steep descent on loose dirt, past the grove of black oaks that gives this trail its name, to the valley floor.

Buckeye, blue elderberry, bay, and willow grace this grassy area, and you soon reach a T-junction with Old Briones Road, just past the 6-mile point. Here you turn right, crossing a tributary of Bear Creek flowing under the road via a culvert, and meander through a level, shady area which soon gives way to open grassland. Continue on a pleasant, level course for about 0.5 mile, at the end of which is a cattle gate. After passing through the gate, you arrive, in about 250 feet, at the junction with the Homestead Valley Trail you passed at the start of this loop. Bear right, now on pavement, and retrace your steps to the parking area.

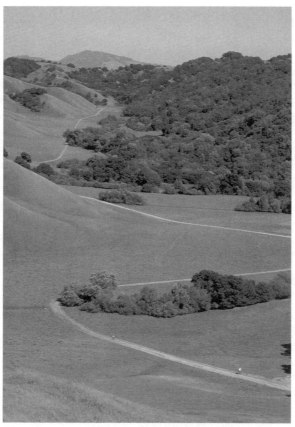

View east across valley and rolling hills toward Mt. Diablo from the Black Oak Trail.

5 Briones Regional Park
DIABLO VIEW

Length: 4.8 miles

Time: 3 to 4 hours

Rating: Moderate

Regulations: EBRPD

Highlights: This loop, which includes all or parts of the Diablo View, Spengler, Pine Tree, and Orchard trails, and part of Old Briones Road gives you a chance to explore the East Bay's largest developed regional park, an area of deep wooded canyons, forested slopes, oak savannas, and open, grassy ridges. The varied habitat attracts a large variety of birds, from chickadees to golden eagles. The plant life along this route is equally diverse, with a wide range of trees, shrubs, and wildflowers.

Facilities: Toilet, water (may not be available due to contamination); horse staging.

Trailhead: Southeast corner of the parking area.

Directions: From Hwy. 4 in Martinez, take the Alhambra Avenue exit and go 0.5 mile south on Alhambra Ave. to Alhambra Valley Rd. Turn right and go 1.25 miles to Reliez Valley Rd. Turn left and go 0.5 mile to the Alhambra Creek Valley entrance, marked by a sign. Turn right and follow the entrance road 0.8 mile to the parking area.

From the southeast corner of the parking area, pass through a gate next to an information board, turn immediately left onto the Diablo View Trail, a dirt road, and follow it on a gentle uphill climb. Another dirt road, heading straight from the gate, is the Alhambra Creek Trail, part of your return route. This is open, rolling country, the realm of grassland and oak savanna. Soon after leaving the parking area, you pass the Tavan Trail, left, and now the slope changes to moderate as you ascend via well-graded S-bends toward the top of a ridge, where a fine view of Mt. Diablo awaits you. Along the way, you pass an unsigned dirt road, left. From the ridgetop you also can see Concord, Highway 4, and the west delta.

The oaks up here, mostly valley oaks, are full of large clumps of mistletoe, easy to see when the limbs are bare or just getting their beautiful yellow-green foliage in late winter. In late winter and early spring, the surrounding hillsides are dotted with color from California buttercup, blue dicks, and Henderson's shooting stars. Other trees and shrubs here

include California bay laurel, California buckeye, blue elderberry, coffeeberry, and hillside gooseberry.

After about 0.5 mile you reach a fork marked by a trail post. Here you
stay on the Diablo View Trail, now a dirt path, as it bends left and makes
a gentle climb along a ridgetop that splits two deep valleys. The route
enters the shade of coast live oak, valley oak, and blue oak, and begins to
climb steeply over several rises, with short descents in between. Soon in
the open, you reach a fence with a gate; just beyond is a **T**-junction, where
you turn right onto a dirt road.

Because of its diversity of habitat—shady canyons, oak savanna, open
grassland—this regional park attracts a wide variety of birds, each suited
to a different environment. The tiny chestnut-backed chickadee, for example, is at home in the trees, where it often hangs upside-down on branches,

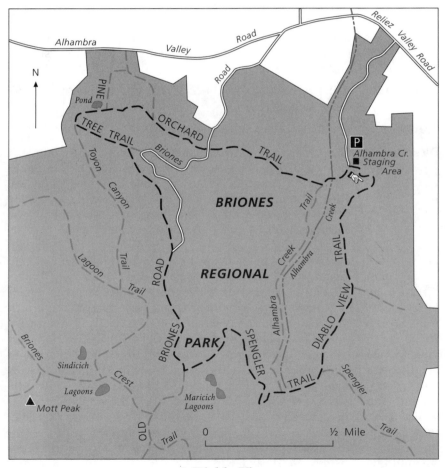

5. Diablo View

picking off insects. Look in the trees also for woodpeckers, warblers, and dark-eyed juncos. The lark sparrow is a bird of open, grassy fields, sharing this terrain with the western meadowlark and the horned lark. Raptors—large birds of prey such as red-tailed hawks, red-shouldered hawks, and vultures—spend most of their time hunting from the air. The golden eagle, a raptor seldom seen in the East Bay, has been spotted here.

As you continue on a rolling course through the oaks, accompanied only by the twitter of birds, you pass an overgrown road leading left and downhill. From time to time you will also see dirt paths diverging from the main route; ignore these. Now the route breaks into the open, with a steep hillside dropping left, and a stunning view of Mt. Diablo, east. Soon you come to a four-way intersection and the end of the Diablo View Trail. Here the Spengler Trail crosses in front of you left to right, and a dirt path continues straight and climbs uphill. Turning right on the Spengler Trail, an eroded dirt road, you descend moderately to a shady area of coast live oak and bay, where the forest floor is carpeted with miner's lettuce, whose tiny white flowers appear in late winter and last through May.

After passing through a gate, you continue to descend over easy and then moderate ground to the Alhambra Creek canyon. At the bottom of the canyon, two creeks merge on your left and flow as one through a culvert under the road. Just past the creek crossing is a junction, where the Alhambra Creek Trail heads right and downhill, and your route, the Spengler Trail, bears left and begins its climb out of the canyon on a moderate grade. Bay limbs arch over the dirt-and-gravel road, giving shade to embankments where ferns and blackberry vines thrive. About 0.1 mile past the previous junction, your route swings sharply right. Here an unsigned path continues straight, following the creek upstream past a lovely series of small waterfalls which tumble over large tree roots instead of rocks.

Where the bay canopy—joined by bigleaf maple, buckeye, and coast live oak—gives way and allows sunlight to penetrate, shrubs such as black sage, bush monkeyflower, blue bush lupine, and toyon have taken hold. Just after the 2-mile point, you pass a dead-end road, right, and continue to climb through alternating sections of sun and shade. The route then breaks abruptly into the open, leading you through a gate, and, in about 100 yards, to a fenced-off lagoon, one of two Maricich Lagoons shown on the EBRPD map, left, where cows may be grazing nearby. At a T-junction here with Old Briones Road, turn right onto it and walk downhill, coming in about 250 feet to another gate and a junction with an unsigned path, left. Now you go through the gate and continue descending north on Old Briones Road, passing several more paths along the way, and soon reaching the edge of a steep and wild-looking canyon, left. California sagebrush, lupine, Indian paintbrush, and madrone cling to the canyon's sheer west-facing wall. A short while ago

View northwest across one of the Sindicich Lagoons from the Briones Crest Trail.

you were in a cool, shady canyon; now the route is open and exposed, a different environment entirely. Across the canyon rises the main crest of the Briones Hills, which you can explore another day by following the "Briones Crest" route description on p. 48.

Following the road downhill, past clearings where you can see Concord and Mt. Diablo again, you eventually reach a parking area, right, at the end of Briones Road, with an information board and drinking fountain close by. Just past the information board is a gate, and beyond the gate, a paved area. Before reaching the gate, find the single-track trail that begins just left of the drinking fountain and skirts the left side of a wooden fence, which is next to paved Briones Road. Follow this trail for about 200 feet, pass through a gap in the fence, then turn left and walk along the fence until you reach a gate. Go through the gate, and begin an uphill climb, with Briones Road on your right, passing a powerline tower in an area overgrown with chamise.

Now descending, at one point with a very steep dropoff on the left, you soon merge with the Pine Tree Trail, a dirt road, and bear left. Soon you are passing the large grove of pines—Monterey and Coulter—that give this trail its name. Western bluebirds, hummingbirds, and western scrub-jays all frequent this area, and in the spring, red maids add patches of magenta which complement the green grass. Shortly after merging with the Pine Tree Trail, the route passes another junction, where the Toyon Trail heads sharply left. Continuing straight, you pass an unsigned path on the right, and see ahead a fenced pond where you may catch a glimpse of a belted kingfisher, a compact blue-and-white bird with a long bill and a pronounced head crest. The kingfisher makes a dry, rattling sound as it flies from one perch to the next.

At the southeast corner of the pond is a junction; here the Pine Tree Trail turns left and goes through a gate, but your route, the Orchard Trail, a dirt road, bends right and begins a rolling course over open terrain. The road passes close to a barbed-wire fence, left, and a stand of eucalyptus and olive trees. Just before making a swing to the left, you pass a path, right, and then go through a gate and walk in the shade of eucalyptus, pine, and coast live oak.

At about the 4-mile point, you reach a junction marked by a trail post, where an unsigned trail merges sharply from the left, and your route, the Orchard Trail, continues straight, passing a path, left, and a gate. This eroded section of the road, near the Rancho Briones Equestrian Facility, may be muddy in wet weather. Just after passing a stable, you cross Briones Road, go through a gate, and continue following the Orchard Trail, now a dirt path, as it leads directly toward Mt. Diablo, a perfect view marred by powerlines. As you walk downhill on a moderate grade, Mt. Diablo appears to sink behind a ridge; if you look carefully you can make out the Diablo View Trail, the first part of this loop, winding its way up that ridge.

With Mount Diablo completely obscured, you continue to walk southeast through a little valley, following a tributary of Alhambra Creek, left, and passing under a set of powerlines. At a place where the trail bends right and climbs slightly, you may see an entire hillside, left, full of ground squirrel holes, a kind of squirrel condominium with sunny, southwestern exposure. Just past the 5-mile point, you come to a large fenced picnic area, left, and a T-junction with the Alhambra Creek Trail. Turn left here, crossing Alhambra Creek, which flows under the road through a culvert, and walk a short distance to the parking area, passing a junction, right, with the Diablo View Trail.

◆ Briones Reservoir ◆

<table>
<tr><td>6</td><td>Briones Reservoir
BEAR CREEK TRAIL</td></tr>
</table>

Length: 8 miles round-trip; 4 miles with car shuttle.

Time: 3 to 4 hours

Rating: Moderate

Regulations: EBMUD; trail use permit required; no bicycles.

Highlights: This pleasant walk on EBMUD land skirts the south and east shores of Briones Reservoir and ends near Briones Overlook Staging Area. A wide variety of trees, shrubs and flowers makes this an ideal nature-study trip.

Facilities: Toilet; horse staging.

Trailhead: Southwest corner of parking lot.

Directions: From Hwy. 24 in Orinda, take the Orinda exit and go 2.2 miles northwest on Camino Pablo to a junction with Bear Creek Rd. Turn right and go 4.2 miles to EBMUD's Bear Creek Staging Area, left, just past the junction with Happy Valley Rd.

If you are doing this as a shuttle trip, leave a car at the EBMUD Briones Overlook Staging Area, 1.4 miles northeast of Camino Pablo on Bear Creek Rd. Then continue, as above, to the Bear Creek Staging Area.

Just beyond the gate at the trailhead, you will see an EBMUD register and a sign for the Bear Creek Trail. After signing the register, turn left, and descend the Bear Creek Trail, here a gravel path, to a clearing where Bear Creek flows in from the left. All the elements that make this a wonderful hike are present at the start—a wide variety of trees and shrubs, and the proximity of water. Trees here include California bay laurel, coast live oak, and willow. Coyote bush, snowberry, and poison hemlock are also here, along with ferns.

After crossing the creek—this may be tricky during periods of high water—climb steeply up an eroded dirt path, and in about 200 feet reach a trail post indicating the Bear Creek Trail and the Overlook Staging Area,

4 miles distant. You will also see on the trail post an emblem for the Mokelumne Coast to Crest Trail. This 300-mile recreational trail, still in the early stage of development, will one day link the Bay Area to the Sierra Nevada. More than a dozen public and private organizations, including EBMUD, EBRPD, the US Forest Service, and the National Park Service, are working together to complete this ambitious project.

About 75 feet uphill from the trail post you reach a gate; go through it and immediately come to a junction with an old paved road, shown on the Olmsted & Bros. map as Shuetman Rd. Turn right at this T-junction—you are still following the Bear Creek Trail—and walk west on a level grade through grasslands bordered with colorful radish weed. In late spring you will see blue elderberry in flower; look for western meadowlark and red-winged blackbirds in the shrubs, and turkey vultures gliding overhead. Soon you get your first glimpse of Briones Reservoir ahead. To your left is a heavily forested area, but across the water are rolling, grassy hills dotted with oaks. At about the 0.5-mile point, you pass through a gate, and in 125 feet or so reach a fork. Here the pavement continues to the water's edge, but your route, the Bear Creek Trail, now a wide dirt road, veers left into dense woodland.

This part of the route is shady and level, and stays by the water. This is a good spot to stop, look, and listen for birds, from small—chickadees—to large—Canada geese. Trees here include bigleaf maple, bay, California buckeye, black oak, and madrone. You may also see shrubs such as snowberry, coffeeberry, and toyon, and spring wildflowers such as Ithuriel's spear, milkmaids, and California buttercup.

6. Bear Creek Trail

At about the 1-mile point, you pass a rest bench at an overlook, then begin an easy climb. Opposite an upcoming trail post, look left into the trees for a glimpse of the foundation and stone stairway of an old house. Several tall walnut trees stand proudly beside the trail, which soon enters an overgrown area where ferns and mosses give a rain-forest feel. You may see a large bird box or two nailed high on a tree. These are for wood ducks, highly colorful birds which nest locally. This area is also good for sighting northern flickers and spotted towhees.

The trail narrows to single-track width as it rises gently across a steep hillside, where a few clearings, right, offer views of the reservoir and the hills beyond. Sunlight filters through the trees here, giving a dappled effect. At one point the trail comes out of the forest and passes within 50 feet of Bear Creek Road; look here for owl's clover growing low to the ground. After crossing over a drainage ditch you re-enter the forest, where you can add to today's list of trees and shrubs canyon live oak, California hazelnut, madrone, manzanita, and bush monkeyflower. Listen for the western scrub-jay's loud screech and the wrentit's repetitive one-note stutter.

After about 2 miles of easy walking, you enter a clearing and almost join a dirt fire road, closed to the public, running at right angles to your route. But just before reaching the road, a trail post directs you to follow the Bear Creek Trail as it veers right and starts uphill, passing a meadow full of thistle and poison hemlock. Here you climb steeply into an area of chaparral, including coyote bush, California sagebrush, bush mon-keyflower, and blue bush lupine. The route is perched on the side of a steep hill with southern exposure in an area loaded with poison oak. Here you have a good look at the reservoir and the dam at its southwestern edge. Soon you come to a grassy area with a couple of inviting rest bench-es. Watch for hillside gooseberry along this part of the route, its thorny fruit looking like a medieval weapon.

The trail, now swinging around Cutter Point and bending southwest, crosses the fire road you met earlier, and soon comes to an open hillside with sagebrush, coyote bush, and bush monkeyflower. You may also see in bloom blow wives, lupine, Ithuriel's spear and blue-eyed grass. A large powerline tower here is the only intrusion on an otherwise lovely scene. The route now crosses another branch of the fire road and descends slight-ly, soon reaching a dense forest of bay and coast live oak. A large grove of madrone trees grows here on a north-facing hillside overlooking the reser-voir.

At about the 3-mile point, you break out into a clearing and walk under a set of powerlines. Here are more chaparral plants, including manzanita, bush poppy and chamise, both of which bloom in late spring. The trail passes through a grove of pines, then moves into the open, where you encounter the powerlines again. The reservoir is on your right, and your destination, the Briones Overlook Staging Area, is straight ahead. From here you descend slightly to water level, with willow, madrone, bush monkeyflower, lupine, and California poppy growing beside the trail. Just a bit farther and uphill from here is an unsigned fork in the trail. If you are doing this hike with a car shuttle, bear left and continue uphill to the staging area (there is a toilet there). If not, turn around and retrace your steps to the Bear Creek staging area. If you are going completely around the reservoir, following the "Reservoir Loop" route description, continue straight and begin using that route description now.

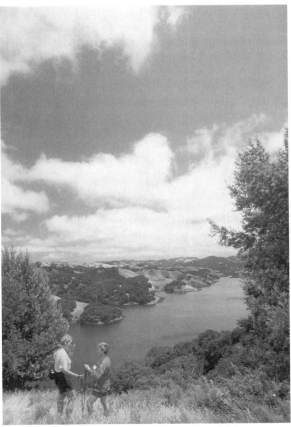

Hikers pause to admire the view east across Briones Reservoir from about the 2-mile point on the Bear Creek Trail.

7	Briones Reservoir
	RESERVOIR LOOP

Length: 14 miles

Time: 6 to 8 hours

Rating: Difficult

Regulations: EBMUD; trail use permit required; no bicycles.

Highlights: This loop, combining the Bear Creek and Oursan trails, is one of the longest in this guide, taking you completely around Briones Reservoir. The route passes through a variety of terrain, from dense oak and bay forest near the reservoir's shore to open grassland high atop Sobrante Ridge. Along the way you will encounter grand vistas, an assortment of trees and shrubs, spring wildflowers, and birds by the dozen. Except for about 3 miles of the Bear Creek Trail, all of the walking is on well-graded dirt roads, which were in good shape in mid-March after a wet winter.

Facilities: Toilet; horse staging.

Trailhead: West side of parking area.

Directions: See the directions for "Bear Creek Trail" on p. 58.

The first 4 miles of this route are described in the "Bear Creek Trail" hike. When you reach a fork in the trail at about the 4-mile point, just below EBMUD's Briones Overlook staging area, continue straight on a level grade, passing through an area of coast live oak, madrone, and pine. You will also notice some large powerlines on your right. Soon another connector to the staging area merges on the left, and a paved road appears on your right, running parallel to the trail. After a short distance the trail joins this road, and about 30 feet farther you come to a T-junction with another paved road, one that comes from Bear Creek Road and heads northwest across the dam that impounds Briones Reservoir.

At this point you leave the Bear Creek Trail, turning right to cross the dam. (Use caution, as this road is traveled by trucks.) Out in the open now, you have a wonderful view of the reservoir, which is surrounded by rolling hills. Overhead you may see vultures circling, while closer at hand, if it's spring, western bluebirds and swallows dart through the air hunting insects. (If you see bird boxes with small holes, they are probably for the bluebirds. Large-holed boxes are generally for wood ducks.) As you cross a bridge over the spillway and get on the dam, you have a deep valley on your left, where San Pablo Dam Road skirts the southwest edge of

San Pablo Reservoir, several hundred feet below. The dam also affords you a fine view, southwest, of San Pablo Ridge and the Berkeley Hills.

On the other side of the dam, the paved road changes to dirt and gravel, bends right, and passes an unsigned junction with a gated dirt road, left. Ahead are several boat houses near the reservoir's shore. (This poorly signed and not particularly attractive section of the route is near a dumping area for clean fill.) Follow the road as it turns left and climbs uphill, past the boat houses. You will notice several side paths as you walk northwest, away from the reservoir; ignore them all. Keep the dumping area to your right as the road levels and begins to descend. Soon the road splits at a fork; here you bear right, and in about 200 feet pass a connector to the left-hand road.

You are now on the Oursan Trail, which you follow as it climbs more and more steeply toward a set of large powerline towers. The terrain is mostly open and rolling, with some groves of California bay laurel and coast live oak. Passing through a gate, you continue to gain elevation, now on a gentle grade, giving you an opportunity to pick out landmarks such as Inspiration Point (southwest), Vollmer Peak (south), and Round Top (just east of south). The Briones Overlook staging area is just across

7. Reservoir Loop

the reservoir to the southeast. The route now turns northeast and begins to climb Sobrante Ridge, passing an unsigned junction with a road climbing steeply left. A wonderful display of spring wildflowers—California poppies and blue dicks—decorates a rocky road cut, and clumps of California sagebrush claim footholds on the open hillside.

At about the 6-mile point, the route swings north, away from the reservoir, to run along the crest of Sobrante Ridge. Coffeeberry and hillside gooseberry are here, along with soap plant and Henderson's shooting stars. As the route levels, you pass a restricted access road, right, and then begin to climb again, getting a

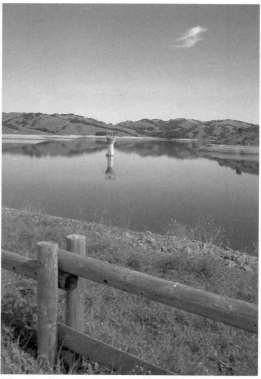

View northeast across Briones Reservoir from the dam.

glimpse of Mt. Tamalpais, west, peeking over San Pablo Ridge. Below and left is Sather Canyon, a deep gash in the landscape with a creek at the bottom that drains into San Pablo Reservoir. Almost due east is Mt. Diablo, and to the southeast rise Las Trampas and Rocky ridges, the latter topped by a single antenna, forming the parallel walls of Bollinger Canyon.

Spring wildflowers put on a beautiful display here, as poppies, California buttercup, and blue-eyed grass color the grassy slopes with dabs of orange, yellow, and blue, sharing the limelight with blue bush lupine. Once on top of the ridgecrest, the route is mostly level, but drops slightly to pass through a shady tunnel of bay and coast live oak. The far end of this tunnel frames a lovely view north toward the Carquinez Strait and Suisun Bay, across an area of open space checkered with densely packed housing developments. In the far distance rises Mt. St. Helena, visible on a clear day.

Now the route makes a 180-degree bend right and begins to work southeast toward Briones Reservoir across open terrain, some of it prone to landslides. Fault Creek flows into the reservoir through a deep valley to your right. As the route turns east and heads directly toward Mt.

Diablo, you pass a junction, marked by a trail post, with a road that heads south. In 100 yards or so, you pass another road, this one restricted access. You are descending on a gentle grade, and soon pass a wooded area, right, on your way to a T-junction with a paved road, the Hampton Trail. Just before reaching the junction, at about the 8.5-mile point, you pass through a gate, directly under a set of powerline towers.

From here, the Hampton Trail heads north, and in about 0.5 mile becomes Hampton Road. Your route, the Oursan Trail, turns right and follows broken pavement downhill on a gentle grade, soon reaching a fork, where you bear left, pass through a gate, and begin to climb on a dirt road. A narrow path, right, leads to a corral and an inviting grove of trees, a good spot for a picnic. From here back to the Bear Creek Staging Area, your route follows the ins and outs of the reservoir's shoreline, often rising to cross a small ridge, then descending to a little gully, where a creek may flow through a culvert under the road and into the reservoir. At the first of these gullies, where Scout Creek flows into Boy Scout Camp Cove, you pass another restricted access road, left, and then cross the creek. Near the creek, willows grow in a wet area, downhill and right, and California poppies decorate a hillside, left. You may see a wedge of Canada geese flying across the reservoir, keeping a tight formation and honking to each other.

A moderate climb takes you through a little notch and over a shoulder, and then you descend in the shade of coast live oaks to another creek, where bay and California buckeye flourish in the moist soil. Leaving the trees, you start climbing again, away from the reservoir and over a rise, where a gate lets you pass through a fence that crosses the road. Now the route descends, then levels out and again follows the shape of shoreline. If the water level is low, you may see large marshy areas with dried-out bulrushes. Your route leads into Bearinda Cove, at about the 10-mile point, past a junction, left, with a restricted access road. After crossing a creek, you veer right as the route heads back toward the reservoir, passing a hillside overgrown with blackberry vines and snowberry, and shaded by bay and buckeye. The occasional shady areas, interspersed with long stretches of open terrain, are welcome on a warm day.

Your course is now generally east, along the north shore of the slender eastern arm of the reservoir. At Pereira Cove, you pass a path heading uphill and left, closed to hikers and horses, as the route swings right, toward the water. In the open parts of the route, you may see red-tailed hawks, red-shouldered hawks, or turkey vultures circling above, but in wooded areas be on the lookout for the varied thrush, which resembles its cousin, the American robin. Just past Pereira Cove, in an open area, you pass a path going left and uphill; bear right and enter an oak woodland where you may be greeted by raucous western scrub-jays.

Climbing for the first time in a while, the route veers north into the first of two narrow, north-pointing ravines, with a finger of the reservoir below and right. After a short, steep climb, you descend on a moderate grade, past a hillside covered with long strands of vine honeysuckle and low-growing periwinkle, to a creek. As the route levels out after its climb up from the creek, you pass a restricted access road, left; here you bear right and begin a gentle descent in the open, toward the reservoir. This process is repeated at the second of the two ravines. Along the way, you may be startled by the loud flapping of wings as a flock of band-tailed pigeons departs from the nearby oaks. These are closely related to rock doves, our common urban pigeons, but are a few inches larger, uniformly patterned, and much more elegant.

Now out in the open, the route crosses an area that may be flooded in wet weather, then climbs over a shoulder on a moderate grade near the east end of the reservoir. Here the terrain drops steeply toward the reservoir's shoreline, right, at the inflow of Bear Creek. After a few more ups and down, you reach a junction with the Bear Creek Trail, just before the Bear Creek staging area. Turn right, pass through a gate, and go past the EBMUD register to the parking area.

Change in the water level leaves a marshy area near Bearinda Cove high and dry.

◆ Carquinez Strait Regional Shoreline ◆

Carquinez Strait Regional Shoreline
FRANKLIN RIDGE

Length: 2.75 miles

Time: 1.5 to 2 hours

Rating: Moderate

Regulations: EBRPD

Highlights: Circling a high ridge overlooking Carquinez Strait, this route has some steep sections, but your efforts are rewarded by terrific views of the strait, Suisun Bay, the west delta, Mt. Diablo, and the hills of Napa and Solano counties. Using the Franklin Ridge Loop Trail, your route explores open grassland, oak savanna, and shady, tree-lined ravines. Parts of this loop may be extremely muddy during and after wet weather.

Facilities: Picnic benches, toilets, horse staging.

Trailhead: West end of upper parking area.

Directions: From Hwy. 4 in Martinez, take the Alhambra Avenue/ Martinez exit and go north 2 miles to Escobar St. Turn left, go 0.1 mile to Talbart St. and turn right. Follow Talbart St. for 0.1 mile, veer left onto Carquinez Scenic Dr. and go 0.3 mile to the John A. Nejedly Staging Area, left. The lower parking area has some shade; the upper area has spaces for horse trailers.

From the west end of the upper parking area, go through a gate and walk west across a large, grassy field, coming after about 200 feet to a trail post. The emblems on the post indicate you are on the Bay Area Ridge Trail and the California Hiking and Riding Trail. The Bay Area Ridge Trail is a proposed 400-mile multi-use trail, about half of which has been completed, that will pass through nine counties and completely circle the Bay Area. The California Hiking and Riding Trail was a similar idea on a state-wide scale, conceived in 1945, but only 16 miles of it are in use in the East Bay today.

Two other routes also begin here. The Rankin Park Trail leaves from the south side of the upper parking area, near picnic tables, and climbs west to the top of a ridge, joining the Bay Area Ridge/California Hiking and Riding trails. And just past the gate, an unnamed dirt road heads right and steeply uphill, climbing to the top of the same ridge. Beyond the trail post, you are on a single-track trail, walking through stands of California bay, California buckeye, coast live oak, and eucalyptus. There is a creek on your left, and this part of the route, in a cool, shady ravine, may be muddy. The trail widens and begins a moderate climb, soon turning away from the creek on a switchback and crossing an open, grassy hillside. Another switchback takes you through a wonderful area of blue elderberry, California sagebrush, and bush monkeyflower. As the trail heads back into the trees, a mourning dove's plaintive call may fool you into thinking you've heard an owl.

A steep climb in the shade of large bay trees, which soon give way to open grassland, leads at last to a T-junction, marked by a trail post, at the summit of a ridge. Here you turn right onto the Franklin Ridge Loop Trail, a dirt road, and follow it north, enjoying magnificent views, right, of Martinez, Suisun Bay with its mothball fleet of W.W.II Navy ships, the west delta, and in the far distance, the Central Valley. From here you can

8. Franklin Ridge

The Franklin Ridge Loop Trail leads to vantage points overlooking Carquinez Strait, the Benicia–Martinez Beach, and Suisun Bay.

even see all the way to the snow-capped peaks of the Sierra. Ahead are the housing developments that surround Benicia, and beyond are the hills of Napa and Solano counties. About 60 feet past the **T**-junction, you pass a road, right, leading to a viewpoint and a rest bench; this is the same steep dirt road you passed earlier as you left the parking area.

Now that you are on the ridgetop the walking is easy, because the trail is mostly level. Here you have splendid views of Mt. Diablo, southeast, and Mt. St. Helena, northwest. The Martinez Regional Shoreline, with its small lake and marshes, and the Martinez marina lie just in front of the Benicia–Martinez Bridge. As you round a bend in the trail, you can see ahead and below to the waters of Carquinez Straight, a narrow passage between Suisun and San Pablo bays. When you reach an unsigned fork, bear left, passing a rest bench where you can sit and enjoy the view, slightly marred by powerlines. You may be visited by a hummingbird here, especially if you are wearing red. Now descending northwest over eroded and perhaps muddy ground, you lose the dramatic vistas, and gain instead more intimate scenes of rolling hills, stately oaks, and circling redtailed hawks.

Passing another rest bench and a watering trough for animals, you get a good look at Carquinez Strait before the road drops off the ridge via a big **S**-bend. As you reach a saddle, you pass a path leading right and uphill to an oak-adorned summit. Below and right you can see the Carquinez Scenic Drive, which used to link Martinez and Port Costa until a 1982 landslide severed the road. Here your route bends left and continues to descend. At the next junction, an unsigned fork, bear right and enter an oak woodland—coast live oak, valley oak, and blue oak—where you may see nuthatches and woodpeckers. A steep downhill pitch brings you, at about the 1.4-mile point, to a creek and a T-junction marked by a trail post.

Here you turn left, continuing on the Franklin Ridge Loop Trail, and begin a gentle uphill climb on a dirt road, with a creek to your right. This is a wonderful area, with a mixture of bay and oak providing shade. In places you may find the road flooded by small rivulets running from a spring on the hillside, left, into the tree-lined creek. As the grade steepens you pass a fence and a restricted area, left, leaving the trees behind and coming again into open country. At a four-way junction marked by a trail post, just past the 2-mile point, you turn left and walk uphill, still on the Franklin Ridge Loop Trail. (The other two roads at this junction lead to the park boundary and private property.) At the end of a valley, right, you can see Highway 4, about 0.5 mile away.

You are now heading east, and after a moderate climb you reach a flat spot and a T-junction marked by a trail post. Running left to right in front of you is the Bay Area Ridge/California Hiking and Riding Trail, a dirt road. To finish your loop, turn left and walk about 250 feet to the junction, marked by a trail post, with the trail coming from the parking area; here you turn right and retrace your steps.

View southeast to Mt. Diablo from the Franklin Ridge Loop Trail.

◆ Coyote Hills Regional Park ◆

This is one of the most user-friendly of the East Bay parks. It has a visitor center with informative displays and helpful staff; a lovely, shaded picnic area; rewarding but not-too-taxing trails; ample opportunity for nature study; and a rich history dating back thousands of years. Children will enjoy the Muskrat Trail, a self-guiding nature walk through the park's Main Marsh, as well as special cultural programs presented by descendants of Native Americans who lived in this area for more than two thousand years. There is a paved pathway, the Bayview Trail, which circles the Coyote Hills on a mostly level course, and connects at its north end with the paved Alameda Creek Trail (see Appendix A).

The Coyote Hills themselves are the tips of an ancient mountain range, composed of iron-rich Franciscan chert, which lies between the Hayward Hills, east, and the Coast Range on the west side of San Francisco Bay. Mud, gravel, and silt washed down from the Hayward Hills created the flat plain at the Bay's southern end. One of the best views of this area is from the summit of Red Hill, just a few minutes from the visitor center. At the end of the last ice age, when sea levels rose and the Bay filled, the Coyote Hills became islands. Gradually, sedimentation deposited by Alameda Creek created marshlands around the islands—on the west side, a salt marsh; and on the east, a marsh flooded with freshwater from the creek.

Wetland areas in the park today consist mostly of brackish marshes, dominated by cattail and bulrush. These areas provide important habitat for many species of birds and aquatic animals. The Coyote Hills bird check list, revised in 1990, contains 210 species in more than 40 categories, including grebes, pelicans, cormorants, herons, egrets, geese, ducks, raptors, shorebirds, gulls, terns, and songbirds. One wetland area, called the DUST (Demonstration Urban Stormwater Treatment) Marsh is a research project, begun in the early 1980s, to study the effectiveness of using marshes to remove pollutants from urban runoff.

Coyote Hills Regional Park was opened to the public in 1968, and the area has a colorful history. The building that today houses the visitor center served in the 1960s and early 1970s as a lab where Stanford Research Institute scientists studied seals and other marine animals. (After the park opened, tours of the lab for the public were arranged.) In the 1950s the building served as an Army barracks for Nike missile crews; the missiles themselves were atop the hills.

Like other regional parks, Coyote Hills has a long ranching history, going back to an 1844 land grant establishing *Rancho Potrero de los Cerritos* (pasture of the little hills). This 10,000-acre parcel, owned by Augustin

Alviso and Tomas Pacheco, included land that became today's 976-acre park. After California became a state in 1850, the US Congress allowed challenges to the land-grant system, and many owners were forced to sell their land to pay legal fees; this fate befell the rancho. One of those who purchased a part of the rancho was George Washington Patterson, who eventually came to own nearly 6,000 acres of farm land, including the current park. The Patterson family, whose farm can be visited at nearby Ardenwood Regional Preserve, and whose name is on the park entrance road, held the land until 1968.

The original occupants of the Coyote Hills area were the Ohlone Indians, whose village sites can be visited on naturalist-led tours. The sites, raised areas that were created by the debris of everyday life, are called "shell mounds," or "kitchen middens," because they contain mostly shells, animal bones, and ashes. But archaeological excavations of village sites have also uncovered jewelry, pieces of mortars and pestles, and remnants of hearths and house floors, along with human remains. Native people lived in willow-framed huts thatched with tule, and navigated the Bay's waterways in kayak-like crafts made of bundled tules. Park naturalists and volunteers have built replicas of Indian buildings at the shell-mound site, and in 1979 they constructed a tule boat, which they paddled across San Francisco Bay. The Spanish referred to all Indians west of the Diablo Range from the Bay Area to Big Sur as Costanoans, or coast people, but today's East Bay descendants prefer the term Ohlone.

Hikers stop to take a photo from the boardwalk near the visitor center.

Park gates open: 8 A.M. to 8 P.M., April–October;
8 A.M. to 6 P.M. November–March

Visitor center: (510) 795-9385

open 9:30 A.M. to 5 P.M.; closed Mondays, Thanksgiving, and Christmas.

9 Coyote Hills Regional Park
LIZARD ROCK

Length:	0.75 mile
Time:	1 hour
Rating:	Easy
Regulations:	EBRPD; fees for parking and dogs; hikers only on the single-track Lizard Rock Trail.
Highlights:	Short and easy, this loop uses the Bayview, Lizard Rock, and Chochenyo trails to give you a quick sample of what this park has to offer, including an overview of the Main Marsh. If you have more time to spend here, consider also doing the "Red Hill" route.
Facilities:	Visitor center, picnic tables, water, toilet.
Trailhead:	West end of parking area, at its entrance.
Directions:	From Hwy. 84 at the east end of the Dumbarton Bridge in Fremont, take the Thornton Avenue/Paseo Padre Pkwy. exit, and go north 1.1 miles on Paseo Padre Pkwy. to Patterson Ranch Rd. Turn left, and go 0.5 mile to the entrance kiosk. Another 1.0 mile brings you to the parking area for the visitor center.

From the west end of the parking area, where the entrance road makes a 180-degree bend, head northwest on the paved Bayview Trail, passing the Quail Trail, a dirt road, left. The Bayview Trail is gated just beyond the parking area; after passing the gate you have the Main Marsh on your right and beautiful grassy hills rising up on your left. The Main Marsh, a brackish body of water overgrown in places with cattails and bulrushes, is a haven for birds; there are several vantage points along the Bayview Trail to look for herons, egrets, ducks, and shorebirds. Black-necked stilts, which nest in marshes around San Francisco Bay, are sometimes here in flocks of 20 to 30. Besides a few willows and London planetrees, introduced hybrids related to sycamores, the vegetation is mostly scrub—coyote bush, fennel, and poison hemlock.

When you reach a junction with the Nike Trail, about 0.1 mile from the trailhead, continue straight on the Bayview Trail. Across the Main Marsh is Lizard Rock, a large pinnacle of light-colored chert, reached by the single-track trail that bears its name. Chert was used by local Native Americans for arrowheads and spear points when they could not obtain obsidian. After about 0.25 mile you reach a junction with the Lizard Rock Trail, where you turn right and then climb on a gentle grade to the rock, passing it on the left. This is a wonderful vantage point from which to look out over the marsh, where herons, egrets, waterfowl, and shorebirds congregate. In late spring, look for flocks of black-necked stilts—showy black-and-white shorebirds with shocking pink legs.

You might also take a moment here to scan the eastern skyline, picking out such landmarks as Mission Peak and, to its right and beyond, Mt. Hamilton. Once past Lizard Rock, the trail descends gently across an open hillside of grass mixed with clumps of California sagebrush. Soon you see ahead the Chochenyo Trail, a dirt-and-gravel road that lies about 40 feet past a junction where an unsigned single-track trail merges with your route from the left. At a T-junction with the Chochenyo Trail, turn right and follow the road back toward the visitor center, passing deeper water where white pelicans sometimes float lazily about. The marsh wren, a chickadee-sized bird mostly heard but not seen, is likely to keep track of your progress with its raspy, buzzing call.

9. Lizard Rock

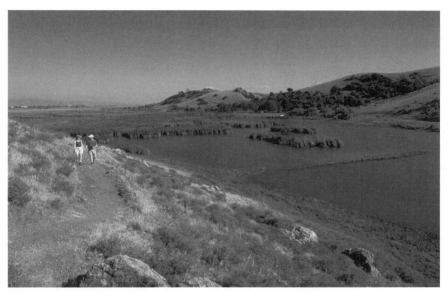

Hikers approach Lizard Rock, which overlooks the Main Marsh. View is to the east.

Here is a good opportunity to learn the difference between cattails and bulrushes, both of which are found along this stretch of the route. Cattail (genus *Typha*) is a familiar perennial marsh plant, found where there is at least some fresh water, best identified by its brown, cigar-like flower clusters held aloft on tall stems. Bulrush, also called tule, refers to plants of the genus *Scirpus*, which has 9 species in coastal California and 17 throughout the state. The ones found here have tall, round stems tapering to a sharp point, and tipped during late spring and summer with brown flower clusters. Red-winged blackbirds share the cattails and bulrushes with the marsh wrens: the blackbird is a vocal wizard, keeping up a constant refrain of odd gurgles, chortles, whistles, and other sounds.

At the south end of the Chochenyo Trail is a gate, and beyond, at a T-junction, a paved path that parallels the park entrance road. If you look left here, you will see also a short paved path leading to a boardwalk that goes out into the marsh, a route followed by the self-guiding Muskrat Trail. To return to the parking area, turn right, and follow the paved path west.

10

Coyote Hills Regional Park
RED HILL

Length: 1.5 miles

Time: 1 hour

Rating: Moderate

Regulations: EBRPD; fees for parking and dogs; hikers only on the Quail Trail.

Highlights: Combining portions of the Bayview, Nike, Red Hill, Soaproot, and Quail trails, this short loop over the summits of Red and Glider hills offers more scenery per calorie expended than any other hike in the East Bay. Besides open summits, which provide 360-degree views that extend from San Francisco to the Santa Cruz Mountains, this park contains an extensive brackish marsh, habitat for waterfowl and shorebirds. If you have more time to spend here, consider also doing the "Lizard Rock" route.

Facilities: Visitor center, picnic tables, water, toilet.

Trailhead: West end of parking area, at its entrance.

Directions: See the directions for "Lizard Rock" on p. 73.

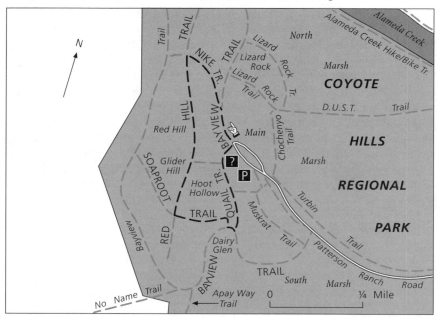

10. Red Hill

This route has the same start as "Lizard Rock," but when you reach the Nike Trail, about 0.1 mile from the trailhead, you climb left, leaving the Bayview Trail to its straight and level course. (The Nike Trail is named for the missiles perched atop these hills during the cold war, not the running shoe.) As you gain elevation on a moderate grade, take a moment to look back and admire the view, which takes in Mt. Diablo, the hills of Garin and Dry Creek Pioneer regional parks, Sunol Ridge, Mission Peak, and Mt. Hamilton. In late spring, the grasses of the Coyote Hills turn a rich, golden brown, especially pleasing an hour or two before sunset; after the autumn rains arrive they become lush green.

Soon you reach a flat spot—a saddle between Red Hill and an unnamed hill to the north—and a four-way junction. Now you can see across San Francisco Bay, with its system of levees and salt ponds, to the hills of San Mateo County. Turning left here onto the Red Hill Trail, a dirt road, you continue your ascent over open terrain, with views of the marshes that compose much of this regional park. To the northeast lies Alameda Creek, which gets its start high on the flanks of Mt. Hamilton, flows through the Sunol Wilderness, and empties into San Francisco Bay northwest of here. The Alameda County flood-control channel, which diverts water from the creek, borders the north side of Coyote Hills Regional Park, where the 12-mile Alameda Creek Regional Trail—actually two trails, one on each side of the channel—connects to the Coyote Hills trail system.

As you reach a short, steep pitch just below the summit of Red Hill, you may see California poppies, blue bush lupine, wild radish, and wild mustard in bloom, their bright colors contrasting with the red dirt underfoot. The only trees up here are acacias, imports from Australia. The summit itself is studded with rock outcrops of Franciscan chert, giving you a pleasant perch to take in the 360-degree view. In terms of scenery per calorie, Red Hill tops the list, being a relatively easy summit to attain, and commanding a superb vantage point. To the northwest is the faint outline of San Francisco, with the dark hulk of Mt. Tamalpais looming behind. Oakland is also in view, beyond Hayward, San Leandro, and Alameda, and just north of this park vast tracts of new housing push almost to the shoreline. To the south, the vista extends past the Dumbarton Bridge and the Don Edwards San Francisco Bay National Wildlife Refuge, all the way to the Santa Cruz Mountains.

While on Red Hill, you may find yourself distracted from the view by the flutter of large yellow and black butterflies. These are swallowtails; there are several species, including one associated exclusively with fennel. Only hearty plants take root on this windy site, where California sagebrush and poison oak sprout from the red, rocky soil. After crossing the level summit, you descend steeply to a saddle between Red Hill and Glider Hill, the next rise south. Just as the route begins to climb once more, you arrive at a four-way junction. From here, single-track trails take off left and right (but only the left-hand one, the Glider Hill Trail, is shown on the EBRPD map). Continuing your climb over moderate and then steep ground, you soon reach the top of Glider Hill, where the views equal those from Red Hill. The open, grassy summit even has a convenient picnic table; from here another unsigned single-track trail heads left.

Now a short, steep descent brings you to another saddle and a four-way junction. At this point, the Red Hill Trail, which continues straight, is crossed by the Soaproot Trail, a dirt road. Turn left and begin a gentle descent: from here you can see the paved Bayview Trail, downhill and right; and ahead, Dairy Glen picnic area and South Marsh. What looks like a continuation of the Bayview Trail, a paved path heading southeast, is called Apay Way; it climbs over South Red Hill and continues to the San Francisco Bay National Wildlife Refuge. The area you are passing through

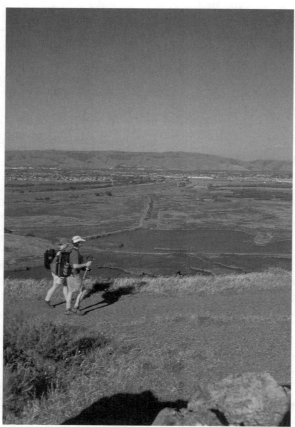

Hikers nearing the summit of Red Hill, with the Main Marsh far below. View is to the northeast.

Mt. Diablo Globe tulip.

is sheltered from the breeze which almost always blows from the Bay, so you may find it much warmer than the exposed summits you just visited.

Your route soon swings left, then bends sharply right and goes moderately downhill. At the bend, you may notice several single-track trails heading north. Pass these by and continue descending to a junction with the Bayview and Quail trails. Turn left onto the Quail Trail (called the Soaproot Trail on older maps), a wide dirt-and-gravel road that climbs north. Just after the road crosses a rise, a single-track trail, right, offers you an easy side trip to Castle Rock, a jumble of pinnacles made from the same red chert as Red Hill.

Following the Quail Trail downhill, you may see and hear its namesake, the California quail. On your way, you pass the Hoot Hollow Trail, left, and the Hoot Hollow picnic area, with its beautiful assortment of trees and shrubs, including acacia, California buckeye, coast live oak, madrone, toyon. Late spring bloomers, buckeyes in flower resemble fireworks, with exploding white blossoms tinged pink and beige against bright green leaves. After the picnic area, you pass an unsigned path heading left up some wooden steps, and a paved path, right, that leads to the visitor center. About 200 feet downhill from these paths you reach a gate and the entrance to the parking area.

◆ Del Valle Regional Park ◆

11

Del Valle Regional Park
EAST SHORE TRAIL

Length: 8 miles

Time: 3 to 4 hours

Rating: Moderate

Regulations: EBRPD; fees for parking and dogs.

Highlights: Located on the flanks of the hot, dry Livermore Valley, Lake Del Valle is a man-made impoundment on Arroyo del Valle, and the lake's surrounding parklands contain many hiking trails, including connectors to the Ohlone Wilderness Regional Trail. The East Shore Trail is the longest of Del Valle's trails, running for more than 6 miles along the lake's indented shoreline. This route explores the trail's first 4 miles, a fine combination of level shoreline, oak woodland, and hilly uplands.

Facilities: Picnic tables, water, toilet.

Trailhead: Northwest end of parking area.

Directions: From Interstate 580 in Livermore, take the North Livermore Avenue/Central Livermore exit, and follow N. Livermore Ave. south through Livermore, where it becomes S. Livermore Ave., and then, at a sharp left-hand bend on the outskirts of town, Tesla Rd. At 3.7 miles from I-580, you reach a junction of Tesla and Mines roads. Turn right and go 3.6 miles to a junction with Del Valle Rd. Bear right and follow Del Valle Rd 3.2 miles to the entrance kiosk. Just past the kiosk, turn right and go 0.7 mile to a large parking area at the end of the paved road.

From the northwest end of the parking area, past a boat ramp, information board, and gate, begin your hike on the East Shore Trail, a dirt road that leads you on a level grade past stands of gray pine, oak, and white alder. The lake is on the left, and rock cliffs, home to California sagebrush and Indian paintbrush, rise steeply from the road, on the right. Raucous western scrub-jays raise their alarm calls from the trees, tiny Bewick's wrens flit through the underbrush, and sleek cormorants fly low over the water. From time to time on this route, narrow paths diverge from the road; unless indicated in the description, ignore them.

Lake Del Valle is popular with boaters and fishermen, while hikers, equestrians, and bicyclists share trails along the shoreline or in the surrounding hills of this 3,998-acre park. Because of its location—Del Valle is one of the easternmost of the East Bay regional parks—you are likely to find yellow-billed magpies and western bluebirds here, along with more com-

11. East Shore Trail

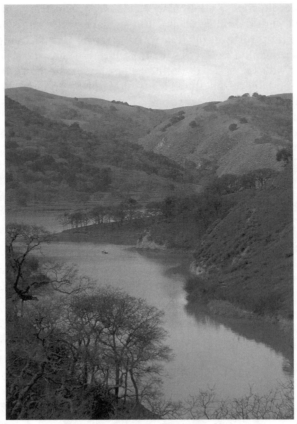

*View southwest across Lake Del Valle from the head of
Badger Cove.*

mon birds such as western meadowlark, Brewer's blackbird, American coot,
and killdeer. At Hetch Hetchy Camp, a clearing with a water fountain and
toilets, you pass the Hetch Hetchy Trail, right, and continue near the lake,
whose level fluctuates by about 25 feet during the year. Across the water, a
high, forested ridge guards access to the Ohlone Wilderness, reached via a
steep climb from the lake's southwest shore.

The route now rises moderately to cross a ridge jutting toward the lake,
and soon reaches a junction with the Ridgeline Trail, right. Continuing
straight, you pass Venados Group Camp, a level area atop another low
ridge, then descend again almost to water level. Early spring wildflowers,
such as California buttercup and Henderson's shooting stars, brings bursts
of color to the grassland here. Just past the camp site, a single-track trail
climbs right, toward a barbed-wire fence, while the road descends to the
lake. Here you turn right, and after passing through a gate, begin a mod-

erate climb through a beautiful, shady savanna of blue oak, coast live oak, and tree-sized redberry buckthorn. The hillside drops steeply left, and as you gain elevation you can look northwest to the far reaches of the lake.

The route descends gently as it follows Badger Cove—a narrow, northeast-pointing finger of the lake—to a T-junction, where you turn left and continue downhill, now on a dirt road. After crossing a creek flowing under the road through culverts, you begin a steep climb in the open, soon reaching a promontory that divides Badger Cove and Swallow Bay. This lovely grassy area, shaded by oaks at about the 2-mile point, is a perfect spot for a picnic. As the route descends from the promontory, you see ahead a large cove, Swallow Bay, where the road swings away from the water and begins to climb into rolling, oak-dotted hills. California ground squirrels scamper across the grass, perhaps communicating with each other in short, high-pitched whistles.

The route climbs on a moderate grade through a road-cut, then descends and bends right, following another narrow finger of the lake to a creek crossing. Now comes a long, steep climb with no shade, on a rutted stretch of road. Your reward, upon reaching a high point, is a grand view of Lake Del Valle, silver water set amid wooded, dark-hued hills. After enjoying this well-earned vista, follow the road as it descends moderately, then levels out in a quiet area of rolling hills and groves of oak. A narrow ravine, left, may hold running water, and the road climbs away from the lake to cross it. There is a stock pond here, and a creek that drains through a culvert under the road, which may be muddy and cut up by cows and horses.

The route bends left, and now a moderate climb to a ridgecrest puts you in view of the lake again, with the dam clearly visible in the distance. Here, at about the 4-mile point, you reach a junction with a single-track trail heading left and downhill to a promontory at the entrance to Heron Bay. If you wish to explore farther, you can stay on the road until it reaches a restricted area near the dam, or turn left and follow the trail through shady groves of California buckeye and oak toward the water's edge. Otherwise, retrace your steps to the parking area via the East Shore Trail, or follow the description in "Ridgeline Loop" below for an alternate return route.

DEL VALLE REGIONAL PARK
RIDGELINE LOOP

Length: 4.8 miles

Time: 2 to 3 hours

Rating: Moderate

Regulations: EBRPD; fees for parking and dogs. (Bicyclists wishing to ride this loop should follow the East Shore Trail to its junction with the Ridgeline Trail, turn right, and then follow the Ridgeline Trail as described below.)

Highlights: Although boating and fishing on man-made Lake Del Valle are the prime attractions of this regional park, there are also fine trails to explore in the surrounding hills. This loop follows the East Shore and Ridgeline trails, taking you from the water's edge through oak savanna to grassy ridgetops, where views extend north to the Livermore Valley, and south to the Ohlone Wilderness.

Facilities: Picnic tables, water, toilet.

Trailhead: Northwest end of parking area.

Directions: See the directions for "East Shore Trail" on p. 80.

Follow the route description in "East Shore Trail," and when you reach the first **T**-junction, before crossing the creek that feeds into Badger Cove, turn right and climb uphill via nicely graded **S**-bends on a wide dirt trail

12. Ridgeline Loop

View north across Lake Del Valle from the Lichen Bark Picnic Area.

through oak woodland. Forest birds such as nuthatches and titmice may be in evidence, although you may hear many more birds than you actually see, especially if the trees have leafed out. The moderate grade soon brings you to a cattle gate; after passing it you reach an open area atop a ridge and a T-junction with the Ridgeline Trail. Turning left, you follow the Ridgeline Trail, a dirt road, as it passes stands of California buckeye and redberry buckthorn, and then reaches a high vantage point with 360-degree views of the lake and its surrounding hills.

Just before going through the next cattle gate, you pass the Hetch Hetchy Trail, right, which connects with the East Shore Trail. Continuing straight, generally level or climbing slightly, the route passes an unsigned road, left, goes through another gate, and passes a connector to the Hidden Canyon Trail, right, at about the 2-mile point. Now you enjoy a peaceful ridgetop stroll, far removed from the lakeshore hubbub of picnickers and power boats; the lake itself is hidden from view here. At the next junction, the Eagle Crest Trail goes right, but you continue climbing to a low point on the ridge ahead, where several paths lead to a viewpoint, right. Bear left and continue to climb, soon reaching a fork. Here you stay to the right, following the Ridgeline Trail on a mostly level course, punctuated by a moderate descent on loose dirt, with a steep ravine to your right.

Now on a narrow ridgecrest, you regain your view of the lake as you drop to a T-junction, where the Eagle Crest Trail heads right, and the Ridgeline Trail, your route, turns sharply left and continues descending on a gentle and then moderate grade. A short rise in the road puts you at a cattle gate; once through, you pass the Squirrel Gulch Trail, right, and continue straight, gaining back some lost elevation. The route hugs the ridgetop for a while, giving you a view east to the park entrance road, but soon begins a moderate and then steep descent to a marshy area where you may be greeted by a chorus of frogs. Here water flows under the road through a culvert and into a steep ravine, right. Now descending gently, you pass a road to the park boundary that joins sharply from the left. This is a moist, shady area where colorful plants such as blue witch and narrow-leaf bush sunflower thrive.

A short, steep pitch brings you to a four-way junction: here your route, the Ridgeline Trail, turns right and continues a gentle descent through oak savanna toward the lake. Following a lovely ravine, right, you pass two entrances to a loop road that circles a water tank, and, continuing your descent, soon reach a gate and the paved East Shore Road. Here you turn right and walk a short distance to the parking area.

◆ Don Edwards San Francisco Bay ◆ National Wildlife Refuge

| 13 | Don Edwards San Francisco Bay National Wildlife Refuge **TIDELANDS TRAIL** |

Length: 1.3 miles

Time: 1 to 2 hours

Rating: Easy

Regulations: Pets are permitted only on the Tidelands Trail and must be leashed at all times. Pets are prohibited inside the visitor center and elsewhere on the refuge.

Highlights: This easy loop, with habitat ranging from upland to salt marsh, is a perfect introduction to the amazing variety of plants and animals, especially birds, found in the refuge. Fall, winter, and spring, when bird populations are highest, are the best months to visit; avoid afternoons, when wind and glaring sunlight may make viewing difficult. Binoculars and/or a spotting scope, along with bird and plant guides, are recommended. Consider also taking one of the guided walks, offered by refuge personnel and volunteers, that concentrate on either birds or plants. Just north of the refuge, across Hwy. 84, is Coyote Hills Regional Park; it would be easy to explore both areas on the same day.

Facilities: Visitor center with interpretive displays, books, maps, and information about guided nature walks and other programs; picnic tables, water, toilet, phone.

Trailhead: On the west side of the parking area, just below the large flagpole.

Directions: From Hwy. 84 at the east end of the Dumbarton Bridge in Fremont, take the Thornton Avenue/Paseo Padre Parkway exit, and go south 0.5 mile to Marshlands Rd., the refuge entrance. Turn right and go 0.5 mile to a stop sign, then left into the parking area.

On the west side of the parking area, there are a large American flag and a sign with information about the refuge. This is our nation's largest urban wildlife refuge, more than 20,000 acres of open space set aside to protect wildlife. Three hundred species of birds and other wildlife, including a number of threatened and endangered species, live here year-round or pass through on migration. The refuge extends from Newark to Alviso and contains a variety of habitat, including open water, salt ponds, mud-flats, salt marshes, and upland areas. The refuge was renamed to honor Don Edwards, a congressman from San Jose, now retired, who was instrumental in creating the refuge through an act of Congress, and then in 1988 expanded it through another act of Congress.

As you walk up the stairs from the west side of the parking area toward the visitor center, you pass a native plant garden containing coyote bush, black sage, toyon and bush monkeyflower. When you reach a **T**-junction with a paved path, turn left and continue uphill to the visitor-center entrance, passing eucalyptus, coast live oak and coast silk tassel on the way. After exploring the visitor center, with its many exhibits, books, and other publications, walk back outside to an observation area overlooking San Francisco Bay.

Looking southwest, the section of the refuge in front of you extends roughly to the middle of the Bay, and includes salt ponds enclosed by levees, as well as Newark Slough, a river of tidewater flowing through the salt marsh just below the visitor center. Salt ponds, remnants of an extensive salt industry that flourished here in the mid-1800s, still exist on the Bay today. Water moves from pond to pond via channels, the salinity

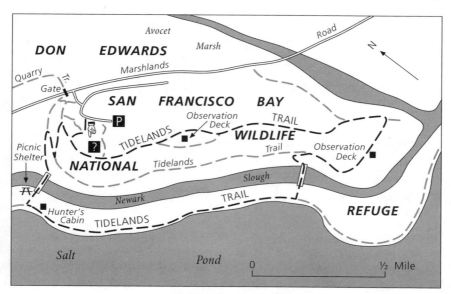

13. Tidelands Trail

concentrates through evaporation, and the highly saline water is eventually processed into salt.

Walking uphill from the visitor center, you follow the self-guiding Tidelands Trail, a loop that will take you through an upland area, beside a salt marsh, across Newark Slough, and along the shore of a salt pond. Gaining elevation on a gentle grade, you can see east to a large salt marsh bordering Marshlands Road, a good area to search for shorebirds on a rising or falling tide. As you climb to a high point, you pass some of the plants growing on the refuge, including toyon, California sagebrush, curly dock, pearly everlasting, and California buckwheat.

A few hundred yards from the visitor center you reach a fork: the left fork goes uphill to an observation deck perched on a bluff overlooking Newark Slough, and the right fork stays level, bypassing the top of the bluff. Bear left, and when you reach the observation deck via steps on your right, take a moment to enjoy a 360-degree view that encompasses much of San Francisco Bay, one of the world's great wildlife areas. Approximately 250 species of birds can be found here, including more than one million shorebirds and waterfowl that use the Bay as a wintering area. Descending from the observation deck on a gentle grade that soon steepens, you pass some picnic tables and then the bypass trail, merging from the right.

As you descend, the route bends left and heads toward the marsh. Shorebirds, terns, ducks, and grebes are the main avian attractions of this refuge, but there are other birds to watch for, including raptors, hummingbirds, and song birds. A dried fennel stalk may offer a perch for the tiny Anna's hummingbird, while the tall spike of a century plant, seen later on, may hold a white-tailed kite. Descending past beautiful acacia trees, which bloom in mid-winter, and a grassy area brightened by yellow Bermuda buttercups, you reach the edge of the marsh, flooded at high tide, where a trail joins from the left.

As the route turns right and heads toward the Bay, you pass a trail heading left into the marsh. Tide and time of year will determine the level of bird activity here, especially for shorebirds, a family that includes oystercatchers, avocets, stilts, plovers, willets, curlews, godwits, small sandpipers, dowitchers, and phalaropes. Most of these birds breed elsewhere, usually during May and June, and arrive here as either migratory visitors or winter residents. At low tide, shorebirds will be dispersed along the many miles of mudflats around the Bay that provide fertile feeding grounds, and at high tide, rising water will force them to congregate in elevated roosting areas, just above the flood. Thus a rising or falling tide is best for viewing shorebirds.

If shorebirds are present, you are almost certain to see one of their tribe called a willet. With its long legs and long bill, this large, drab gray sandpiper transforms itself in flight into a thing of beauty, flashing a bold black-and-white wing pattern as it skims low over the marsh. As you begin to climb through a rocky area, you pass some large century plants, residents of southern California, whose tall stalks offer perches for winged hunters in this treeless part of the refuge. At a rest bench, the route levels and bends right, leading you to another observation deck.

Here the route forks, the right-hand path staying level and the left-hand path dropping past a tangle of blackberry vines to a bridge over Newark Slough. Descend to the bridge, which makes a great vantage point for observing birds as they fly over the marsh and swim in the slough. You can also study the marsh plants—pickleweed, cordgrass, salt grass, alkali heath—spread out below and adapted in varying degrees to their salty surroundings. In the late summer and early fall, marsh gum-plant sports bright yellow flowers, pickleweed adds touches of red and magenta, and dodder, a parasitic plant, paints everything it touches a garish orange.

After crossing the bridge, you reach a T-junction with a dirt path running along the top of a levee next to a salt pond. If the pond is flooded, you may see shorebirds such as western and least sandpipers, dunlin, and black-necked stilts scampering along its edge, probing for invertebrates or picking brine flies off the water's surface. Turning right, you come to a picnic bench and another observation deck, a good vantage point from which to observe the Bay's salt ponds. Although definitely a drastic alteration of the natural habitat, salt ponds have created a unique environment, similar to saline Mono Lake in the eastern Sierra, that supports a breeding population of American avocets, black-necked stilts, and Forster's terns, along with phalaropes and California gulls. Another local

Bridge over Newark Slough.

breeder, snowy plover, is federally listed as a threatened species, prompting the closure, from April through approximately the end of August, of Marshlands Road beyond the visitor-center parking area.

Endangered species, such as brown pelican, peregrine falcon, least tern, clapper rail, and salt marsh harvest mouse, call the refuge home or pass through on migration; despite habitat loss, they have survived thanks to efforts by conservationists, scientists, and government agencies. Other animals, such as grizzly bear and tule elk, are no longer found here. Stories of the Bay's huge supply of waterfowl attracted sportsmen and market hunters to these marshes beginning in the late 1800s. A low red hunting shack, right, was built in the 1930s by Joe Pine of Niles, California, and was occupied by him until the 1960s. A nearby sunken blind, left, offers a hidden site for bird observation and photography. Just past the blind, the route turns right to cross Newark Slough on a long wooden bridge. (The Newark Slough Trail, a 5-mile circuit, starts here and follows the slough west into the marsh.)

Partway across the bridge, another shack, left, has a picnic table and information about the creatures—brine flies and brine shrimp—that live in salt ponds. Once across the bridge, you switchback right, passing a trail leading left to a small amphitheater used for outdoor meetings and programs, and climb to an observation deck flanked by picnic tables in the shade of a eucalyptus. At a T-junction you turn left, joining the path coming from above the first bridge. As you come over a low rise, you reach the paved path leading right and uphill to the visitor center. With the large flagpole directly ahead, follow a dirt-and-gravel path straight to the parking area.

◆ Dry Creek Pioneer Regional Park ◆

14 Dry Creek Pioneer Regional Park
TOLMAN PEAK

Length: 9.6 miles

Time: 4 to 6 hours

Rating: Difficult

Regulations: EBRPD; fees for parking and dogs when entrance kiosk is attended; no bicycles on the South Fork or Dry Creek trails.

Highlights: This route, combining the High Ridge Loop, Tolman Peak, South Fork, Meyers Ranch, and Dry Creek trails, explores a regional park gem—a 1,563-acre oasis in the middle of one of the East Bay's most heavily industrial and residential areas. Scenery, views, and variety of habitat combine to make hiking to Tolman Peak more than just a challenging workout. Mileage and commitment, rather than steepness of terrain, earn for this hike its "difficult" rating.

Facilities: The visitor center in a restored barn has displays of antique farm equipment and information about Hayward's ranching and farming history; toilets nearby in a separate building; picnic tables, water, phone.

Trailhead: From the northeast corner of the lower parking area, turn east and cross a creek on a wooden bridge, then continue straight on a path into a picnic area. The route starts at the visitor center, a big red barn several hundred yards north.

Directions: From Interstate 580 eastbound in Castro Valley, take the Hayward/Route 238 exit and follow signs for Hayward. From the first traffic light, continue straight, now on Foothill Blvd., for 1.7 miles to Mission Blvd, staying in the left lanes as you approach Mission Blvd. Bear left onto Mission Blvd. and go 3.5 miles to Garin Ave. Turn left and go 0.9 mile uphill to the entrance kiosk. At the kiosk bear right and proceed to parking areas; park in lowest one if space is available.

From Interstate 580 westbound in Castro Valley, take the Strobridge exit and go 0.2 mile to the first stop sign. Turn right, go 0.1 mile to Castro Valley Blvd., and turn left. Follow Castro Valley Blvd. 0.5 mile to Foothill Blvd., turn left, and follow the directions above.

From just south of the visitor center, find a dirt path heading east across a large meadow. When you come to a four-way intersection with a north–south gravel road, continue straight and begin climbing the High Ridge Loop Trail, a dirt road, through an open area of tall grass and weeds, leaving behind the trees—sycamore, willow, fig, and California buckeye—that line the creek by the park's picnic area. As you gain elevation, turn around from time to time to appreciate the expanding view of San Francisco Bay. In spring, before the hills begin to turn brown, look for wildflowers such as California poppy, red maids, Ithuriel's spear, and Mariposa tulip. Along the way uphill you may be accompanied by red-winged blackbirds, turkey vultures, or a kestrel hovering overhead. A

14. Tolman Peak

recently built trail connects this part of the High Ridge Loop Trail with the Newt Pond Wildlife Area.

The route levels, turns southeast, and at the 1.1-mile point reaches a junction with the Meyers Ranch Trail, right. This area is used by cows, and you may notice several stock ponds along the way. Continuing straight, you are just east of and below the crest of a ridge that blocks your view of the Bay. But in a few minutes a grand scene is revealed—San Francisco Bay National Wildlife Refuge, Coyote Hills, the Dumbarton and San Mateo bridges, Fremont, Newark, and Union City. A short climb to a notch between two low hills earns your first view of Mission Peak to the southeast, and the southern end of San Francisco Bay.

Just past the 2-mile point, you reach a junction with the Gossip Rock Trail, which heads left. There is a rest bench here, but on a hot day you may want to walk the short distance to Gossip Rock and enjoy the shade of the large California bay laurel trees growing there. Western mead- owlark, western scrub-jay, wrentit, and horned lark are all possible sight- ings in this area. Keep your ears as well as your eyes alert: you will often hear birds before spotting them. Leaving the junction, the road descends through open grassland dotted with rocks and boulders. As the route steepens, notice the large western sycamore trees in a gully on your right. While the gully itself may be dry most of the year, there is enough mois- ture underground to support these large, water-loving trees. California sagebrush, a plant suited to dry areas, grows here on an east-facing slope above the gully.

Bear right at the next junction, unsigned, and continue steeply down- hill through a weedy area of thistle and poison hemlock. Soon you reach a shady stretch where bay, coast live oak, California buckeye, blue elder- berry, snowberry, and vine honeysuckle thrive. The route descends to a lovely valley with a seasonal stream on the right. Just before the 3-mile point, the Pioneer Trail takes off to the right, and your route continues straight. Bigleaf maple joins sycamore in a wet area on the right. Hear a scratching sound in the dry leaves? It could be a spotted towhee, or per- haps even a skunk.

At 3.5 miles you reach a T-junction; here the High Ridge Loop Trail turns right, but your route, the Tolman Peak Trail, goes left. (To shorten this route by omitting the hike to Tolman Peak, turn right and follow the directions below to the parking area.) Turning left on a dirt-and-gravel road, you pass a stock pond and walk through Black Creek Valley, a low- land area of sycamore, eucalyptus, willow, bigleaf maple, coast live oak, and blue elderberry. While the grassy meadow bordering a creek on your right looks inviting, be careful: cows use this area and their pies are every- where. A bit farther, past a cattle pen, left, there is a place to sit and rest in a shady grove of tall eucalyptus.

Pass through a gate, and with a creek on your right, leave the eucalyp- tus grove behind. The route soon crosses the creek on a small bridge, then comes into the open. Farther on, you may have to hop from rock to rock across flooded areas. Soon the Tolman Peak Trail turns left, but you continue straight on the dirt road you have been following, now called the South Fork Trail. Just before reaching the regional park boundary, the South Fork Trail, now a single track, turns left and climbs across a steep hillside into a shady, overgrown area.

As you gain elevation in the shade of bay and coast live oak, the route veers left at about the 5-mile point and comes out of the forest to cross a grassy hillside. Here the trail may be completely overgrown and hard to spot: look for a line of matted grass. As you continue to climb across the southwest slope of Tolman Peak, you begin to see the southern end of San Francisco Bay and the Santa Cruz mountains. As the grades eases, you leave the single-track trail and regain a dirt road, heading northwest. A rest bench provides you with another opportunity to sit and admire the view of San Francisco Bay, and if you look northwest, you can see the trail to Gossip Rock you passed earlier.

As you begin to descend, look for a trail post with a sign for the Tolman Peak Trail. From here, a faint path in the grass leads uphill to the right, heading for Tolman Peak, its summit topped by a grove of bay, buckeye, and bigleaf maple. (The 0.2-mile side-trip to the summit is fun but does not gain you any better views.) As you wind downhill from the trail post on a moderate and then steep grade, you follow a small creek through an area of sycamore, coast live oak, and eucalyptus to a junction, where you turn right and retrace your steps through Black Creek Valley, perhaps to the sound of a woodpecker drumming on a tree.

Hikers northbound on the Meyers Ranch Trail, near the site of Meyers Ranch.

At about the 7.3-mile point, you return to the junction with the High Ridge Loop Trail. Here you continue straight, climbing in the open on a gentle grade, with a creek downhill and on the left. Soon an unsigned road heads left, but you turn sharply right and descend past stands of willow and coast live oak, which give shade that is welcome on a warm day. About 0.5-mile past the previous junction, the route forks: here a dirt road goes left to a fence at the end of Tamarack Dr., but you veer right toward a trail post. This trail post marks the intersection of the High Ridge Loop Trail and the Meyers Ranch Trail. From here, the High Ridge Loop Trail curves left and uphill, and the Meyers Ranch Trail, your route, continues straight and slightly downhill. Dry Creek, which flows into San Francisco Bay via Alameda County's flood-control channel, is on your right, and you are walking upstream. Meyers Ranch Trail, a dirt road, crosses Dry Creek on small bridges several times as the route ducks in and out of trees. Along the way you will notice many narrow paths diverging from the main road; ignore them.

If you hear a bird making a sound like a chickadee, you may glimpse instead its cousin, the plain titmouse, a small gray-brown bird with a small crest and a long tail. Chickadee and titmouse belong to the same genus (*Parus*). Feeding mostly on insects, these lively birds are amusing to watch as they search branches and limbs, sometimes hanging upside down, for their supper. Just past the 8-mile point, you come to a sign for Meyers Ranch; here you will see antique farm equipment, rusted, lying in the grass to your right. Planted poplars and fruit trees show this was once a homestead. In fact, Garin and Dry Creek Pioneer regional parks were once occupied by two cattle ranches. Garin Ranch was obtained by EBRPD in the 1960s, and in 1978 the District received a gift of the 1200-acre Dry Creek Pioneer Ranch from the three Meyers sisters, granddaughters of settlers who came here in 1884. After leaving the Meyers Ranch site, look for a trail post on your left indicating the Dry Creek Trail. Turn left and descend a narrow path, which may be muddy in the spring. After about 100 feet, an unsigned path joins from the left, and just ahead is a narrow wooden bridge over Dry Creek.

Approximately 150 feet past the bridge, you come to a barbed-wire fence and cattle gate. Go through the gate and walk about 75 feet to a trail post and T-junction with the Dry Creek Trail, a single track. Left are wooden steps which the trail climbs on its way to a junction with the High Ridge Loop Trail. Your route, toward Jordon Pond and the visitor center, goes right. Along the upcoming section of the Dry Creek Trail, you will see numbered markers for the park's self-guiding nature trail, a great excursion for children and parents. (A booklet keyed to the numbers can be bought or borrowed at the visitor center.) Your route now winds through a shady area and crosses the creek on another wooden bridge. Dark-eyed juncos frequent this area, and you may spot a western bluebird here, or get buzzed by a hummingbird.

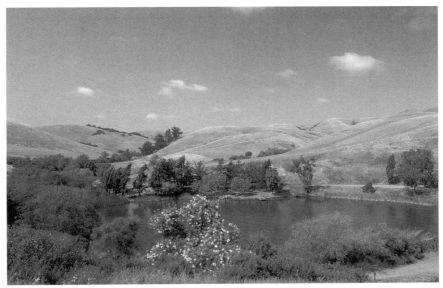

View north across Jordon Pond from the High Ridge Loop Trail.

After crossing a low ridge, you come to a grove of tall bay trees. Here one branch of the trail leads straight to a horse crossing at the creek, but you turn left and cross the creek on a wooden bridge. A dark shape gliding through the trees in this area may be a Cooper's hawk, a crow-sized raptor sporting a streaked breast—reddish in adult birds—and a long, black-and-white striped tail. Once across the creek, turn right and, at a big rock, join the path coming from the horse crossing. Now your route bends sharply left and soon reaches an open area, which may be muddy. Here a path heads left uphill, but you continue straight through a willow thicket, and in 150 feet reach a fork in the trail: right for horses, straight for hikers. Another bridge takes you over the creek, and soon, heading straight, you come to a T-junction at man-made Jordon Pond.

Here a trail post indicates the High Ridge Loop Trail to the left, but you turn right and begin circling the pond on a dirt road, through an area of picnic benches and fire grates. Keep an eye out for birds in this part of the park too; songbirds, such as Bullock's oriole, favor the tree branches, with occasional forays into the open. As you near the end of the pond, you come to a fork in the route: left to a picnic area, right to the visitor center and parking area. Bear right, and just before reaching the visitor center, you will see the start of the High Ridge Loop Trail, right. Turn left here and retrace your steps to the parking area.

◆ East Bay Skyline National Recreation Trail ◆

The East Bay Skyline National Recreation Trail was the nation's first nonfederal national recreation trail, a designation granted by the US Department of the Interior to publicly owned or controlled routes that are close to an urban or metropolitan area; have scenic value; are wide enough to provide for hiking, horseback riding, nature study, and, in some cases, bicycling; and do not allow motor vehicles. The Skyline Trail certainly fulfills all of these requirements and more: it is one of the gems of our East Bay parklands.

When the Skyline Trail opened in 1970, it ran through only Anthony Chabot and Redwood regional parks. Today the 31-mile route stretches from Alvarado Staging Area in Wildcat Canyon Regional Park to Proctor Gate in Anthony Chabot Regional Park, meaning it is possible to walk or ride a horse on an unbroken path from Richmond to Castro Valley. (Bicycles are not permitted on a 6.3-mile section from Lomas Cantadas in Tilden Regional Park to Skyline Gate in Redwood Regional Park.) The Skyline Trail passes through six EBRPD regional parks and preserves: Wildcat Canyon, Tilden, Redwood, Anthony Chabot, Sibley Volcanic, and Huckleberry Botanic. The route also briefly crosses EBMUD land between Tilden Regional Park and Sibley Volcanic Regional Preserve.

While it is possible to hike or jog the entire trail in one day, most people do it in stages; I have broken it into four segments, each of which is easily completed in a day, with a not-too-difficult car shuttle. Be sure to take plenty of water and snacks; there is only limited water along the way. Food, drinks, and cold beer are available at the Willow Park Golf Course,

The official emblem of the trail.

near Proctor Gate, the trail's southern end. There is currently only one overnight camp for individuals and groups, at Anthony Chabot Campground near the southern end of the route. For campground information call (510) 636-1684.

15 East Bay Skyline National Recreation Trail
WILDCAT CANYON TO LOMAS CANTADAS

Length:	10.2 miles
Time:	4 to 6 hours
Rating:	Difficult
Regulations:	EBRPD
Highlights:	This northernmost segment of the 31-mile East Bay Skyline National Recreation Trail uses the Wildcat Creek, Belgum, San Pablo Ridge, Curran, Sea View, Lupine, and Vollmer Peak trails, along with Nimitz Way, to traverse Wildcat Canyon and Tilden regional parks. Although there is steep climbing at the outset, much of the route is along the top of San Pablo Ridge, a generally level course, and views are among the best in the East Bay.
Facilities:	Water and picnic tables are available in the Alvarado Area picnic grounds, northwest of the parking area in Wildcat Canyon, and at Lomas Cantadas near Tilden Regional Park's Steam Trains parking area. Toilets are available at the Alvarado Staging Area, Inspiration Point, and Lomas Cantadas.
Trailhead:	East end of the parking area.
Directions:	This is a car shuttle trip, starting at **Alvarado Staging Area** in Wildcat Canyon Regional Park, and ending at **Lomas Cantadas**, near the Steam Trains in Tilden Regional Park. Drive first to Lomas Cantadas, leave a car there, and proceed to Alvarado Staging Area.
	To reach **Lomas Cantadas**: From Hwy. 24 just east of the Caldecott Tunnel, take the Fish Ranch Rd. exit and go uphill 1.0 mile to a four-way intersection with Grizzly Peak Blvd. Turn right and go 1.1 miles to Lomas Cantadas Dr. Turn right and then immediately left onto a road signed for Tilden Regional Park's Steam Trains, Fire Station, and Corporation Yard. Pass the entrance to the Steam Trains, left, and at a fork bear right and slightly uphill to a large gravel parking area.

15. Wildcat Canyon to Lomas Cantadas

To reach **Alvarado Staging Area**: From Lomas Cantadas, return to Hwy. 24 and follow it west to Interstate 580 westbound, then get on Interstate 80 eastbound. From Interstate 80 eastbound in Richmond, take the Solano Avenue exit, which puts you on Amador St. Go 0.4 mile north to McBryde Ave. Turn right and follow McBryde Ave. 0.2 mile, staying in the left lane as you approach a stop sign. (Use caution at this intersection; traffic from the right does not stop.) Continue straight, now on Park Ave., for 0.1 mile to the parking area, left.

From the east end of the parking area, head uphill past stands of coast live oak, eucalyptus, acacia, and Monterey pine on paved Wildcat Creek Trail, a remnant of Wildcat Canyon Road, which was closed in the early 1980s by landslides. After about 0.25 mile the pavement ends, and you continue on a rocky and eroded dirt road, past an unsigned path, left. Willows signal the presence of Wildcat Creek, downhill and right, which gets its start high on Vollmer Peak and empties into San Pablo Bay north of the Richmond–San Rafael Bridge.

At about the 0.5-mile point, you come to a junction with the Belgum Trail, here a paved road, where you turn left and begin to climb. There is a trail post at the junction with an emblem for the East Bay Skyline National Recreation Trail. As you walk uphill, you pass an area, left, that has been invaded by cardoon, an artichoke relative in the thistle family. A program by EBRPD to control this non-native pest is underway. Passing through a gate, you stay on pavement for about 100 feet and then the Belgum Trail continues as a dirt road. There is a large eucalyptus grove ahead, and if you turn and look west, you have a beautiful view of Mt. Tamalpais.

The route alternates between wooded and open areas, and at one point passes several large palm trees. As you gain elevation on a moderate grade, the view gets even better, taking in Angel Island and the Golden Gate Bridge. Open areas here, mostly grassland, will be decorated in spring with blue bush lupine and California poppy. Beyond another large stand of eucalyptus, the route stays in the open, passing occasional groves of California bay laurel. With every step, more of the Bay Area is revealed, including the San Francisco skyline, which on a clear day appears etched on a background of hills and blue sky.

After reaching a shoulder, the route passes a rest bench, bends left and continues its climb, aiming for the high ground of San Pablo Ridge, just east across an open valley. As the route levels and then drops slightly, the vista extends north across San Pablo Bay to the hills of Napa and Sonoma counties and Mt. St. Helena. At the next flat spot, several junctions sprout trails in different directions. The first junction is a fork; here an unsigned road heads straight but you veer left, reaching a trail post in about 50 feet.

At the post, the Clark-Boas Trail heads left and downhill, a faint trail climbs right, and your route, the Belgum Trail, continues straight. A field of California buttercup brightens the scene here, and nearby is an active California ground squirrel colony. You may see an American kestrel hovering overhead, on the lookout for small reptiles and rodents.

Soon you reach the next junction, a fork marked by a trail post, where you veer right and steeply uphill on the San Pablo Ridge Trail, a rough dirt road. As you crest San Pablo Ridge, you have your first view today of Mt. Diablo, dead ahead. The route now climbs over several high summits, each one affording 360-degree views of almost the entire Bay Area; this park provides some of the best vantage points in the East Bay hills. As you head southeast along the ridgetop, the side of San Pablo Ridge drops steeply left to the narrow valley filled by San Pablo Reservoir. Ahead in the distance lies Tilden Regional Park, crowned by Vollmer Peak (1913′), a forested summit with communication towers; a parking area just south of the peak is your goal for today.

Now descending in open terrain, you reach a junction, at about the 2.75-mile point, with the Mezue Trail, right. Ahead is a large cattle pen. Whatever trees and shrubs grow here, mostly bay and coyote bush, are kept low and flat-topped by the wind, which usually blows from the west. About 100 yards past the Mezue Trail, you pass a dirt road, left, and a trail post that indicates Nimitz Way is straight ahead. Some 50 feet farther, you pass Old Nimitz Way, another dirt road merging from the left. Now on Nimitz Way, you continue southeast on a mostly level course and soon

View southwest to San Francisco from the Belgum Trail.

View east across Nimitz Way and San Pablo Reservoir to Mt. Diablo from the Conlon Trail.

reach a **T**-junction at the base of a hill used during the Cold War as a Nike missile site.

Here a gravel road heads left to the Nike site, and your route, Nimitz Way, now a paved road, goes right. As you curve around the hill Oakland's skyline appears, and you begin to get views toward the south end of San Francisco Bay. In spring, poppies, red maids, and other wildflowers color the grassy hills beside Nimitz Way. A short distance beyond the Nike site you pass a junction, right, with the Havey Canyon Trail. Soon a rest bench beckons, and you can enjoy a glorious view of Mt. Diablo and, to its right, Las Trampas and Rocky ridges, the high walls that form Bollinger Canyon. A bit farther, the Eagle's Nest Trail, a segment of the Bay Area Ridge Trail, joins from the left. From here to near the south end of Anthony Chabot Regional Park, the Bay Area Ridge and East Bay Skyline National Recreation trails follow the same route.

Continuing on Nimitz Way, a poplar route for hikers, bicyclists, in-line skaters, equestrians, and joggers, you next pass the Conlon Trail, which goes straight and uphill to the edge of Tilden Regional Park, then switches back and descends to the Wildcat Creek Trail. At about the 5-mile point, you cross into Tilden Regional Park and enter the shade of a large eucalyptus grove. Soon the Peak Trail joins Nimitz Way from the right, and if you look up the trail you can see a planted stand of cone-shaped trees, giant sequoias, called the Rotary Peace Grove. (These trees achieve their giant status only on the western slope of the Sierra Nevada, their natural habitat.)

Bicyclists gather at Inspiration Point for a ride on paved Nimitz Way.

Now you are walking in filtered sunlight and shade, thanks to the eucalyptus and bay trees that line the route. Beside the road you may find snowberry, blackberry, vine honeysuckle, and much poison oak. At the next junction, the Laurel Canyon Road leads right and downhill through the Tilden Nature Area. As you continue on Nimitz Way, you pass several large stands of mostly Monterey pine, right, and a seasonal wetland bordered with willows, left. Another collection of giant sequoias, right, called the Redwood Grove, was planted by the Berkeley Hiking Club.

The route soon swings left and follows a set of powerlines, and now, rounding a bend, you can see Inspiration Point and its parking area ahead. Rest benches on this part of Nimitz Way are strategically placed to take advantage of the best views, especially of Mt. Diablo and Mt. Tamalpais. Just before reaching Inspiration Point, a little past the 7-mile point, Nimitz Way bends left and comes to a gate. Before the gate, just past some toilets, look for a trail post, right, with the Bay Area Ridge Trail and East Bay Skyline National Recreation Trail emblems. Here you turn right, descend a dirt-and-gravel path, and in about 30 feet turn right again on the Curran Trail, a dirt road.

Continuing to descend over rough ground, you enter an area shaded by bay, coast live oak, and pine. A few hundred yards down the road you pass the Meadows Canyon Trail, right, and in about 50 feet come to a junction with a single-track trail going left and uphill. Climbing up it on a moderate grade across a brushy hillside, you soon reach Wildcat Canyon Road, a paved thoroughfare that runs through the heart of Tilden Regional Park. Cross the road carefully and find the Sea View Trail, a dirt road, taking off left and uphill. This rocky road makes a sweeping **S**-bend to gain altitude on a moderate grade. Eucalyptus trees, which here shade the route, look and smell lovely, but besides being a fire hazard they can fall during wind storms.

As the route bends left you pass a trail, right, to the Quarry picnic area, then continue on a moderate uphill grade, with views extending from Mt. St. Helena to the San Francisco skyline. If you look carefully, you can even pick out your earlier route along San Pablo Ridge in Wildcat Canyon Regional Park. Soon you pass the Big Springs Trail, right; afterwards the uphill grade eases somewhat as you enter a stand of Monterey and Coulter pines. The view now extends west past the Golden Gate Bridge to the Pacific Ocean, and east to Briones Reservoir and the hills of Briones Regional Park. On this stretch you will pass several paths that head left to viewpoints, but your route continues straight and soon begins to climb steeply over rocky, eroded ground.

Reaching a high point, you are rewarded by a 360-degree panorama and a conveniently placed picnic table. In spring, large sunflower-like blossoms of mule's ear appear, giving a festive appearance to the grassy slopes, which are also decorated with lupine and fiddleneck, sporting yellow-orange flowers along a coiled stem. Now the route descends, in preparation for the final push up Vollmer Peak. Reaching a flat spot at about the 9-mile point, you pass the Big Springs Trail, unsigned, heading right and downhill. Beginning to climb again on a moderate grade, you pass a west-facing hillside covered with clumps of California sagebrush

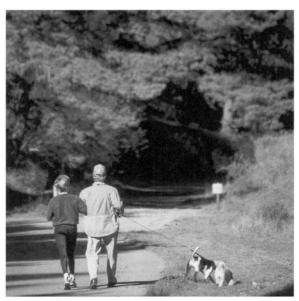

The Sea View Trail is open for dogs.

and black sage, chaparral plants that seem out of place in the fog belt. The road now makes a series of **S**-bends to gain elevation, and soon reaches a junction marked by a trail post.

Here the Lupine Trail, a single track, goes right, bending away from Vollmer Peak, and the Sea View Trail continues over the peak, then descends to the Lomas Cantadas parking area. (Bicyclists must use the Sea View Trail.) Turning right, you pass in about 20 feet a junction with the Arroyo Trail, right, but you continue straight on the Lupine Trail. After several hundred feet, you pass an unsigned trail, right, and then climb through a brushy area to a clearing and a **T**-junction marked with a trail post. Here the Lupine Trail turns right, but you turn left onto an unsigned trail and continue to climb, now on a rocky path. In about 150 feet you reach another trail post and a junction; at this point the rocky path, signed here as the Vollmer Peak Trail, continues uphill, but your route veers right and holds a contour around the west side of the peak. Crossing a steep hillside brightened by buttercups, lupine, mule's ear, and poppies, you soon reach a junction; here the Vollmer Peak Trail turns right, but you veer left and enter a dense bay forest. After about 200 feet you emerge at the Lomas Cantadas parking area.

East Bay Skyline National Recreation Trail
LOMAS CANTADAS TO SKYLINE GATE

Length:	6.3 miles
Time:	3 to 5 hours
Rating:	Moderate
Regulations:	EBRPD; no bicycles; horses and dogs in Huckleberry Regional Preserve are allowed only on the East Bay Skyline National Recreation Trail.
Highlights:	This segment of the East Bay Skyline National Recreation Trail, here also part of the Bay Area Ridge Trail, heads southeast from Tilden Regional Park, crosses EBMUD land and the Caldecott Tunnel, and then traverses Sibley Volcanic and Huckleberry Botanic regional preserves on its way to the northwest corner of Redwood Regional Park. A trip of many ups and downs, from open grasslands to deep wooded canyons, its rewards include dramatic views of Mt. Diablo and a wonderful assortment of trees, shrubs, and wildflowers.
Facilities:	Water and toilets are available at Lomas Cantadas in the Steam Trains parking area; at Sibley Volcanic Regional

16. Lomas Cantadas to Skyline Gate

Preserve visitor center (about half-way); and at Skyline Gate. There are picnic tables across the road from the Steam Trains entrance. A phone is available at Skyline Gate.

Trailhead: At the southeast end of the Lomas Cantadas parking area.

Directions: This is a car shuttle trip, starting at **Lomas Cantadas**, near the Steam Trains in Tilden Regional Park, and ending at **Skyline Gate** in Redwood Regional Park. Drive first to Skyline Gate, leave a car there, and proceed to Lomas Cantadas.

To reach **Skyline Gate**: From Hwy. 24 just east of the Caldecott Tunnel, take the Fish Ranch Rd. exit and go uphill 1.0 mile to a four-way intersection with Grizzly Peak Blvd. Turn left and go 2.5 miles to Skyline Blvd. Turn left and follow Skyline for 2 miles, staying left at an intersection with Snake Rd., to Skyline Gate, on the left, 0.1 mile beyond Shepherd Canyon Rd.

To reach **Lomas Cantadas**: From Skyline Gate, return on Skyline and Grizzly Peak boulevards to the junction of Grizzly Peak Blvd. and Fish Ranch Rd. Continue straight 1.1 miles to Lomas Cantadas Dr. Turn right and then immediately left onto a road signed for Tilden Regional Park's Steam Trains, Fire Station, and Corporation Yard. Pass the entrance to the Steam Trains, left, and at a fork bear right and slightly uphill to a large gravel parking area.

From Hwy. 24, see the directions on p. 99.

From the southeast end of the parking area, walk along the entrance road—passing a paved road that climbs Vollmer Peak, left, and a road to the Steam Trains, right—until you reach Lomas Cantadas Dr. Cross carefully and look left for a trail post with emblems for the East Bay Skyline National Recreation Trail and the Bay Area Ridge Trail. Here you get on a single-track trail and follow it downhill, passing through several gates into a weedy area overgrown with coyote bush, cow parsnip, vine honeysuckle, and poison oak. You are now on EBMUD lands, and the view, when you reach a clearing, extends east toward Orinda and Mt. Diablo. The trail is rough and eroded in places, lined with California sagebrush, bush monkeyflower, toyon, and thimbleberry, and shaded by California bay laurel and California buckeye.

The route levels, then climbs, and soon reaches a T-junction with the deLaveaga Trail, a dirt road. Here you turn right, climb a short steep section, and then enjoy a level walk with a beautiful view, left, of Mt. Diablo.

(Another beautiful, if startling, sight when I hiked here was a large male peacock, perhaps someone's pet.) The road bends sharply left, descends slightly, then levels off and comes to a four-way junction, poorly signed, with a dirt road. To the right and uphill the road reaches a gate and then Grizzly Peak Blvd.; to the left, closed to hikers and horses, the road descends steeply toward the California Shakespeare Festival grounds. Here you proceed straight, finding a single-track trail that leads through a brushy area decorated with Chinese houses, mule's ear, and woodland star.

The trail crosses a steep hillside that drops to your left, and then alternates between open and wooded areas, where blackberry, coffeeberry, and hillside gooseberry grow in the shade of bay and coast live oak. Passing the Berkeley Hills Reservoir, a large EBMUD water tank, you come to a fork marked by a trail post, where a faint trail goes left and uphill and your route continues straight. Soon you reach an open grassy area where the trail turns sharply west toward the Golden Gate Bridge. Below you is Fish Ranch Road, which you will soon cross. Entering a stand of eucalyptus, you pass another faint trail heading right and uphill, but here your route bends sharply left and goes downhill over rough ground. Then, at about the 1.5-mile point, you reach two gates and a paved path leading, in approximately 200 feet, to Fish Ranch Road.

Fish Ranch Road is a busy, high-speed thoroughfare, so take care when crossing. Once on the other side, you will see signs for the East Bay Skyline and Bay Area Ridge trails. Now on a wide dirt trail, you wind on mostly level ground through a wooded area of coast live oak, bay, and blue elderberry. Soon the route begins a moderate descent, then rises slightly to a four-way junction with an overgrown dirt road. The Caldecott Tunnel, built in 1937, runs through the Berkeley Hills near this spot. Here you continue straight, descending past bigleaf maple, California hazelnut, and madrone, on a trail lined with French broom, coyote bush, and poison oak. Several tight S-bends take you downhill quickly, but then a short climb wins back some of the lost elevation.

Reaching a paved road, right, you join it briefly, then continue straight as the road makes a sharp left bend. You are now on a dirt road, heading southeast and climbing on a gentle grade. Willows beside the road indicate water is near; in fact it may be flowing across your path. Soon the road narrows, crosses several eroded gullies that may have water in them, and then begins a gradual climb beside a creek nestled in a shallow ravine, right. This is a beautiful area, deep in a shady forest. A wooden bridge takes you across the creek, and now the route climbs on a moderate grade below a high ridge, right, topped with eucalyptus.

After a long, steady climb, you arrive at the Sibley Volcanic Regional Preserve visitor center, just a few paces north of a small parking area off Skyline Blvd. Here you will find water, toilets, and an interpretive display with information about the preserve's geology, plants, and animals. You have come about 3.4 miles, and have approximately 2.9 miles more to reach Skyline Gate at Redwood Regional Park. Walk on a paved path around the west side of the visitor center; just before reaching a gate you will see a dirt single-track trail, signed for the East Bay Skyline/Bay Area Ridge Trail and the Round Top Loop Trail, climbing right.

Turn right and follow the trail northeast through a wooded area, parallel to and just above a paved road that climbs Round Top (1763'), an extinct volcano and one of the highest peaks in the Oakland and Berkeley hills. As you emerge into a clearing, you pass a trail, left, and in about 100 feet come to a confusing four-way junction. Left, the dirt-and-gravel Round Top Loop Trail, described elsewhere in this book, leads to the volcanic area. Right, a paved path leads downhill, and, in about 50 feet, joins a paved road that goes uphill to a well-hidden EBMUD water tank. Your route continues straight, crosses the water-tank road, and now as a single track heads southeast through a corridor of tall Monterey pines. Your trail soon crosses the paved road to Round Top's summit and in about 125 feet reaches a junction where you leave the Round Top Loop Trail. Here you bear right and follow the East Bay Skyline/Bay Area Ridge Trail.

On a gentle descent through eucalyptus and pine, the route makes a sharp bend right and passes tangled thickets of blackberry, coyote bush, and evergreen huckleberry, then switchbacks on a steeper grade into a dense forest of bay and coast live oak. Soon a clearing brings dramatic views of Mt. Diablo and the high ground around Bollinger Canyon, including Las Trampas and Rocky ridges. More switchbacks over rocky and eroded terrain lead you down a ridge with steep drop-offs on either

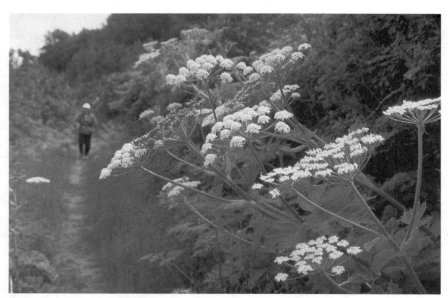

Cow parsnips in flower beside the trail, near Los Cantadas.

side, and eventually you reach the bottom of heavily wooded San Leandro Creek canyon.

Beyond a wooden bridge, a short walk brings you to San Leandro Creek; after fording it, climb about 100 yards to a T-junction, marked with a trail post, and turn right. This is a lush and possibly muddy area, shaded by curving bay trees, home to California hazelnut, creambush, and western sword fern. Now in the Huckleberry Botanic Regional Preserve, you turn sharply left at the next junction and follow the Huckleberry Path, a self-guiding nature trail described elsewhere in this book, on a moderate uphill course. The route traces the indentations of a steep, northeast-facing ridge, trying to maintain a steady elevation. After passing junctions, about 0.4 mile apart, with the Huckleberry Path and Huckleberry Trail, right, the route enters a eucalyptus grove and soon emerges in civilization—Oakland's Montclair neighborhood—where Skyline Blvd. and Pinehurst, Shepherd Canyon, and Manzanita roads all converge.

Pinehurst Road is the paved road you reach first. After crossing it, look left and uphill for a trail leading to a fence marked with the East Bay Skyline Trail and Bay Area Ridge Trail emblems. After passing through the fence, follow a dirt trail uphill across a clearing that opens toward Mt. Diablo, with private homes on your right. Now back in trees, the route levels and then descends to meet the East Ridge Trail, a dirt road. Here you turn right, and perhaps in the company of bicyclists, dog-walkers, and other hikers, proceed a short distance, the last bit of it paved, to Skyline Gate.

17

East Bay Skyline National Recreation Trail
SKYLINE GATE TO MACDONALD GATE

Length: 5 miles

Time: 3 to 4 hours

Rating: Moderate

Regulations: EBRPD; no bicycles on the Golden Spike or MacDonald trails. Bicyclists must follow the West Ridge Trail to the Fishway Interpretive Site, then take the park entrance road south to Redwood Rd., turning right to reach MacDonald Gate.

Highlights: This section of the East Bay Skyline National Recreation Trail, here part of the Bay Area Ridge Trail, follows the West Ridge Trail through Redwood Regional Park for almost that trail's entire length, then uses the Golden Spike and MacDonald trails to reach the northern edge of

17. Skyline Gate to MacDonald Gate

Anthony Chabot Regional Park. While not particularly scenic, the West Ridge Trail gives you an opportunity to see a wide variety of trees and shrubs, including impressive coast redwoods, and, in spring, songbirds and butterflies. The West Ridge Trail spends much time in the open, a consideration on a hot day, but is considerably less strenuous than the alternate East Bay Skyline route, the well-shaded French Trail.

Facilities: Water and toilets are available at Skyline Gate and Redwood Bowl; there are picnic tables at Redwood Bowl, and phones at Skyline Gate and in the parking area near the archery range; horse staging at MacDonald Gate.

Trailhead: At the south side of Skyline Gate parking area.

Directions: This is a car shuttle trip, starting at **Skyline Gate**, Redwood Regional Park, and ending at **MacDonald Gate**, Anthony Chabot Regional Park. Drive first to MacDonald Gate, leave a car there, and proceed to Skyline Gate.

To reach **MacDonald Gate**: From Interstate 580 eastbound in Oakland, take the 35th Avenue exit, turn left and follow 35th Ave. east into the hills. After 0.8 mile 35th Ave. becomes Redwood Rd., and at 2.4 miles it crosses Skyline Blvd., where you stay in the left lane and go straight. At 4.3 miles from Interstate 580 you reach MacDonald Gate, right.

From Interstate 580 westbound in Oakland, take the Warren Freeway/Berkeley/Hwy. 13 exit and go 0.9 mile to the Carson Street/Redwood Road exit. From the stop sign at the end of the exit ramp, continue straight, now on Mountain Blvd., 0.2 mile, and bear right onto Redwood Rd. Go 2.9 miles to MacDonald Gate, right.

From Hwy. 13 southbound, take the Redwood Road/Carson Street exit, turn left onto Redwood Rd. and follow the directions above.

To reach **Skyline Gate**: From MacDonald Gate, return on Redwood Rd. to the junction of Redwood Rd. and Skyline Blvd. and turn right. At the 0.6-mile point, Skyline Blvd. makes a sudden right turn. Follow Skyline Blvd. for a total of 3.7 miles to Skyline Gate, right.

Three of Redwood Regional Park's many trails—East Ridge, West Ridge, and Stream—can found at Skyline Gate. Your route is the West Ridge

Trail, a dirt road that heads south from the parking area and follows a
level course past stands of California bay laurel, coast live oak, coast redwood, eucalyptus, and Monterey pine. (This route is very popular with
dog walkers, and while most clean up after their pets, as required, the few
who do not can make hiking here an unpleasant experience for everyone.)
Butterflies are the prime attraction in late spring along this part of the
hike, filling the air with moving patches of color and landing on thistle
that borders the road. This is also a good spot to listen for birds: you may
hear the chestnut-backed chickadee saying its name, the wrentit giving a
staccato trill, or the mourning dove making its sad call.

The variety of trees and shrubs here makes this an ideal place to learn
about the plants of the East Bay. Besides the common trees already mentioned, you are likely to find blue elderberry, California hazelnut, and
madrone, along with shrubs such as creambush, evergreen huckleberry,
snowberry, and toyon. Coyote bush and poison oak, present throughout
the East Bay, are here too. Where the road makes a sharp right-hand bend,
at about 0.6 mile, you pass the French Trail, left, an alternate and considerably more challenging East Bay Skyline route that is closed to bicycles.
(The French Trail is described elsewhere in this book.)

Staying on the West Ridge Trail, you enter a shady corridor of redwoods, then emerge to find a rest bench with a view east toward Las
Trampas Wilderness and Mt. Diablo. Now the road climbs slightly; where
it crests and starts to descend, you pass an unsigned trail, right, and then
a junction, left, with the Tres Sendas Trail. A short distance beyond is a
path to Moon Gate, right, beside busy Skyline Blvd. Here your route
swings left and climbs in the open, with improving views of Mt. Diablo
and soon your first glimpse of San Francisco Bay. It is said that mariners
entering the Bay would steer a safe course between Yerba Buena and
Alcatraz islands by sighting on two of the tallest redwoods in these hills,
some of which grew to more than 20 feet in diameter.

Those giants are long gone, felled by loggers from 1840 to 1860 to build
the Bay Area's cities. Now redwoods and other native trees compete for
survival with eucalyptus, an fast-growing import from Australia. A program to control the eucalyptus is underway in Redwood and Anthony
Chabot regional parks, and you may see areas that have been logged.
About 0.5 mile past Moon Gate you come to a metal gate across the West
Ridge Trail; just beyond is a large clearing, with an archery range to your
left. Continue straight across the clearing, passing several dirt roads, and
about 100 yards past the gate you meet a paved road leading to a small
paved parking area, which serves the Chabot Observatory and Science
Center offices. (There is a telephone beside the parking area.) Continue
straight and follow the West Ridge Trail, here a dirt path, as it passes
under tall redwoods, climbing and then descending to a fork. Bear left at
the fork, passing the Redwood Bowl picnic area, downhill and left, a convenient rest stop with water, picnic tables and toilets.

Just past the picnic area, at about the 2-mile point, you reach a signed junction where you turn left and follow the West Ridge Trail downhill, soon meeting a dirt road, left, and then a fork. Here the Graham Trail heads right, but you bear left, still on the West Ridge Trail, heading southeast. Several hundred yards past the fork, you pass a short connector trail, left, to the Redwood Peak and Madrone trails. (A short side-trip from here climbs Redwood Peak, at 1619 feet the park's highest point.) Continuing straight through a corridor of Monterey cypress, you soon reach an open, brushy area bordered by eucalyptus and acacia, and begin a descent over rocky and eroded ground. When you reach an unsigned fork bear right on a wide dirt trail lined with French broom—the left-hand trail rejoins your route after several hundred yards. After the two trails rejoin, you come to another fork, this one signed, where the Baccharis Trail branches right, and your route, the West Ridge Trail, bears left.

Soon you pass the Fern Trail, left, and continue to descend, sometimes over bare rock. Near the end of a large clearing, you pass the Chown Trail, left, and, after more bare rock, meet the other end of the Baccharis Trail merging from the right. Now you enter a corridor of eucalyptus, then emerge into an area of chaparral, mostly chamise and manzanita. Here you pass junctions with the Tate Trail, right, and the Orchard Trail, left. (If you are using the French Trail as an alternate route, you will arrive at the West Ridge Trail via the Orchard Trail.) An unsigned path climbs from the Orchard/West Ridge junction through a grassy field, right. As you enter a wooded area the route descends past the Toyon Trail, right, and soon steepens, following a big S-bend down through bay, coast live oak, eucalyptus, and madrone. Use caution here: the eucalyptus capsules scattered beneath your feet are like ball-bearings and can cause a fall. As the grade eases and the route begins to bend left, at about the 4-mile point, look for a trail post with emblems for the East Bay Skyline and Bay Area Ridge trails. Here you turn right onto a short connector trail, and in a few hundred feet come to a T-junction with the Golden Spike Trail.

Turning right on this single-track trail, you descend into a heavily wooded canyon filled with redwood and bay. After leveling out, the route begins to climb on a gentle and then moderate grade, hugging the edge of a steep hillside that falls away left. Now the route levels and begins to descend, bringing you to a brushy area of coyote bush, blue bush lupine, canyon gooseberry, and bush monkeyflower. Passing a closed trail, right, your route bends sharply right, then climbs gently through a lovely, open stretch decorated with Indian paintbrush and California sagebrush. This is a hidden corner of Redwood Regional Park, less traveled and more like a wilderness, with an intimate feel.

Soon you reach a junction, marked by a trail post, where the Golden Spike Trail continues straight, and your route turns left and drops to a flat area, surrounded by bigleaf maple, next to Redwood Road. After crossing a bridge over a tributary of Redwood Creek, carefully cross Redwood

Road, walk through the Big Bear Gate parking area, and find the MacDonald (on the trail post MAC DONALD) Trail, and overgrown single-track, heading southeast. The creek you just crossed comes under the road through a culvert, merges with another that flows under the trail, and now is to your left as you walk downstream. About 100 yards past the Big Bear Gate parking area, you pass the Big Bear Loop Trail, right, and after several hundred more yards reach MacDonald Gate.

View east to Mt. Diablo from just north of Skyline Gate.

East Bay Skyline National Recreation Trail
MacDonald Gate to Proctor Gate

Length: 9.3 miles

Time: 4 to 6 hours

Rating: Difficult

Regulations: EBRPD

Highlights: This lengthwise exploration of Anthony Chabot Regional Park is the southernmost leg of the East Bay Skyline National Recreation Trail, using the MacDonald, Grass Valley, and Brandon trails. The Bay Area Ridge Trail also uses most of today's route, leaving it near the end via the Willowview Trail. The beginning and end of the route are mostly on open ridgetops, and the middle third passes through open Grass Valley and then enters mixed woodland on the slopes above Grass Valley Creek and Lake Chabot. In spring, wildflowers add color to the grasslands, and birds, especially hummingbirds, are everywhere. The only overnight campground currently available for individuals and groups using the Skyline Trail is located on Marciel Rd., near Lake Chabot; for information call (510) 636-1684.

Facilities: Water is available at the Bort Meadow picnic area, a short distance northwest of the junction of the MacDonald and Grass Valley trails; and at the Willow Park Golf Course. Toilets are at Bort Meadow Staging Area on Redwood Rd.; the junction of the Brandon Trail and Marciel Rd.; the golf course; and Proctor Gate. There are a phone and cold beer at the golf course. Horse staging at MacDonald Gate, Bort Meadow, and Proctor Gate.

Trailhead: The east side of MacDonald Gate parking area.

Directions: This is a car shuttle trip, starting at **MacDonald Gate** and ending at **Proctor Gate**. Drive first to Proctor Gate, leave a car there, and proceed to MacDonald Gate.

To reach **Proctor Gate**: From Interstate 580 eastbound in Castro Valley, take the Redwood Rd. exit and go north 2.4 miles to a small unsigned parking area, left.

From Interstate 580 westbound in Castro Valley, take the Castro Valley exit, turn left onto E. Castro Valley Blvd. (which soon becomes Castro Valley Blvd.) and go 1.1 miles

18. MacDonald Gate to Proctor Gate

to Redwood Rd. Turn right and go 1.8 miles to a small unsigned parking area, left.

To reach **MacDonald Gate**: Continue north on Redwood Rd. 8.6 miles from Proctor Gate to MacDonald Gate, left.

From the east side of the parking area, you follow the MacDonald Trail, a dirt road shaded here by California bay laurel and willow, and in about 100 yards pass a trail post and the Bird Trail, right. Immediately after this junction, you cross a creek that flows under the road through a culvert, and begin to climb on a gentle and then moderate grade. Trees and shrubs in this beautiful, lush area include coast live oak, madrone, California sagebrush, creambush, and toyon. The route alternates between open and wooded areas as it winds uphill to the top of a ridge. French broom, bush monkeyflower, and blue bush lupine add color in spring and summer.

Once atop the ridge the route maintains a mostly level course above a deep canyon, right, beyond which rises a forested slope dotted with private homes. At about the 1-mile point, you pass a road, right, leading to a residential area along Parkridge Road, off Skyline Blvd. Now the view improves dramatically, taking in the rest of this regional park and extending southeast all the way to the Sunol/Ohlone Wilderness, Mission Peak, and the Santa Cruz Mountains. Tall Monterey pines nearby make ideal perches for birds of prey such as the American kestrel, the smallest North American falcon. The route here is in the open, crossing rolling grassland studded with clumps of coyote bush. Soon you pass a path, left, that

Climbing trail just south of the MacDonald gate.

Equestrians near Bort Meadow, Anthony Chabot Regional Park.

climbs a grassy hill to a viewpoint; continuing straight, you enjoy a superb vista which now includes EBMUD lands to the east and the high ground around Rocky Ridge.

Passing the Brittleleaf Grade, left, a short trail to a high point, you begin to descend over easy ground, soon reaching a gate. Along today's route you will see unsigned paths leaving the main trail; ignore them. Passing through the gate, you now have a view of the Upper San Leandro Reservoir, left, nestled in a narrow valley. The route continues its descent via several sweeping bends, still along the crest of a ridge. You may be visited here by hummingbirds, especially if you are wearing red, and you may hear California quail calling from a valley, right. (You may also hear the annoying sound of rifle fire from the Chabot Marksmanship Range, which, thankfully, is closed Mondays and Tuesdays.)

Reaching a sparsely wooded area—coast live oak, eucalyptus—you pass a grove of acacia trees, fragrant when in bloom, and then reach a gate. About 100 feet past the gate is a junction marked by a trail post. Here the MacDonald Trail, signed with emblems for the East Bay Skyline and Bay Area Ridge trails, continues straight. But your route, similarly signed, turns right, toward Bort Meadow and Grass Valley. Descending on an eroded single-track trail a hundred yards or so to a junction, you turn left and follow the trail a short distance to reach a trail post and then a gravel road. Once on the road, you turn left, toward Grass Valley, and in about 50 feet reach a confusing intersection, where one road heads left and uphill to the Bort Meadow Staging Area off Redwood Rd., and another goes right, to a parking area and the Brandon Trail.

Continue straight across the intersection to a gate. Your route, the Grass Valley Trail, heads southeast past the gate and through Grass Valley, staying east of willow-lined Grass Valley Creek. (On a hot day, consider taking the Brandon Trail, a shaded route west of the creek; the two trails merge in about 1.5 miles at the Stone Bridge.) Grass Valley, being wide and open, is a good place to observe birds that might otherwise stay hidden in trees. Depending on time of year, you may see, in addition to other species, gold-crowned sparrow, northern flicker, California towhee, and western scrub-jay. Listen for the repeated staccato call of the wrentit, often heard but seldom seen. After passing a cattle gate and a stock pond—Grass Valley is a grazing area—you begin to see a forest of tall eucalyptus, right; an occasional coast live oak gives the trail some much-needed shade on a hot day.

Passing the Redtail Trail, left, you soon enter a forest of eucalyptus, coast redwood, bigleaf maple, bay, and willow, with a tangled understory of poison oak and blackberry vines. Going through another gate and past a possibly muddy area, you reach a T-junction with the Brandon Trail, just a few feet east of the Stone Bridge, a shady rest stop at about the 4.3-mile point. Here you turn left on the Brandon Trail, part of the Lake Chabot Bicycle Loop (a circuit of either 12.42 or 14.41 miles, depending on choice of route). Now on a moderate uphill grade, your route alternates between opens areas and eucalyptus forest, some of which is being thinned to reduce fire danger and allow other species to thrive. Most of Chabot's eucalyptus trees were planted beginning in 1910 by People's Water Company, precursor to the East Bay Water Company, which was later incorporated into EBMUD. On a breezy day, you may enjoy the rustling of the eucalyptus leaves and the strange groaning sounds the trunks make when they rub against each other.

After its climb from the Stone Bridge, the Brandon Trail levels and tries to maintain a contour as it follows the indentations of a hillside above Grass Valley Creek. On this part of the route, you will pass a number of unsigned trails, including the Cottontail Trail and the start of the Escondido Trail. Stay on the obvious main road, which takes you from time to time past lovely patches of spring wildflowers, mostly California buttercup and blue-eyed grass, complimented by colorful clumps of bush monkeyflower, Indian paintbrush, and lupine.

After the Brandon Trail turns uphill again, you reach a connector, left, to the Redtail Trail. Here the Brandon Trail continues straight for a short level stretch, then makes a sharp bend right and begins a gentle climb, giving you the first view today of San Francisco, the Bay Bridge, and Mt. Tamalpais. Just before the 6-mile point, you pass the other end of the Escondido Trail, right, then walk through a heavily logged area where all the eucalyptus has been removed. The route swings sharply right, enters a wooded area, and soon passes a path, left, to the marksmanship range. (A sign here reads CAUTION DO NOT ENTER RIFLE RANGE.)

Next you pass a road to the marksmanship range, clearly marked, and in 100 feet or so come to twin entrances, about 100 feet apart, to the

Loggers Loop Trail, right. Staying on the Brandon Trail, you veer left and descend, crossing a creek, perhaps seasonal, over a culvert and re-entering shade. In about 0.2 mile, you pass the other end of the Loggers Loop Trail and the Mirador Trail, both on the right. Another 0.2 mile brings you to the Two Rocks Trail and a fine vantage point for a view of San Francisco Bay. Here the Brandon Trail turns left and heads east across a open, grassy field speckled with California poppies.

Reaching a gate, you go through it and then cross paved Marciel Road, which runs from Marciel Gate on Redwood Road to Anthony Chabot Campground. Once across the road, continue straight through a paved parking area, past two information boards and onto a dirt path. About 30 feet farther you pass the Redtail Trail, left, and in another 40 feet or so reach a fenced dirt road, the continuation of the Brandon Trail. Pass through an opening in the fence and follow the road southeast on a mostly level grade, past coast live oak and bigleaf maple, to a junction, right, with the Towhee Trail. Continuing straight, the Brandon Trail begins to lose elevation, and crosses an open area where spectacular views extend south to Hayward and the Coyote Hills, and east to Mt. Diablo. At about the 8-mile point, where a rest bench beckons from beneath a coast live oak, the Willowview Trail, part of the Bay Area Ridge Trail, heads left, and your route, the Brandon Trail, swings right.

The route continues to descend, mostly in the open, and now you can see down to Redwood Road and Willow Park Golf Course. To your right, beyond a steep drop-off, are the waters of Lake Chabot. Nearing the end of a ridge, the route makes gentle S-bends downhill, taking its time to reach the golf course. (The golf course, where you will find a restaurant, coffee shop, and bar, is the only place in the East Bay where you can get a cold beer a few paces off the trail.) The Brandon Trail ends at the golf course parking area. To reach Proctor Gate, follow a dirt path that runs just left of and parallel to the golf course entrance road. Before reaching Redwood Road, cross the entrance road, and in about 50 feet you will pass a wooden shed and then come to a fork. Here you bear left and walk parallel to Redwood Road, which is left and just beyond a barbed-wire fence. In several hundred yards you pass an unsigned trail, right, but you continue straight, soon reaching the Proctor Gate entrance road. Turn right and walk about 200 feet to the parking area.

• Garin Regional Park •

19	Garin Regional Park **GARIN PEAK**

Length: 3.25 miles

Time: 2 to 3 hours

Rating: Moderate

Regulations: EBRPD; fees for parking and dogs when entrance kiosk is attended.

Highlights: A perfect introduction to the rolling hills, windy summits, and shaded creeks of 1,520-acre Garin Regional Park, this route uses the Vista Peak Loop Trail to take you past Vista and Garin peaks, from whose summits you will have most of San Francisco Bay displayed for your enjoyment.

Facilities: The visitor center in a restored barn has displays of antique farm equipment and information about Hayward's ranching and farming history; toilets nearby in a separate building; picnic tables, water, phone.

Trailhead: Northeast end of parking area.

Directions: From Interstate 580 eastbound in Castro Valley, take the Hayward/Route 238 exit and follow signs for Hayward. From the first traffic light, continue straight, now on Foothill Blvd., for 1.7 miles to Mission Blvd, staying in the left lanes as you approach Mission Blvd. Bear left onto Mission Blvd. and go 3.5 miles to Garin Ave. Turn left and go 0.9 mile uphill to the entrance kiosk. At the kiosk bear left, find the parking area farthest left, and enter by turning right.

From Interstate 580 westbound in Castro Valley, take the Strobridge exit and go 0.2 mile to the first stop sign. Turn right, go 0.1 mile to Castro Valley Blvd., and turn left. Follow Castro Valley Blvd. 0.5 mile to Foothill Blvd., turn left, and follow the directions above.

At the end of the parking area is a paved, gated road. As you head north on the road, a creek lined with willow and western sycamore will be on your right. The visitor center and picnic areas are across the creek. Soon you pass through a shady corridor of Monterey pine, coast live oak, willow, and white alder. Two very different birds, the California quail and kestrel, may be heard and seen here. The quail, with its repetitive "chi-ca-go" call, is a ground-dweller and travels in flocks, taking flight when flushed. The kestrel, our smallest North American falcon, is a solo acrobat of the skies, hovering and diving on prey, and sometimes giving a shrill "killee, killee, killee" call.

At the end of the paved road you pass a junction with a road heading left to the Arroyo Flats picnic area. About 50 feet past this junction, you reach a cattle gate; now you are on a dirt road. Approximately 100 yards past the gate you reach another junction; here the road continues straight, to the Newt Pond Wildlife Area; but your route, the Vista Peak Loop Trail, shown on older maps as the High Ridge Trail, turns left. Now you climb a dirt-and-gravel road on a moderate grade toward a cattle pen, but

19. Garin Peak

before reaching it, you bear right on a dirt road and continue uphill to a junction with the return part of the Vista Peak Loop Trail, right.

From here you continue climbing through an area of coast live oak and California bay laurel, where a few eucalyptus and olive trees have been planted, and soon you are rewarded by wonderful views, if the day is clear, northwest to San Francisco and Mt. Tamalpais, and south to the Coyote Hills and the Santa Cruz Mountains. Garin Regional Park, and its neighbor, Dry Creek Pioneer, are havens in the midst of bustling commercial and residential areas, some of which press right up to the parks' boundaries. But despite, or perhaps because of, the intense human activity nearby, wildlife, especially birds, finds refuge here. During your hike you may glimpse a small blue and orange bird—the western bluebird—darting out from the trees, hunting for insects. Also here is the western meadowlark, another colorful songbird, with a bright yellow breast, black breast band, and white outside tail feathers.

At about the 1.25-mile point, you reach a junction; here your route, the Vista Peak Loop Trail, turns right and climbs east over open ground. After 150 feet or so, you pass a shortcut, right, that traverses the southwest side of Garin and Vista peaks. Bush monkeyflower and California sagebrush are among the shrubs growing on the high ground around the peaks. As the road reaches the ridgetop just north of Vista Peak (934'), it bends right and heads for the summit of Garin Peak. To reach that peak's 948-foot summit, you leave the road before it starts to descend and walk uphill across a gentle, grassy slope.

Cows graze beside the High Ridge Trail (looking southwest).

From the summit, you have 360-degree views of the Bay Area land-marks, including Mt. Tamalpais (northwest), Mission Peak (southeast), and Mt. Hamilton, the large peak east of and beyond Mission Peak. California poppies, Ithuriel's spear, and yarrow decorate the scene in spring. After admiring the view, return to the road and descend through a gap between Garin Peak and an unnamed peak to the left. As the road makes a gentle descent through open country, the shortcut you passed earlier appears on your right. Now the descent steepens as the route drops into a small valley. Overhead, turkey vultures may be catching ther-mal updrafts or soaring on the breeze.

At about the 2-mile point, in the bottom of the valley, you pass a junc-tion with the Zeile Creek Trail, left. Here the Vista Peak Loop Trail con-tinues straight, then bends right, climbing to a gap between two hills. This is a scenic, more remote section of the park, and the route charts a rolling course across grassy hillsides and through occasional groves of trees. Soon, as the route starts to bend west, you see Newt Pond through some big western sycamore trees, downhill and left. Ahead in the distance are the visitor center and parking areas. If the sun is about to set, listen care-fully here for the "hoo, hoo, hoo-hoo" call of a great horned owl. Just before the 3-mile point, you reach the junction you passed at the start of this loop. Turn left and retrace your steps to the parking area.

20 Garin Regional Park
ZEILE CREEK

Length: 4.25 miles

Time: 2 to 3 hours

Rating: Moderate

Regulations: EBRPD; fees for parking and dogs when entrance kiosk is attended; no bicycles.

Highlights: This route shares the same start and finish with "Garin Peak," but trades the views from Vista and Garin peaks for a quiet stroll along Zeile Creek through a botanically rich, secluded canyon on the park's northeast boundary.

Facilities: The visitor center in a restored barn has displays of antique farm equipment and information about Hayward's ranch-ing and farming history; toilets nearby in a separate build-ing; picnic tables, water, phone.

Trailhead: Northeast end of parking area.

Directions: See the directions for "Garin Peak" on p. 123.

Follow the route description in "Garin Peak" to the junction about 1.25 miles from the trailhead. From this junction, descend just west of north on a dirt road, across open, rolling hills, with the CSU Hayward campus ahead in the distance. With a large barn, left, and a steep hillside dropping right, you pass through a gate and soon reach a junction with a road going

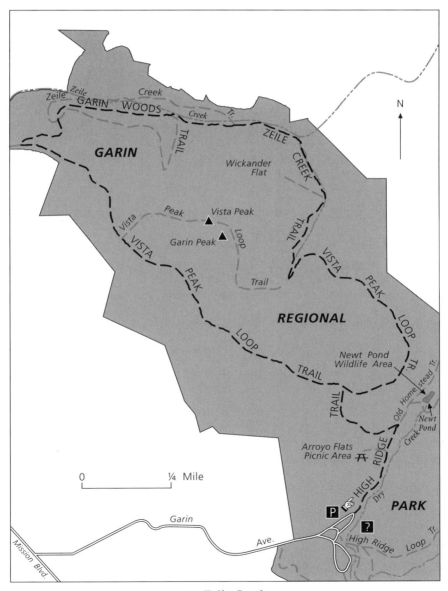

20. Zeile Creek

downhill and right, signed for the Garin Woods and Zeile Creek trails. Turn right and follow the road as it descends into a canyon via several long switchbacks. As the road bends left, you reach a junction with the Garin Woods Trail, a single track for hikers only, heading right. The Zeile Creek Trail, for horses and hikers, continues straight. The area you are about to enter, a botanical treasure trove, is owned by the California State Research Foundation and managed by EBRPD.

Turn right, and about 50 feet after leaving the road, pass a junction with a single-track trail climbing right. Continue downhill, and in another 50 feet you enter a cool, shady forest of California bay laurel, with toyon, poison oak, blackberry vines, ferns, and mosses growing on the damp hillside. This hidden canyon, at about the 2-mile point, contrasts wonderfully with the open grassland you have been hiking across so far. Zeile Creek is at the bottom of a steep ravine, left. Soon the route levels off, then descends again on a gentle grade. You may notice a faint path coming up from the creek; about 200 feet farther, you come to a fence, with a housing development visible uphill on an open hillside, left. Just past the fence, another path comes in from the left, but you turn right and begin a gentle climb.

This area may be muddy in wet weather, and moisture stored year-round in the soil promotes a wide variety of plants, among them willow, bay, coast live oak, California buckeye, coffeeberry, vine honeysuckle, and canyon gooseberry. As you come over a rise, you pass an unsigned trail, right, and soon after, the Zeile Creek Trail joins from the left. The area you are now in, Wickander Flat, may be flooded during and after wet weather, because the trail is right beside the creek. Now you climb away from the creek on a moderate grade, past another fence, and soon come out of the trees, making an abrupt transition back to grassland.

After passing an unsigned road, right, the route, now a dirt road, bends left and continues uphill. Just before the 3-mile point, you reach a T-junction with the Vista Peak Loop Trail. Turn left and follow the route description in "Garin Peak" from the 2-mile point back to the parking area.

◆ Hayward Regional Shoreline ◆

<table>
<tr><td>21</td><td>Hayward Regional Shoreline
COGSWELL MARSH</td></tr>
</table>

Length: Approximately 3.3 miles

Time: 2-3 hours

Rating: Easy

Regulations: EBRPD; no dogs.

Highlights: The Hayward shoreline is one of the best places in the East Bay to view shorebirds. The trails are easy and bring you close to the water. The birds are used to people and will generally stay put. The route goes through a restored marsh—a great example of how nature, with a little help, can reclaim areas previously altered by human intervention. The area gets windy in the afternoon, especially during spring and summer.

Facilities: A small visitor center, open 10 A.M. to 5 P.M., closed Mondays, with toilets, water, books, maps, and information.

Trailhead: Behind the visitor center.

Directions: From Hwy. 92 eastbound at the east end of the San Mateo Bridge in Hayward, take the Clawiter Road/Eden Landing Road exit. At a four-way stop, turn left onto Clawiter Rd., cross over the highway, and at the next four-way stop turn left onto Breakwater Ave. Almost immediately, Breakwater Ave. turns left, then veers right and heads west, parallel to Hwy. 92. Follow Breakwater Ave. to the Hayward Shoreline Interpretive Center, about 1 mile from Clawiter Rd. Park on the right side of the road.

From Hwy. 92 westbound at the east end of the San Mateo Bridge in Hayward, take the Clawiter Road/Eden Landing Road exit, and from the four-way stop at the end of the exit ramp go directly across Clawiter Rd. onto Breakwater Ave., then follow the directions above.

From just behind the visitor center, operated by the Hayward Area
Recreation and Park District, take a moment to look out over the system
of marshes around you. To your left are the Oliver Ponds, remnants of a
vast salt-harvesting industry that began during the mid-19th century in
San Francisco Bay and still exists today in limited areas of the Bay. Four
generations of the Oliver family farmed salt on the Hayward shoreline,
and the Hayward Area Recreation and Park District (HARD) purchased
the ponds from the Oliver estate in the mid-1990s. The area directly in
front of you is the H.A.R.D. Marsh, former salt ponds restored to tidal
action in 1986. Beyond lies the fresh and brackish water Hayward Marsh,
an EBRPD project created in 1988 to naturally cleanse and release into the
Bay some one million gallons per day of secondary treated sewage dis-
charge water. To your right is habitat managed for the endangered salt
marsh harvest mouse.

Turn left and begin walking west on a wide, hard-packed dirt path;
your route will be along the levees that criss-cross this area. The 1-mile
trail from the visitor center to the Bay honors Arthur Emmes, a prominent
Castro Valley optometrist and member of the Hayward Area Shoreline
Planning Agency's citizen advisory committee, who championed acquisition and development of trails along the shoreline. After reaching the Bay,
this trail joins EBRPD's trail system, which continues north about 7 miles
to the San Leandro Marina.

As you walk toward San Francisco Bay, following a slough on your left,
scan the marsh to your right for shorebirds, a class that includes oystercatchers, avocets, stilts, plovers, willets, curlews, godwits, small sandpipers, dowitchers, and phalaropes. In just a few minutes you may see
a fine assortment, including black-necked stilts, American avocets,

21. Cogswell Marsh

The Hayward Regional Shoreline Interpretive Center on Breakwater Ave.

long-billed curlews, marbled godwits, dowitchers, and sandpipers, along with other water-loving birds such as egrets, ducks, and gulls.

Once you reach the shoreline, in about 0.8 mile, the route turns north and runs along the water. From here you have terrific views, on a clear day, of San Francisco, Oakland, the Bay and San Mateo bridges, the Oakland and Berkeley hills, Mt. Diablo, and Mt. Tamalpais. If the tide is out, you will see shorebirds during most of the year, feeding on the mud flats at the edge of the Bay. Being migratory, many shorebirds fly north to Canada, Alaska, and the Arctic to breed in May and June, which accounts for their absence from our area during those months. But during the rest of the year, and especially in winter, San Francisco Bay hosts one of the largest concentrations of shorebirds in North America, sometimes more than one million strong. The Bay is also the most important stop on the Pacific Flyway, the aerial route between northern breeding grounds and wintering areas in southern California, Mexico, and Central and South America.

As you turn north, the route crosses another slough, whose water passes under the dike through large pipes, and makes several jogs on its way around the west edge of Hayward Marsh. Two of the most common marsh plants, pickleweed and cordgrass, are evident here. Pickleweed, a low-growing plant with many stubby branches, thrives in the middle marsh, where it is moistened only briefly by the tide's salty flow. Light green in spring and summer, pickleweed brightens marshes in the fall as it turns red and purple, but winter finds it dull brown. Cordgrass, 1 to 4 feet tall and dark green, lives low in the marsh and is well adapted to twice-daily flooding by the tide. Cordgrass, like other plants, is an air purifier, consuming carbon dioxide and carbon monoxide, and releasing oxygen into the atmosphere.

After walking about a mile, you reach a junction with a path going right, which you will use later on your return. But for now, turn left and return to the shoreline at Johnson's Landing, a cove with a small beach and breakwater. John Johnson began harvesting salt from San Francisco Bay by putting levees around natural pools in the marsh. This landing, like others along the shoreline, was built in the 1850s for boats that carried salt, waterfowl, agricultural products, and passengers to San Francisco.

As you turn north and continue walking along the water's edge, a sweeping view of the Alameda County shoreline stretches before you all the way to Oakland. This part of the route is also a segment of the San Francisco Bay Trail, which uses existing trails and roadways owned and maintained by various public agencies and will some day encircle the Bay. About half of the Bay Trail's proposed route has been completed. On your right is Cogswell Marsh, named in honor of Dr. Howard L. Cogswell, a well-known Bay Area shorebird biologist, educator, and member of EBRPD's board of directors from 1971 to 1982. This large marsh consists of several former ponds restored to tidal action by an EBRPD levee-breaching project completed in 1980.

Soon you reach the first of two bridges which span breached levees in this section of the shoreline. Here is an excellent vantage point from which to study shorebirds feeding on the mud flats below. Time your arrival just

Birders explore the Hayward Regional Shoreline near Johnson's Landing.

after high tide, when the water begins to recede and more and more of the flats are being continuously exposed. Different shorebirds have evolved different strategies for feeding, from the avocet's side-to-side swiping motion, to the dowitcher's rapid, machine-like drilling. Our largest North American shorebird, the long-billed curlew, probes deep in the mud for small clams using its long, down-curved bill. The bird will then rinse off its muddy prize before swallowing it whole.

After crossing the first bridge, continue north, with the Bay on your left and the salt marsh spreading out to your right. Soon the route turns right, away from the bay, and heads east. On your left is a large inlet, with the second bridge ahead. On a rising tide, shorebirds feeding in the shallows of this inlet are pushed toward shore, so this is another great vantage point for observing their antics. And because you are facing north as you look out across the inlet, the sun is behind you for most of the day, another plus when viewing birds. Across the Bay to the northwest, the light-colored buildings of San Francisco are thrown into relief by the dark background of Mt. Tamalpais.

At the second bridge, after you've had your fill of birding, turn right and begin your return trip along a dike with a slough and salt marsh to the left. (If you want a longer hike, cross the bridge and follow the route northeast, then west to Triangle Marsh and Hayward's Landing.) Check the slough for ducks; especially pretty are ruddy ducks in bright plumage. After walking south for about 0.5 mile, turn right on a dike leading back to the bay. If the tide is coming in, especially just before sunset, you may see large flights of shorebirds coming to roost in Hayward Marsh, left. Soon you rejoin the original route near Johnson's Landing; turn left here and retrace your steps to the visitor center.

◆ Huckleberry Botanic Regional Preserve ◆

<table>
<tr><td>22</td><td>Huckleberry Botanic Regional Preserve
HUCKLEBERRY NATURE PATH</td></tr>
</table>

Length: 1.9 miles

Time: 1 to 2 hours

Rating: Easy

Regulations: EBRPD; no bicycles, dogs, or horses.

Highlights: This hike, an easy self-guiding loop through a 235-acre botanical treasure trove, is simply not to be missed, especially from late winter through spring, when its shrubs and flowers are in bloom. Among the highlights are two rare plants: western leatherwood, which is hard to find elsewhere in the East Bay; and pallid, or Alameda, manzanita, found only here and in Sobrante Ridge Botanic Regional Preserve, near El Sobrante. **Bold face** numbers in the route description refer to numbered markers along the trail and plant descriptions in "Huckleberry Self-Guided Nature Path," an interpretive pamphlet available at the trailhead. Because this is a short and easy hike, you may also have time to visit nearby Sibley Volcanic Regional Preserve, just 0.4 mile north on Skyline Blvd.

Facilities: Toilet

Trailhead: On the southeast side of parking area.

Directions: From Hwy. 24 just east of the Caldecott Tunnel, take the Fish Ranch Rd. exit and go uphill 1 mile to a junction with Grizzly Peak Blvd. Turn left and go 2.5 miles to a junction with Skyline Blvd. Turn left and go 0.5 mile to a parking area, left.

While a walk in the woods is always enjoyable, Huckleberry Botanic Regional Preserve offers much more: a chance to see and learn about a wide variety of native plants, some only found in a few areas of the East Bay. The soil in parts of the preserve is rocky and lacks nutrition for all but the hardiest chaparral species, such as manzanita. Establishing itself on "barrens," manzanita helps create soil that is then hospitable to other shrubs and trees, a process called "plant succession." As you start out on the dirt hiking trail, pick up a copy of the pamphlet, "Huckleberry Self-Guided Nature Path," published by EBRPD. Keyed to the numbered posts along the trail, this pamphlet will help you identify more than a dozen native plants.

About 100 yards past the trailhead, the Huckleberry Path forks: descend left on a series of switchbacks through a fragrant forest of California bay laurel and coast live oak. Evergreen huckleberry, the plant that gives this park its name, is here, along with two other berry producers, blackberry and blue elderberry. Soon you come to a large madrone, **1**, an evergreen tree with smooth, reddish bark and finely-toothed elliptical leaves. Related to and sometimes mistaken for manzanita, madrone in spring produces lovely white flowers and in fall red berries which are eaten by birds. Also in this area are toyon, vine honeysuckle, and bush monkeyflower.

A short walk brings you to California hazelnut, **2**, a relative of the commercial filbert. The bright green leaves of this shrub, renewed each spring, feel like pieces of soft felt. When you come to the next fork, bear right and begin to climb; here the Huckleberry Path joins the East Bay Skyline/Bay Area Ridge trail, on its way between Sibley Volcanic Regional Preserve and Redwood Regional Park. Be sure to scan the ground for spring wildflowers, such as red columbine, as you walk.

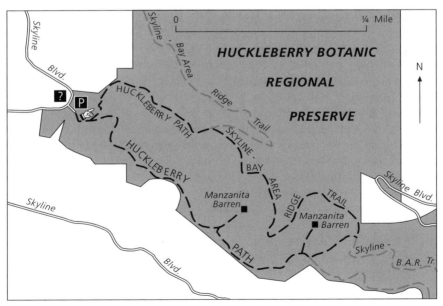

22. Huckleberry Nature Path

Thriving in damp areas beneath California bay laurel and coast live oak is western sword fern, **3**. Long, pointed fronds give this fern its name and distinguish it from wood fern, **4**. To compare the two, find the wood fern, then look across the trail for western sword fern growing on the downhill slope. Now the route swings left to contour around a bulge in a ridge, then continues its southeast course and arrives at a grove of large bay trees, **5**. Here the towering bays have established dominance by depriving their would-be competitors of sunlight. Just past this grove is a junction; here the East Bay Skyline/ Bay Area Ridge Trail continues straight, but your route, the Huckleberry Path, climbs steeply right via wooden steps and switchbacks.

Hikers scan the skies from a perch on a manzanita "barren."

At about the 1-mile point, after a short climb, you reach a T-junction with the upper segment of the Huckleberry Path. Turn right, and almost immediately come to a junction, **6**. Here you turn right and climb a rocky path to a manzanita barren—a dry, gravelly plateau in the early stage of succession from manzanita to huckleberry. Also here are canyon live oak and shrub chinquapin, two plants described in the brochure as numbers **10** and **13**. From this perch your views range northwest to Round Top, one of the highest summits in the Oakland and Berkeley hills, and east to Mt. Diablo, the highest peak in the East Bay.

Back at the main path, you turn right and continue on a shady, rolling course to search for the lavender-to-blue flowers of Douglas iris, **7**, a spring bloomer. At about the 1.3-mile point, turn right at a junction and descend on a side trail through the woods to find markers **8**, **9** and **10**. As you begin walking on this trail, look for a short path leading right and downhill to a rare shrub called western leatherwood, **8**. The yellow flowers of this shrub, which gets its name from the flexibility of the wood, appear in the winter, when its branches are still bare. Climb back to the side trail, turn right, and walk to another manzanita barren, where you will find jimbrush, **9**, and canyon live oak, **10**.

Now retrace your steps to the main trail, where you turn right. Walking past stands of huckleberry, **11**, you soon reach an area, **12**, where the plants are in an intermediate stage of succession. Here manzanitas are being replaced by other, faster-growing plants, such as huckleberry and shrub chinquapin, **13**. Two types of manzanita grow along this exposed stretch of trail: brittle-leaf, **14**, and pallid, **15**. Pallid manzanita is rare, growing only in this preserve and Sobrante Ridge Botanic Regional Preserve, an area described elsewhere in this book. Brittle-leaf manzanita is a small shrub with a burl, or knot, at its base and stiff-pointy leaves with stems. Pallid manzanita is a large shrub whose gray-green leaves tightly clasp its reddish branches, attaching with hardly any stem.

In addition to its notable plants, this preserve is home to many birds. Two species here are often heard rather than seen—wrentit and bushtit. The wrentit's song, given year-round, sounds like someone trying, without luck, to start a car: a series of sharp notes and then a trill. This sparrow-sized brown bird, a member of the thrush family, is usually alone or with a mate. Bushtits, tiny gray birds belonging to their own family, travel in swarms and make high-pitched twittering sounds from the tree limbs where they feed.

A bit farther, you come to coast silk tassel, **16**, a shrub with stiff, curly leaves that are shiny green on top, gray-green underneath. The tassel in its name refers to the flower clusters hanging in winter from male plants. The route now descends via wooden steps into a dense bay forest, where you may hear a spotted towhee rustling in the leaf litter, and then levels off in an area where you can see pink flowering currant, **17**. This beautiful shrub dangles its delicate flowers from bare branches in the winter, then produces fresh green leaves that are somewhat sticky. Just past marker **17** you reach a junction; here you continue straight and retrace your steps to the parking area.

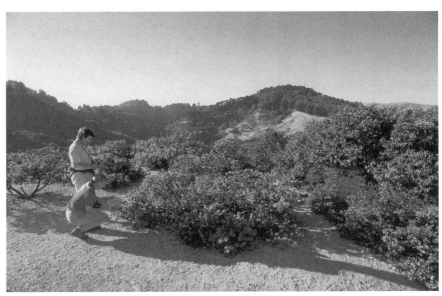

Huckleberry Preserve is an excellent place to study native East Bay plants.

◆ Joaquin Miller Park ◆

<table>
<tr><td>**23**</td><td>Joaquin Miller Park
REDWOOD FOREST</td></tr>
</table>

Length: 3.6 miles

Time: 1.5 to 2 hours

Rating: Moderate

Regulations: City of Oakland, Office of Parks, Recreation, and Cultural Affairs; no dogs in picnic areas; dogs on leash at all times elsewhere; bicycles not allowed on the Wild Rose, Fern, and Ravine trails, or on the Palos Colorados Trail between Sinawik Cabin and Joaquin Miller Court.

Highlights: This park, adjacent to Redwood Regional Park, offers many of its neighbor's attractions in a more intimate and less crowded setting. Using the Sunset, Cinderella, and Sequoia–Bayview trails, this loop explores forests of redwood, Monterey cypress, eucalyptus, and acacia, and offers a fine view of Oakland and San Francisco.

Facilities: Ranger station, with maps, brochures, and displays on the geology and trees of the park, open 9 A.M. to 5 P.M. seven days a week; toilets; water; picnic tables.

Trailhead: In front of the ranger station.

Directions: From Hwy. 13 northbound in Oakland, take the Joaquin Miller Road/Lincoln Avenue exit, bear right onto Joaquin Miller Rd., and go 0.8 mile to Sanborn Dr., the park entrance. Turn left and go 0.1 to the ranger-station parking area, left.

From Hwy. 13 southbound in Oakland, take the Joaquin Miller Road/Lincoln Avenue exit, stay left, and at a stop sign turn left onto Monterey Blvd. Go several hundred feet to Lincoln Ave., turn left and cross over Hwy. 13. Now on Joaquin Miller Rd., follow the directions above.

From the front of the ranger station, leave the parking area and walk south along Sanborn Drive, in a corridor of California bay laurel, coast live oak, madrone, and pine, toward the park entrance. After about 0.1 mile, just before you reach Joaquin Miller Road, you come to a yellow gate, left; beyond it there are two routes. The route heading sharply left, a dirt path, goes downhill to the Lower Meadow and Pinewood picnic areas. The dirt-and-gravel road heading straight, your route, goes downhill toward the Upper Meadow and Greenwood picnic areas.

After a short distance, you reach a flat area where Palo Seco Creek flows under the road. Just past the creek is a T-junction with the Sunset Trail, as well as two paths—one left, the other right—leading to open, grassy meadows. Turn left at the junction and follow the Sunset Trail, a dirt road, northwest past stands of bay and coast redwood, which tower over a tangled understory of ferns, blackberry vines, and woodland strawberry. With a meadow on your left, you enjoy a level walk on a well-maintained road carpeted with pine needles and leaf litter, passing a path going right and uphill to a picnic area, and another joining your road from the left.

Following Palo Seco Creek, left, you descend gradually, and soon pass the Sinawik Trail, a dirt path that crosses the creek on a small stone bridge. About 100 feet farther, you come to a junction where the Sunset Loop

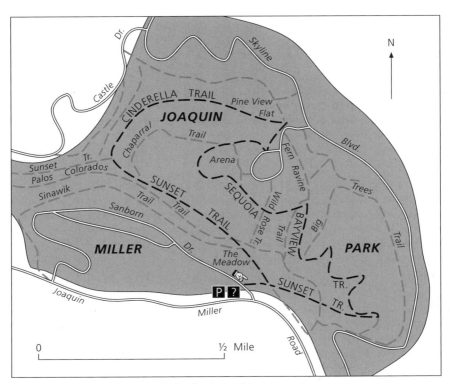

23. Redwood Forest

heads right and steeply uphill. Continue straight on the Sunset Trail, and in another 100 feet or so, you pass a junction, left, with the Palos Colorados Trail. Soon the surrounding dense forest ends, and you emerge into a more open area, where bay and redwood are joined by bigleaf maple, blue elderberry, pine, and toyon. Two non-native plants that thrive along this section of the route are French broom, an invasive member of the pea family enjoyed for its bright yellow flowers, and cotoneaster, a bushy shrub with small oval leaves and bright red berries.

With Palo Seco Creek now in a deep ravine, left, you pass the Chaparral Trail, unsigned, heading right and uphill; here your route narrows to a single track as it crosses a slope prone to landslides. Ahead on a ridge is a forest of eucalyptus, and soon you reach a tributary of Palo Seco Creek, flowing under the trail through a culvert. Where the Sunset Trail swings sharply left, you turn right onto the Cinderella Trail at an unsigned junction and begin climbing steeply uphill. The trail, rocky and eroded, follows a beautiful ravine lined with willows, right, that holds the tributary creek. The grade eases somewhat as you climb mostly in the open, past hillsides of French broom, California sagebrush, and a few bushes of California barberry, a holly-like shrub rarely seen in the East Bay parklands.

This section of the route may be muddy; in one place water may be flowing across the trail from a pipe on the left. As you gain elevation, the eucalyptus on the ridge above and left give way to pines, while closer at hand, blackberry vines replace the French broom. Crossing the creek, which flows under the trail, you begin a series of alternately steep and level sections, past stands of pink flowering currant and thimbleberry. At about the 1.4-mile point, just before you reach Pine View Flat, a level clearing carpeted with wood chips, look for an unsigned junction. Here you turn sharply right and follow the Sequoia–Bayview Trail, a single track, as it skirts below a parking and picnic area, with a restroom above and left.

After several hundred yards you come to a junction marked by a trail post; here you turn right and walk about 100 feet to a T-junction, also marked, with a path that is paved to your left and dirt to your right. Turn right and follow the Sequoia–Bayview Trail on a level course, past an overgrown area of evergreen huckleberry, creambush, and gooseberry. Soon you pass an path, left, leading uphill to the Sequoia Arena, an equestrian facility. A bit farther, you come to a sign on the right side of the trail that reads NATURE TRAIL CONTINUES, and then reach a junction where your route, the Sequoia–Bayview Trail, turns left, and the Chaparral Trail continues straight.

Climbing from the junction on a moderate grade, the route then levels and enters a magical forest—cool, quiet, and secluded—of Monterey cypress, pine, and, farther along, acacia, an import from Australia. At about the 2-mile point, you pass a junction with a trail that heads left and uphill to the horse arena. Now the route maintains a contour as it follows the indentations in a steep, southwest-facing ridge that dominates this park, leading you through a eucalyptus forest and then into the domain of coast redwood, a true East Bay native.

Once in the redwoods, you pass a four-way intersection with the Wild Rose Trail, and then, at the head of a ravine where a stream flows under the trail, are junctions with two branches of the Fern Ravine Trail. Where the Sequoia–Bayview Trail swings sharply right, one branch of the Fern Ravine Trail goes left and uphill. About 75 feet farther, the other branch veers right and downhill. Continuing on a level course, you soon pass a junction, left, with the Big Trees Trail, and also with an unsigned path heading right and downhill. California hazelnut, with fuzzy, toothed leaves, and snowberry, with small round leaves, some of which are irregularly indented, thrive here. Passing another unsigned path, right, you now reach a clearing where a view west across San Francisco Bay allows

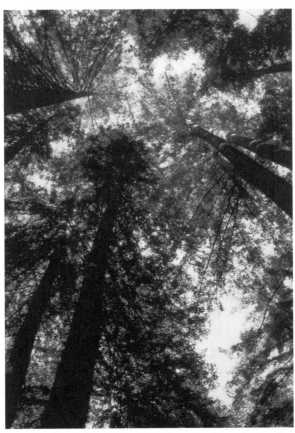

Towering second-growth coast redwoods, descendants of a once-magnificent forest.

the trail to live up to its name: from this vantage point, the skylines of San Francisco and Oakland are aligned one behind the other.

As the route finishes a right-hand bend at the head of a little canyon, at about the 3-mile point, where water may spill across the trail in wet weather, you will find a sign marking a junction, right, with the Sunset Trail, your return route downhill to the meadow area. On this trail the grade is moderate at first, then gentle, and the ground is rough and rocky in places, with magnificent redwoods towering overhead. As you near the end of the descent, you pass a trail post, right, signed for the Sunset and Palos Colorados trails. There are also several paths here joining on the left. About 200 feet past the trail post is a sign, which you must face uphill to read, commemorating Harold Ireland, a nature lover and mountain climber who for more than 60 years led hikes in the Bay Area, and especially on this trail. Resuming your downhill course, you pass two paths heading right and uphill, the first unsigned, and the second signed as the Sunset Loop.

Continuing straight on the Sunset Trail over level ground, you pass the Greenwood picnic area, left, a grassy meadow, and another unsigned path, right. Look for Fremont star lily—spikes of six-petaled white flowers held upright on tall triangular stems—beside the trail here in spring. Soon you reach the junction beside Palo Seco Creek where you began this loop; now retrace your steps uphill to the parking area by the ranger station.

• Lafayette Reservoir •

<table>
<tr><td>**24**</td><td>Lafayette Reservoir
RIM TRAIL</td></tr>
</table>

Length:	4.7 miles
Time:	2 to 3 hours
Rating:	Moderate
Regulations:	EBMUD; parking fee; Trail Use Permit not required; no horses. Roller-skating and skateboarding are prohibited, except bikes and roller skates are allowed: Tuesdays and Thursdays 12 noon to closing; Sunday mornings, opening to 11:00 A.M.
Highlights:	This walk around Lafayette Reservoir on the Rim Trail, with great bird-watching opportunities and several high points affording 360-degree views, is a great introduction to the parklands administered by EBMUD.
Facilities:	Visitor center/boat house, picnic tables, toilet, phone, water.
Trailhead:	Foot of cement staircase at the north end of parking area.
Directions:	From Hwy. 24 in Lafayette, take the Acalanes Road/Mt. Diablo Blvd. exit, and go east 0.8 mile on Mt. Diablo Blvd. to the entrance to EBMUD's Lafayette Reservoir Recreation Area. Turn right and go 0.2 mile uphill on the one-way entrance road, then turn left for the main entrance, or right for the annual-pass entrance. Parking is on top of the dam. There are meters for up to 2 hours; or you can buy an all-day pass at the entrance station, $5 for cars and motorcycles, $12 for vans. (If the entrance station is closed, you can buy an all-day parking pass at the visitor center, 0.25 mile west around the reservoir.)

Lafayette is the smallest of five EBMUD reservoirs in the East Bay that have public trails along their shores. Built in the mid-1920s and designed as a much larger facility to hold water from the Sierra, its size was reduced when, during construction, the dam settled and cracked. For safety's sake the dam was widened and the size of the reservoir reduced. The intake tower, which stands high and dry above the water near the dam, was built before problems arose; its height shows the planned depth of the reservoir. Today the reservoir, with 115 acres of surface area, is a recreation area and emergency water supply.

Birds are plentiful around Lafayette Reservoir, so start looking even before you leave the parking area. Double-crested cormorants roost on the intake tower, great blue herons stalk the shallows near shore, hummingbirds buzz and dart among the shrubs, warblers flit through the Monterey pines and coast live oaks, and California towhees scratch through leaf litter for food. From the trailhead, walk up the cement stairs and continue straight on a wide dirt path through a picnic and children's play area. Below and left is the Shore Trail, a paved road that circles the reservoir—

24. Rim Trail

another fine hike. After leaving the picnic area, you join a dirt road, right, and pass another, left, as you continue uphill on a moderate grade. This area may be muddy in wet weather.

Open grasslands with valley oaks appear as you near a ridgecrest, while overhead a red-tailed hawk may be gliding on the wind. The route turns west and heads for a flat spot on the ridge ahead; turn around here and enjoy a great view of Mt. Diablo, with the reservoir in the foreground, its waters shimmering perhaps in the sunlight. To the southeast is more high ground—EBMUD land around Rocky Ridge, and Las Trampas Wilderness. To the north is busy Highway 24, and beyond, the hills of Briones Regional Park. At several points along the way, trails connecting with the reservoir's Shore Trail drop from the rim.

Easy walking brings you, at about the 0.75-mile point, to the first of these junctions, where the Westview Trail heads left. Now climbing on a moderate grade, you pass a grove of California bay laurel on your way to the next high point, near a residential area at the park's western boundary. Here the route levels, descends into a forested area, and then climbs steeply as it swings south, alternating between sun and shade. Another descent takes you to a rolling section around the 1-mile point, where the trees give way to grass and coyote bush.

A moderate climb, followed by a moderate descent, brings you to a junction with a path that heads left to a viewpoint. Passing that, you soon reach a low point and a path, right, leading to Meadow-Park Court, off Glorietta Blvd. Continuing straight through a possibly muddy area, where animal tracks, especially those of deer, may be evident, you begin a very steep climb, with the reservoir now obscured by a ridge, left. As you walk past groves of pine and coast live oak, the route levels briefly but then plunges steeply to another low spot, with a residential area, right, and a junction with the Canyon Trail, left.

More up-and-down travel brings you to the summit of a high ridge where the grade eases off, and now you pass fine stands of coast live oak, pine, eucalyptus, and California buckeye. Listen carefully and you may hear the sharp cry of a northern flicker as it moves from tree to tree, probing for insects. Southwest from here is Round Top, an extinct volcano in the Sibley Volcanic Regional Preserve, its forested summit topped with communication towers. Mt. Diablo, which resembles a volcano but is actually made from uplifted layers of rock that were originally underwater, still dominates the eastern skyline.

When you reach a large water tank, follow a paved path around it to the right, and pass a paved road heading right, downhill. Continue around the tank, where drinking water is available, and climb uphill on pavement through a pine grove. Now the pavement ends and you are back on a dirt road, walking east through a treeless area of grasses and shrubs. Climbing steeply, you soon reach the route's high point (1038'), and the road divides to go around it. If you spot a small gray hawk, it is probably a white-tailed kite, one of the few birds that can truly hover. This raptor, which feeds on rodents and insects, is expanding its range and increasing in numbers.

This high point affords you 360-degree views: from the Oakland and Berkeley hills to Walnut Creek, Alamo, and Mt. Diablo; from Orinda, Moraga, and Rheem Valley to Briones Regional Park. After enjoying your time on the summit, continue east and immediately begin a steep drop on a dirt fire break, which may be muddy and eroded. Pick your way carefully down this short, steep section, and as the route swings north look for blue bush lupine on your left, and some beautiful oaks. As the grade eases you reach a junction: to your left is a dirt road, missing from the EBMUD and Olmsted & Bros. maps; to your right is a path leading to a gate at the end of Campolindo Drive, off Moraga Road.

As you continue straight the route climbs in the open, reaches a high point, turns northeast, and descends to a junction, just short of the 3-mile point, with the Campolindo Trail, a dirt road heading left. Here you may spot another hovering bird, the American kestrel, the smallest North American falcon. Compare the hovering birds you may have seen so far with the ever-present turkey vulture, a large black raptor that glides and soars on air currents, tipping from side to side, its wings held in a V-position. While some birds hunt from the air, many feed on the ground. Ground feeders that prefer open sites, such as gold-crowned sparrows, flock together for safety, while birds that feed in dense cover, such as

California buckeye in full bloom. The distinctive upturned "candles" of white flowers are a common spring sight in the East Bay Hills.

spotted and brown towhees, can afford to do so singly or in pairs. Check both kinds of habitat here for these birds and others like them.

The route now bends right and climbs, giving you good views of the reservoir, the dam, and Highway 24. As you walk east over level ground, western scrub-jays may announce your arrival with their raucous calls. Turning north and descending gently, you pass a residential area, right, and enjoy a pleasant respite from the constant up-and-down terrain. Just past the 3-mile point, you come to a junction with the Big Oak Trail, heading left. Your route veers right and continues over open, level ground, past stands of pine and eucalyptus. The next junction is with the Lafayette Reservoir Trail to Moraga Road., heading right and uphill.

A short, moderate climb brings you to another high point with 360-degree views, increasing significantly the "scenery per mile" quotient of this hike. As you descend, you reach a junction with the Sunset Trail, heading straight, but your route turns left and continues downhill on a moderate grade, meandering past oaks loaded with mistletoe. At about the 4.3-mile point, you come to a junction with the Shore Trail, the paved path that circles the reservoir. Turn right and walk through a picnic area toward the dam, descending gently before reaching the parking area.

◆ Lake Chabot Regional Park ◆

25	Lake Chabot Regional Park

LAKE LOOP

Length:	9 miles
Time:	4 to 6 hours
Rating:	Difficult
Regulations:	EBRPD; fees for parking and dogs; no bicycles on the Columbine Trail.
Highlights:	This loop—combining the East Shore, Honker Bay, Columbine, Bass Cove, and West Shore trails—takes you around the 315-acre lake that forms the heart of Lake Chabot Regional Park. A wide variety of plant and bird life, along with ever-changing terrain, makes this a rewarding trip. A surprising degree of solitude can be found here, especially on the Columbine Trail. During periods of extreme wet weather the Columbine Trail may be closed where it crosses Grass Valley Creek, making it impossible to complete the loop: call (510) 635-0138, ext. 2571 to check. The East and West Shore trails may be hiked separately for shorter, less strenuous trips. A lake shuttle/tour boat makes stops at various points along the shoreline; see the EBRPD Lake Chabot brochure for more details.
Facilities:	Picnic tables, water, toilets, snack bar; boat and bike rentals; fishing licenses available.
Trailhead:	Northeast side of parking area.
Directions:	From Interstate 580 eastbound in San Leandro, take the 150th Avenue/Fairmont Drive exit. Go through the first light at 150th Ave. and at the next light turn left onto Fairmont Dr. After 1.8 miles, Fairmont becomes Lake Chabot Rd. Continue 0.1 mile and turn left into the Lake Chabot Marina parking area.

From Interstate 580 westbound in San Leandro, take the 150th Avenue/Fairmont Drive exit, turn right onto Fairmont Dr. and follow the directions above.

From Castro Valley Blvd. in Castro Valley, go north 1.8 miles on Lake Chabot Rd. to the Lake Chabot Marina parking area.

As you leave the parking area, walk downhill on a paved road—the East Shore Trail—and immediately come to a four-way intersection with a paved path. To your left is the marina and a launch site for boats, canoes, and kayaks. A sign board with a map and park information is on your right. Continue straight, cross a small creek, and where a dirt path joins from the right, follow the paved road as it swings left, and, in about 50 feet, passes a paved path leading uphill to the Mallard picnic site. Continue straight, passing a small pond on your left, and in another 50 feet or so you reach an intersection with a paved path that leads left and downhill, past the Willow picnic site, to the marina and snack bar.

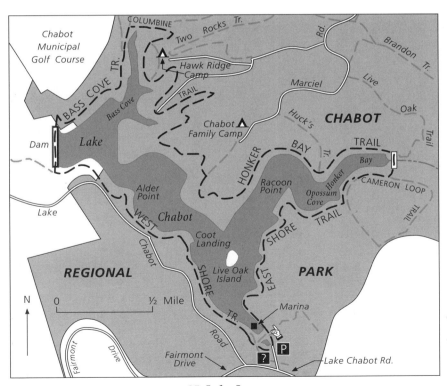

25. Lake Loop

Continue straight and walk northwest through a wooded area of willow, poplar, coast live oak, walnut, and white alder. The East Shore Trail, paved and relatively flat, is very popular with hikers, dog-walkers, joggers, and exercise walkers; as part of the Lake Chabot Bike Loop it is used by bicyclists as well. (Bike loop distance: 12.41 miles via the Live Oak Trail; 14.41 miles via the Honker Bay Trail.) Soon you can see the marina across the water, left. You may also see and hear a large flock of geese on the lawn next to snack bar, begging passersby for food. The route climbs gently, past stands of Monterey and coulter pine, and turns northeast as it follows the contour of the lake.

In sunny areas, you may see blue elderberry, California sagebrush, toyon, coyote bush, poison oak, and bush monkeyflower. But as soon as the route enters shade, following indentations in the shoreline, the vegetation changes abruptly, and you find yourself in a cool, dark forest of coast live oak and California bay laurel, with ferns, creambush, and blackberry vines clinging to the damp hillsides. The route repeats this transition many times as it circles the lake. As you come into the open again, there is a view of Live Oak Island in the middle of the lake, left. Nearby, a wooden staircase leads from the East Shore Trail down to the water's edge.

You may see a plump black bird floating on the water, with white bill and large yellow lobed feet. This is the American coot, a common bird related to rails and gallinules. Another black waterbird—larger than a coot, and with a snake-like neck—is the double-crested cormorant. You will often see cormorants perched on rocks or snags, drying their outstretched wings. Unlike many other waterbirds, cormorants have no waterproofing oil in their feathers. After diving for fish, they must dry out. You also may see or hear Anna's hummingbird, tiny and gray-green, with males displaying a bright ruby-red throat.

At about the 1.25-mile point, you reach a trail post and a trail leading left and downhill to Raccoon Point, a spit of land that marks the entrance to Opossum Cove and Honker Bay. Here the East Shore Trail swings right and begins a moderate climb in the shade of large bay trees. You may also find coffeeberry and snowberry in this shady section. The route descends, then begins a series of ups and downs. Soon you pass a ravine, right, filled with a jumble of rocks and large boulders, dry in summer. In wet weather, however, water cascading down this ravine flows under the road through a large metal culvert. Steller's jays and western scrub-jays favor this area, and your passage may set off their raucous alarms. Look here also for the diminutive ruby-crowned kinglet, a nervous bird about the size of a chickadee, dull yellow-green with white wing bars.

The lake, left, is here shallow and marshy, filled with cattails and bulrushes, also called tule. Great blue herons and great egrets often wade in these shallows or stand on low islands, hunting for small fish. At the other end of the size scale, gold-crowned sparrows may be seen feeding in

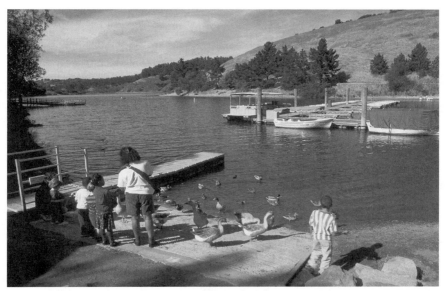

Feeding the waterfowl is popular with children at the Lake Chabot Marina.

flocks on the ground beside the road. Small birds that feed in the open need the protection from predators that is provided by a flock. But other small ground feeders who feed while hidden in dense thickets, like the spotted towhee, can safely feed alone.

At about 1.7 miles, the paved East Shore Trail ends at a metal gate. Here you join the Cameron Loop Trail, a wide dirt road heading sharply right but also straight ahead. Continue straight and climb a gentle grade in dense forest, past stands of willow and bigleaf maple. After about 0.1 mile, you leave the Cameron Loop Trail by turning left, walking down a few wooden steps, and crossing a 200-foot wooden bridge over San Leandro Creek. From the bridge, stop and look for birds in this marshy, wooded area and listen for their calls—the sharp "klee-yer" of the northern flicker, or the plaintive "keeeer" of the red-tailed hawk.

Once across the bridge, you are back on a dirt path, with underbrush and trees on either side. About 100 yards from the end of bridge, just as you begin to emerge from the marshy area, you come to a four-way junction. Your route is the Honker Bay Trail, a wide dirt road heading left. A gated dirt road, right, leads to a restricted area. The Live Oak Trail goes straight and heads uphill; cyclists can choose this route or go left on the Honker Bay Trail. Turn left and walk on a level grade past a brushy area with coyote bush, California sagebrush, fennel, and cotoneaster, a non-native shrub with red berries. This area may be muddy in wet weather. A large expanse of marsh is to your left, and a steep, rocky hillside rises on your right.

At about the 2.33-mile point, you reach a junction with Huck's Trail, a steep path for hikers only, heading right and uphill. (There is a toilet on the left here.) As you round a point, Honker Bay is left, and a large eucalyptus forest graces the ridge ahead and also right. Closer at hand are coast live oak, willow, and white alder. Keep a sharp eye out for deer lurking in the shade. You may be startled by a loud scratching in the underbrush: this may be the California towhee or perhaps a spotted towhee searching for food. Look high in the tree branches to find yellow-rumped warblers.

The sight of small boat dock (and another toilet) indicates you've reached the start of the route's hilly section. Here the Honker Bay Trail turns right, away from the lake, and begins to climb uphill on a moderate grade, passing coast live oak, bay, and blue elderberry along the way. The grade levels off, then climbs steeply to an area of low shrubs—coyote bush, toyon, bush monkeyflower, and California sagebrush. Ahead on a ridge, you will see a large eucalyptus forest, perhaps with hawks or vultures soaring above. Views of the lake, looking back toward the marina, are soon left behind, but with the trees comes shade, welcome on a warm day. The route switches back and continues to climb, soon reaching a junction with the Columbine Trail.

From here the Honker Bay Trail continues its climb to the Anthony Chabot Campground, at the end of Marciel Road, but your route, the single-track Columbine Trail, closed to bicycles, heads left around the lake. The air here on a warm day is wonderfully fragrant with the smell of eucalyptus and bay. The route now meanders, trying to hold a contour as it follows ridges and inlets along the lake's indented east shore. California hazelnut and vine honeysuckle can be added to your list of today's plants.

At about the 4-mile point, you reach a junction with fenced-off trail leading left and downhill. Your route goes right and stays level, then drops on a series of switchbacks to a streambed which may be dry in summer. In an area overgrown with blackberry vines and poison oak, cross the streambed and climb on a gentle grade, soon reaching open terrain on the side of a ridge. As you round the ridge, you pass the trail to Lost Ridge Campground, taking off sharply right. From here you can look northwest, across an arm of the lake, to Chabot Municipal Golf Course. And if you look southwest you get your first look at the dam that formed Lake Chabot.

After walking almost another mile, you reach an unsigned fork in the trail; here you stay left, now enjoying the shade of coast live oak and bay. Soon you pass the Hawk Ridge Trail, leading right and uphill via several wooden steps. The Columbine Trail continues straight, then bends right to cross a streambed, and swings left toward a junction with the Cascade Trail. At about the 6-mile point, you reach a sandy, brushy area, sometimes dry, where Grass Valley Creek flows into Lake Chabot. In extreme wet weather the Columbine Trail may be closed here. After crossing the creek bed, you come to a T-junction and several trail signs. From here the Cascade Trail goes right, but your route, the Bass Cove Trail, goes left and continues around the lake to the dam. The signs at this junction list mileages to various points around the lake, but the figures do not exactly match mileages given on the EBRPD or Olmsted & Bros. maps.

Following a line of willow and bay, you turn left onto the Bass Cove Trail, a dirt road, and walk south, past a rest bench, soon leaving the trees and coming into the open. The lake is to your left, and soon the road swings back to the shade of an oak and bay enclave. Now in the sun again, the route starts a short, moderate climb, passes a junction, right, with the Goldenrod Trail, and then another with an unsigned dirt road going right and uphill. As you descend toward the lake, you get good views of the dam, and to its left, forested Fairmont Ridge, topped by a communication tower.

The route meanders in and out of little coves as it contours and climbs along the lakeshore. At one point, with the dam in sight, a hidden inlet forces you to jog north, then south. Soon, in an area where large pines and coast redwoods reach for the sky, you reach a junction with a road heading left. Continue straight, and almost at once you come to another junction, this time with a paved road. Here you will find a trail post with a sign for the Bass Cove Trail, and a toilet. Turn left and walk downhill on pavement, which leads you across the dam.

The earthen dam you are crossing was built in the 1874-75 by Anthony Chabot, founder of the Contra Costa Water Company. With Oakland and surrounding cities facing a water shortage, Chabot decided to dam San Leandro Creek, which flows west from here and empties into San Leandro Bay at the Martin Luther King Jr. Regional Shoreline. According to Malcolm Margolin, author of *East Bay Out*, Chabot used hydraulic techniques developed for California gold mining. Chabot's crews used high-pressure streams of water to wash thousands of tons of dirt into San Leandro Creek, and then brought in herds of wild horses to compact the dirt into a dam. Construction began in 1874, and in 1876 the first water entered the reservoir's pipelines. A filter plant was added in 1890. The dam, originally called San Leandro Dam, was acquired along with the reservoir and filter plant in 1928 by EBMUD, which renamed the facilities to honor Chabot. The lake was opened to recreation in the 1960s and now serves as an emergency water supply for the East Bay.

Just after crossing the dam, now on the West Shore Trail, you can visit an observation deck, left, with fine views of the lake and dam, a California historic civil engineering landmark. Proceeding southeast, you come to a wonderful, shady part of the route, thick with all the now-familiar trees and shrubs. Here you may see a gray sparrow-like bird with a black head, pink bill, and white along the outer edge of its tail. This is the dark-eyed junco, usually found in flocks in wooded areas or at backyard bird feeders, where it comes readily. A highly variable bird found across the US and Canada, the dark-eyed junco was formerly divided into four species; our variety was known as the Oregon junco.

At about the 7.5-mile point, you come to an unsigned junction; here the West Shore Trail turns left and goes downhill, while another path continues straight to Lake Chabot Road. When you reach the lake shore, your route bends right, passing a dirt trail that heads left to Alder Point. Soon you pass another trail going left, this one to Coot Landing; a nearby rest bench beckons from beneath a coast live oak. From here you can glimpse your goal, the marina, ahead and left. Before you reach it, however, the route climbs until it is high above the lake. From a vantage point, you can see familiar landmarks—Live Oak Island, the East Shore Trail, and Honker Bay.

Just before reaching the marina, the route crosses a ledge which was cut from the steep hillside, exposing layers of rock. When you reach the marina, you may be surrounded by ducks and geese begging for food. Among the domestic geese may be Canada geese, large gray-brown birds with black head and neck, and white throat patch. These "honkers" are often seen during spring and fall migration, flying in a classic V-formation over wetlands and marshes. From the marina, follow the West Shore Trail as it passes right of the snack bar on its way to the parking area.

Cattails line the shore near Bass Cove.

◆ Las Trampas Wilderness ◆

Las Trampas Wilderness, 3,798 acres of convoluted, oak-studded hills and wind-swept, chaparral-cloaked ridges, is one of the great undeveloped parks in the EBRPD system. The park is dominated by two high ramparts, Las Trampas Ridge and Rocky Ridge, guarding the deep slash of northwest–southeast trending Bollinger Canyon. The high point on Las Trampas Ridge, Las Trampas Peak, is 1,827 feet in elevation. The top of Rocky Ridge, a little more than a mile south, stands at 2,024 feet. Rocky Ridge, once used as a Nike missile site, now sports a communication tower on its summit. Fine views of Mt. Diablo can be had from the top of Las Trampas Peak or along the "Corduroy Hills" route. From the top of Rocky Ridge, the vista extends southwest across EBMUD lands to Upper San Leandro Reservoir. The twin walls of Rocky and Las Trampas ridges, rising between the Oakland and Berkeley hills and Mt. Diablo, are landmarks easily seen from many vantage points in the East Bay.

Las Trampas in Spanish means "The Traps," perhaps a reference to the Ohlone Indian practice of trapping deer and elk by driving them into the area's steep box canyons, or perhaps, as Erwin G. Gudde writes in *California Place Names*, a reference to traps set in chaparral to catch elk. Like many other East Bay parks, Las Trampas was at one time a large rancho, but after California became a state, its lands fell into American hands. The names of nearby valleys and canyons—Bollinger, Cull, Hunsaker, Stone, and Tice—commemorate the early settlers who benefited from the misfortunes of the rancho's original owners, the Romero brothers. The East Bay Regional Park District purchased the parklands in the 1960s, using state bond money and federal grants.

Las Trampas is one of the finest places in the East Bay to study chaparral, and it is one of the few places to see scrub oak, the plant whose Spanish name, *chaparro*, gives us the word for this hearty plant community. The park, which contains the Las Trampas and Bollinger faults, is also of great interest to geologists and paleontologists: its high ridges were at one time part of the ocean floor, and the sandstone outcrops and cliffs of Rocky Ridge and Las Trampas Ridge contain shells and fossils of animals long extinct, such as primitive camels, a three-toed horse, and a four-tusked elephant-like animal. Present-day mammals that may be seen in the park, according to the EBRPD brochure, include raccoons, foxes, opossums, bobcats, skunks, squirrels, and deer. Sightings of mountain lions have been reported in recent years.

Las Trampas is best enjoyed during cool weather, but mud can be a problem after rainy periods. Parking-area gates are open from 8 A.M. to dusk; be careful not to get locked in, especially if you are doing the long "Corduroy Hills" hike.

26 Las Trampas Wilderness
CORDUROY HILLS

Length:	6.1 miles
Time:	4 to 6 hours
Rating:	Difficult
Regulations:	EBRPD; no bicycles or horses.
Highlights:	This rugged loop joins all or parts of the Chamise, Las Trampas Ridge, Corduroy Hills, Madrone, Virgil Williams, Del Amigo, Sulphur Springs, Trapline, and Mahogany trails, leading you through an amazing variety of terrain, from sun-baked chaparral to shady forest. Some of the best views in the East Bay of Mt. Diablo are to be found on this loop, which passes through a stunted forest of scrub oak and other interesting plant communities. Bring plenty of water and start early; the parking area gate may be locked at 5 P.M.
Facilities:	Picnic tables, toilet, water (may not be available year-round).
Trailhead:	On the northeast side of Bollinger Canyon Road, about 0.1 mile southeast from the parking area.
Directions:	From Interstate 680 in San Ramon, take the Crow Canyon Road/San Ramon exit and go west 1.1 miles on Crow Canyon Rd. to Bollinger Canyon Rd. Turn right and go 4.5 miles to the end of the road, past the first Las Trampas Wilderness entrance, and turn left into the parking area.
	From Interstate 580 eastbound in Castro Valley, take the Center Street/Crow Canyon Rd. exit, go left over the free-way, then right on Castro Valley Blvd., which soon becomes E. Castro Valley Blvd., 0.7 mile to Crow Canyon Rd. Turn left and go 7.5 miles to Bollinger Canyon Rd., then follow the directions above.
	From Interstate 580 westbound in Castro Valley, take the Castro Valley exit, turn left onto E. Castro Valley Blvd. and go 0.1 mile to Crow Canyon Rd. Turn right and follow the directions above.

From a turn-out on Bollinger Canyon Road, go through a gate, and follow the single-track Chamise Trail as it climbs southeast across an open hillside to a junction with the Bollinger Canyon Trail. Here your route turns left and begins a series of well-graded switchbacks. As you look southwest across Bollinger Canyon, you can see the southern segment of Las Trampas Wilderness, dominated by the steep escarpment of Rocky Ridge, worth exploring on another day. As you gain elevation you may see turkey vultures circling overhead, or hear the sharp cry of a northern flicker. Wet weather may bring mud and even landslide activity to parts of this route.

The Chamise Trail takes its name from a hearty, widespread shrub, also known as greasewood, which grows here in the company of two other chaparral plants, buckbrush and black sage. Looking like a small ever-green tree, chamise sports white flowers in late spring, then turns brown when its rust-colored fruit appears. As the trail bends left, you pass a junc-tion with the Mahogany Trail, part of your return route, heading straight and steeply downhill. To the northeast is Las Trampas Ridge, a rugged, chaparral-covered barrier you will cross later today. Continuing to climb moderately along the crest of a narrow north–south ridge, you pass through a corridor of chaparral—a great place to study the plants up close—and, in a grove of coast live oak, reach the other end of the Mahogany Trail, right.

Now in the open, the route climbs a grassy hill and approaches the northwest–southeast spine of Las Trampas Ridge, right, guarded by massive rock cliffs. In addition to the chaparral plants, another shrub to

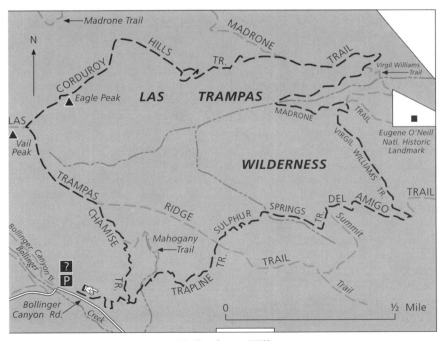

26. Corduroy Hills

admire here is a thorny relative of the flowering currants, hillside gooseberry, whose delicate white-and-purple flowers appear in late winter. A
flat area and a T-junction mark the point where the ridge you are on
intersects Las Trampas Ridge. The Chamise Trail ends here, and you
bear left on the Las Trampas Ridge Trail, enjoying views of Mt. Diablo,
northeast, and Rocky Ridge, sporting a lone communication tower,
southwest.

Just past the junction, you will encounter a large grove of scrub oak,
right, a low-growing shrub with light bark and small, pointed leaves. The
Spanish word for scrub oak, *chaparro*, gives us "chaparral," but chaparral
in the East Bay almost always contains a wide variety of shrubs adapted
to dry conditions. One of these, also found here, is redberry buckthorn,
whose round, prickly leaves make it resemble a small live oak.

Passing through a fence, you descend a steep, narrow track, muddy at
times, past more scrub oak, soon reaching a clearing where the route levels off. Back in chaparral, with occasional pockets of shade offered by oak
and California bay laurel, the trail follows a rolling course on the edge of
a steep canyon, right. The designation of this area as a "wilderness" is
appropriate; except for the trail, human intervention is nowhere to be
seen. In one of the shady areas, just east of Vail Peak (1787'), you reach a
fence, right, and a junction with the Corduroy Hills Trail. Here your route,
a single track, turns right and steeply downhill, following at first some
wooden steps, then switchbacks, to an open, grassy hillside. A small
divide, which you cross, separates two canyons, the left one formed by
two ridges, Las Trampas and Nordstrom. Just ahead is Eagle Peak (1720'),
a high point on the southeast end of Nordstrom Ridge.

A steep ascent, in places a scramble over rocky ground and boulders,
puts you atop a cliff just west of Eagle Peak, a nice rest stop. The view
from here is spectacular, taking in Walnut Creek, Concord, Suisun Bay,
and the west delta. Once on level ground, you reach a trail junction where
the Corduroy Hills Trail continues left and downhill, via wooden steps,
and a spur trail to Eagle Peak heads right and uphill. After turning left
and descending the steps, you traverse the north side of Eagle Peak on a
trail carved in a steep cliff, enjoying a terrific view of Mt. Diablo. Soon you
begin to descend steeply, then less so, through a wooded area along the
crest of a ridge.

In a grassy meadow the route levels out, bends right, and begins to
climb through oak and chaparral. This dramatic part of Las Trampas
Wilderness, the Corduroy Hills, is characterized by deeply convoluted
canyons and ridges. Black oak makes an appearance here, favoring
warmer, drier slopes. Now beginning a long, moderate descent, you break
out of the trees and wind down through open grassland to a T-junction,
just after some switchbacks, with a wide dirt road. Turn left—the arrow
pointing straight on a trail post here is confusing—and continue your descent, following the road as it heads first toward Mt. Diablo, then zigzags

down a ridge, soon joining a road coming from the right-hand branch of the previous junction.

At about the 2.5-mile point, the Corduroy Hills Trail ends, and you merge with the Madrone Trail, coming from the left. Here you go straight, passing an area that may be quite muddy in wet weather, and continue to descend. As the road makes an almost 180-degree bend right, you pass a narrow, unsigned trail veering left. Stay on the road, and soon you reach a dense forest with a creek on your left, where the route begins to climb southwest on a moderate grade that soon eases. This area too may be muddy or even flooded in wet weather. Trees thriving here in the cool, moist soil include California buckeye, bigleaf maple, and white alder, along with the usual bay and coast live oak. With trees that lose their leaves in winter, it is sometimes easier to identify them by looking down at the leaf litter, instead of up at their bare branches.

The road bends left and crosses the creek, which flows through two large culverts, and continues to climb, soon reaching a gate and the end of the Madrone Trail. At this point, the Virgil Williams Trail, a narrow dirt track, crosses the road, heading left and right. Here you turn right and climb uphill through dense forest on moderate and occasionally steep grades, glimpsing left through the trees Tao House, the one-time home of playwright Eugene O'Neill, preserved by the National Park Service as a National Historic Site. It was in Tao House, where he lived from 1937 to 1944, that O'Neill wrote *The Iceman Cometh* and *A Long Day's Journey Into Night*, two of his best-known dramas. (Arrangements to visit Tao House can be made by calling (925) 838-7546.)

As the route levels off, you pass through an area of chaparral, then make another steep climb, and descend to a junction with the Del Amigo Trail, a wide dirt road. Turning right, you come to the steepest part of the route, a climb that helps earn for this hike its "difficult" rating, putting it in company with Ramage Peak and several trips on Mt. Diablo as the most challenging in this book. Speaking of Mt. Diablo, it is worth turning around from time to time as you grunt and sweat your way uphill to view its hulking form across the Interstate 680 corridor. On your way up the steep slope, you will encounter shrubs such as coffeeberry, bush monkeyflower, California sagebrush, and blue bush lupine, growing here in the company of black oak and bigleaf maple. As the grade eases, the route enters a lovely clearing, bends sharply left, and reaches a junction on level ground with a trail signed as the Summit Trail, straight, and the Sulphur Springs Trail, right.

As you begin to follow the Sulphur Springs Trail, a steep dirt road, you will notice a narrow path, right, leading through the grass to a group of boulders, shaded in the afternoon and conveniently sized for sitting. This area makes a good rest stop. After you are again underway, descend into a beautiful, shady canyon, then follow a creek, which may be flowing across the road in more than one spot, downstream to several horse watering troughs in a grove of coast live oak. Here your route, the Sulphur Springs Trail, turns left, crosses the creek at a trail post, and, as an eroded single track, begins climbing uphill on a moderate grade.

A pleasant climb through oak woodland and past a meadow, possibly flooded, wins back some of the elevation you recently lost and soon brings you to a four-way junction and the end of the Sulphur Springs Trail. Here the Las Trampas Ridge Trail crosses left to right, and your route, the Trapline Trail, goes straight. In about 100 feet you reach a saddle on the crest of Las Trampas Ridge, where an opening in a barbed-wire fence allows you to pass through. Directly

Hiker closely examines a cocklebur bur.

ahead, about 0.5 mile away, is Bollinger Canyon, with Rocky Ridge rising up behind, a sure sign you are nearing the finish. Now you follow the Trapline Trail, here a rock-and-dirt path, down through a corridor of chaparral, where you may find mountain mahogany, a large shrub with silver-gray bark and small, translucent green leaves, serrated at the ends.

Soon chaparral gives way to open grassland, then forest, as you lose hard-won elevation, finally reaching the end of the Trapline Trail. Here you join the Mahogany Trail, an single track merging from the right, and continue to descend beside a creek in a steep ravine, right. What a contrast with the dry chaparral of a few minutes ago! Here everything is cool and lush, and you are surrounded by the soothing sound of running water. Most of the East Bay's common oaks—blue, black, canyon live, coast live—are represented in Las Trampas Wilderness, along with one that is rare in our area, Garry oak. This commercially valuable tree, growing from Central California to British Columbia, resembles valley oak, but its leaves are slightly larger and have fewer lobes.

After a steep descent, in places on wooden steps, you reach a bridge over the creek near a small waterfall. Once across, you begin to climb a narrow path through an area where bay and toyon, normally a shrub but here a small tree, compete for sunlight. An unusual plant growing in this wooded area is California pipevine, whose flowers, appearing in late winter, resemble miniature saxophones. A steady climb brings you to a fence, and just beyond, a junction with the Chamise Trail, where you continue straight and retrace your steps to the parking area.

Las Trampas Wilderness
LAS TRAMPAS PEAK

Length: 3.8 miles

Time: 2 to 4 hours

Rating: Moderate

Regulations: EBRPD; no bicycles on the Chamise Trail or single-track segment of the Las Trampas Ridge Trail. (Bicyclists wishing to ride to Las Trampas Peak must follow the Bollinger Canyon Trail uphill to the multi-use part of the Las Trampas Ridge Trail.)

Highlights: Exploring Las Trampas Peak via the Chamise, Las Trampas Ridge, and Bollinger Canyon trails is the goal of this semi-loop hike, which passes through oak and bay forest, chaparral, and grassland, on its way to high grounds with great views.

Facilities: Picnic tables, toilet, water (may not be available year-round).

Trailhead: On the northeast side of Bollinger Canyon Road, about 0.1 mile southeast from the parking area.

Directions: See the directions for "Corduroy Hills" on p. 156.

Follow the route description in "Corduroy Hills" on pages 156–158 to a junction, just past the 1-mile point and near Vail Peak, where the Corduroy Hills Trail leaves the Las Trampas Ridge Trail. From here you follow the Las Trampas Ridge Trail as it bends left and climbs through a dense forest of trees and shrubs, including coast live oak, canyon live oak, California bay laurel, toyon, and hillside gooseberry, a thorny bush with lovely white-and-purple flowers. Farther up the trail, you may see gooseberry's relative—pink flowering currant, a shrub with pink flowers and no thorns. With a deep canyon on your right, follow the trail as it tops a small rise and begins to descend around the north side of Vail Peak (1787'). Big, beautiful madrone trees with reddish bark stand at the edge of an area of chaparral, mostly chamise and buckbrush, where you have a view of Rocky Ridge, topped by a communication tower, left across Bollinger Canyon. Through the trees, right, Mt. Diablo rises behind Alamo, Danville, and the Interstate 680 corridor. In a clearing, lupine and bush monkeyflower soak up the morning sun.

As you come to a clearing at about the 1.4-mile point, a connector to the Bollinger Canyon Trail heads left. (If you do not want to continue to Las Trampas Peak, turn left here, descend about 0.2 mile to the Bollinger

Canyon Trail, and follow the directions given later in this route description back to the parking area.) Continue straight, walking northwest, with spectacular views ahead across Moraga Valley to the Oakland and Berkeley hills, topped by Round Top and Vollmer Peak, and behind them in the distance, Mt. Tamalpais. Now passing through a corridor of chaparral, the route begins to climb an ever-narrowing ridge with steep dropoffs on both sides. Nordstrom Ridge rises from a deep, forested valley, right, and behind it looms the hulking form of Mt. Diablo.

After reaching a high point, the route descends to meet the Bollinger Canyon Trail, a dirt road, left. Your route, the Las Trampas Ridge Trail, now also a dirt road, continues straight, with the summit of Las Trampas Peak (1827') about 0.5 mile ahead. (To shorten the hike, you have the

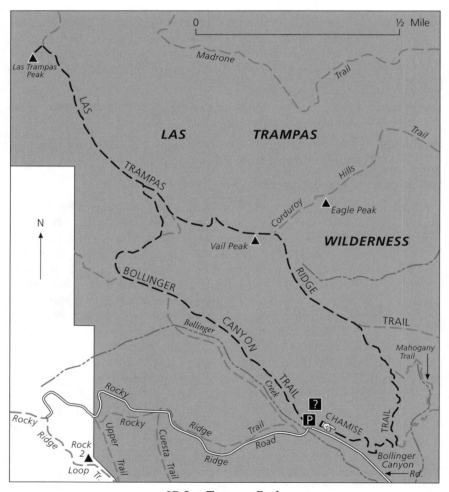

27. Las Trampas Peak

option of turning left here and following the Bollinger Canyon Trail back to the parking area.) Continue straight on a gentle and then moderate grade, past stands of madrone, manzanita, and coast silk tassel. Descending to a saddle, the route makes a final push steeply uphill to surmount Las Trampas Peak. At about the 2-mile point, you reach a junction with a road heading left to the peak's summit. The road you have been on bends right and drops over the edge of a grassy plateau on its way to the park boundary. Before climbing to the summit, walk to the edge of this plateau to enjoy a fine view which extends north toward Walnut Creek, Concord, Mt. Diablo, Suisun Bay, and the west delta. Now turning back toward Las Trampas Peak, you climb on a moderate grade to its summit for another vista, this one south along Las Trampas Ridge to Pleasanton and beyond.

From the summit, retrace your steps to the junction of the Las Trampas Ridge and Bollinger Canyon trails. Bear right and follow the Bollinger Canyon Trail, a dirt road, downhill on a moderate grade through chaparral—manzanita, chamise, toyon, black sage, and buckbrush. As the route steepens and bends right, you pass the connector to the Las Trampas Ridge Trail, left. Soon you come to an unsigned fork: bear right and continue the descent into Bollinger Canyon. Western scrub-jays and California towhees are two of the most common birds you may see here. The former is one of three species of scrub-jays found in North America; the latter is one of five species of towhees. Ornithologists are constantly learning more about the birds they study, and sometimes this results in birds being renamed or reclassified. Until recently, scrub-jays all belonged to a single species, and the California towhee was called brown towhee. At about the 3-mile point, you pass an unsigned road, right, and continue to descend through open areas that may be flooded, muddy, eroded or all three. Bollinger Creek, bordered by trees, is on your right, and soon you come to a junction with the Creek Trail, also very muddy at times. Continuing on the Bollinger Canyon Trail, you come after about 0.5 mile to a fence at the end of Bollinger Canyon Road and the entrance to the parking area.

Blue bush lupine.

28 Las Trampas Wilderness
ROCKY RIDGE

Length: 3.8 miles

Time: 2 to 3 hours

Rating: Moderate

Regulations: EBRPD; no bicycles; trails may be closed to horses when wet and muddy.

Highlights: This short but scenic loop, via Rocky Ridge Road and the Cuesta and Upper trails, takes you atop 2,000-foot Rocky Ridge, the border between Las Trampas Wilderness and EBMUD lands of the Upper San Leandro Reservoir watershed. Rocky Ridge, a Nike missile site during the Cold War, rises midway between Redwood and Anthony Chabot regional parks and Mt. Diablo State Park, making it a commanding vantage point with great views.

Facilities: Picnic tables, toilet, water (may not be available year-round).

Trailhead: Northwest corner of parking area, at the green cattle gate.

Directions: See the directions for "Corduroy Hills" on p. 156.

After passing through the cattle gate, you begin a steep uphill walk on paved Rocky Ridge Road. After a while the grade eases somewhat, but a cattle gate ahead signals another steep section, bordered by coast live oak and California bay laurel. In wet weather, water may be running here in channels on both sides of the road. If you are here late in the day, listen for the "hoo, hoo, hoo-hoo" of a great-horned owl, but don't be fooled by a mourning dove's plaintive cooing. After climbing about 0.5-mile, you reach a junction with a single-track trail heading left and steeply uphill. Turn left, and immediately you come to a fork with a trail post in the middle. Here the Rocky Ridge Trail heads right and the Cuesta Trail, your route, goes left.

Turn left and climb south and then southeast across an open hillside, enjoying views of Bollinger Canyon, Mt. Diablo, and your goal, Rocky Ridge, right. The trail, climbing on a gentle grade, may be muddy and damaged by cows. Along the way uphill you pass many paths joining your route; ignore these and stay on the Cuesta Trail, a well-defined path. Watch for red-tailed hawks soaring overhead and dark-eyed juncos darting from tree to tree. Bigleaf maple joins bay and oak to offer some occasional shade, but the route stays mostly in the open.

Now the route bends right, heads toward Rocky Ridge, and starts to climb past a hillside dotted with boulders and clumps of blue bush lupine. Soon you turn left and descend over rough and eroded ground to a fence; here the grade levels and then begins to climb again. The hillside sweeping up to your right is getting steeper, and across Bollinger Canyon, left, Mt. Diablo rises majestically behind Las Trampas Ridge. The route finally begins a steep climb, via switchbacks, to Rocky Ridge, and now you can see a communication tower on the ridge's high point (2024'). Across Bollinger Canyon in the distance, just right of the antenna, is Las Trampas Peak (1827'), a great destination for another day.

Just before the 2-mile point, after the final switchback, you reach a four-way junction with the Upper Trail, a dirt road running southeast to northwest, and a path heading southwest. Turn right and follow the Upper Trail as it climbs in the open over several high points, each with terrific views, especially southwest to EBMUD lands around Upper San Leandro Reservoir. Ramage Peak (1401') stands watch in front of the reservoir, and

28. Rocky Ridge

left of the peak you can see Hideaway Ranch, on private lands at the end of Cull Canyon Road. Descending briefly from these heights, you reach a flat spot and a junction with the Sycamore Trail, a faint trace heading left across the grass. Soon back on the ridgecrest, you come to a fence, left, guarding EBMUD's watershed. Here the road goes through a locked gate and becomes part of EBMUD's Rocky Ridge Loop Trail (Trail Use Permit required), but your route, the Upper Trail, continues as a single-track trail on the right side of the fence. Heading northwest, you now have views extending north past Walnut Creek and Concord to Suisun Bay and the west delta. You can also see the parking area where you started this hike, right and downhill.

At about the 2.75-mile point, you reach a gate in the fence, left, marking a junction with EBMUD's Rocky Ridge Loop Trail. As you continue straight, still on the Upper Trail, you cross a steep hillside which falls away to your right; ahead is paved Rocky Ridge Road, which you will soon reach after a moderate descent on rough, eroded trail. Just before reaching the road, you pass the steep Rocky Ridge Trail, right, leading down to the Cuesta Trail. Continue straight, and in a few feet you come to Rocky Ridge Road, gated uphill to your left, with another EBMUD access point on the other side of the road. Turn right and begin a moderate descent on the paved road. At about the 3.3-mile point, you reach a junction with the Cuesta and Rocky Ridge trails, right. From here, retrace your steps to the parking area.

• Martin Luther King Jr. Regional Shoreline •

29 Martin Luther King Jr. Regional Shoreline
ARROWHEAD MARSH

Length: 3.7 miles

Time: 2 to 3 hours

Rating: Easy

Regulations: EBRPD; dogs on leash.

Highlights: The San Leandro shoreline, in one of the East Bay's busiest industrial corridors, hosts a wonderful array of water-birds, from long-legged waders such as the great blue heron, to small shorebirds like the least sandpiper. This hike follows a level, paved pathway that runs from Garretson Point to Swan Way, passing San Leandro Bay, Elmhurst Creek, San Leandro Creek, Arrowhead Marsh, and Airport Channel, all productive birding areas. Birds will be most numerous in fall through spring, because the San Francisco Bay, on the Pacific Flyway, attracts large numbers of migrating and wintering species, many of which are on northern breeding grounds during the summer. Plan your hike for a rising or falling tide when the birds are active but not too far away to identify.

Facilities: Picnic tables, water, toilet, phone.

Trailhead: Southwest edge of parking area.

Directions: From Interstate 880 in Oakland, take the 66th Avenue/Coliseum exit and go briefly west on 66th Ave. to Oakport St. Turn left and go 0.6 mile to Hassler Way. Turn right and go 0.2 mile to Edgewater Dr. Turn right again and go 0.25 mile to the end of Edgewater Dr. Continue straight 0.1 mile on the entrance road to the Garretson Point parking area.

With binoculars and a bird guide or note pad handy, walk toward the water from the parking area and find the Garretson Point Trail, a paved pathway leading left and right along the shoreline. (This pathway may be signed as the Elmhurst Creek Trail, which you actually reach farther on.) In front of you is San Leandro Bay, nestled between Oakland International Airport and Alameda. To your left, jutting northwest into the bay, is 50-acre Arrowhead Marsh, a wildlife sanctuary that attracts large numbers of coots, ducks, grebes, herons, egrets, gulls, terns, and shorebirds. Arrowhead Marsh is part of the Western Hemisphere Shorebird Reserve Network, a collection of sites identified as critical to shorebird survival. To your right is the much smaller Damon Marsh, also a wildlife sanctuary.

Turn left, walk past the toilet, drinking fountain, and, at Fred (Skip) Garretson Memorial Point, a picnic area with white alder, western sycamore, eucalyptus, and acacia trees. The late Fred Garretson was a reporter for the *Oakland Tribune* whose stories inspired shoreline conservation efforts. Although this park is situated in a heavily industrial area, it is one of the best places to observe waterbirds in the East Bay. Looking south across the bay with binoculars or a spotting scope, you should be able, depending on the tide and time of year, to pick out a wide variety of birds, including common ducks such as American widgeon, mallard, northern pintail, ruddy duck, scoter, and scaup, and shorebirds such as American avocet, dowitcher, and willet. Benches and picnic tables along

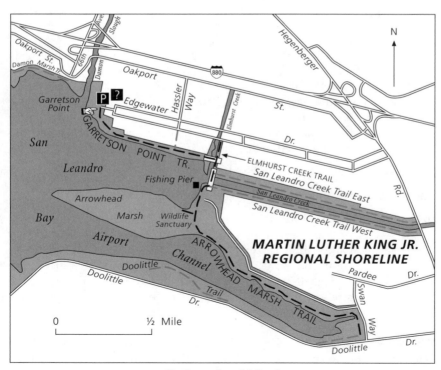

29. Arrowhead Marsh

the way make this an ideal route for a picnic, with plenty of opportunities to sit, watch birds, and enjoy the view. Perhaps a great blue heron will pay you a visit, landing silently on a nearby rock.

Where there are ducks and shorebirds, especially in the fall, there may be falcons—merlin and peregrine—hunting them. Be alert for something "putting up" the birds: when panicked, great clouds of waterbirds will lift from the mud flats or water in a noisy attempt to evade and confuse their predators. Nothing sets a birder's heart pounding like the glimpse of a dark shape, wings swept back, streaking seemingly out of nowhere in hot pursuit of a meal.

At about 0.7 mile, the paved path bends left, away from the water. Here a set of railroad tracks dead-end at an exercise station, and a small spit of land juts southwest into the water beside Elmhurst Creek. At high tide, look for large numbers of shorebirds roosting at the end of this spit. Species here may include American avocet, black-necked stilt, willet, marbled godwit, dowitcher, and small sandpipers. Roosting is a crucial part of a shorebird's daily activity, when the rising tide covers feeding areas and forces the birds to seek out protected high ground. Disturbing roosting or feeding birds threatens their delicate, life-and-death struggle to balance energy, rest, and food requirements. It may be fun for kids or dogs to chase birds, but it is cruel sport.

After crossing Elmhurst Creek on a bridge, and scanning its banks for more birds—perhaps a greater yellowlegs—you reach a T-junction with the Elmhurst Creek Trail. Turn right and follow it back toward the marsh.

Some birders use heavy equipment.

Soon you reach another bridge, this one across the mouth of San Leandro Creek, here a wide channel. Just before the bridge, you pass a junction on your left with San Leandro Creek Trail East; just after the bridge is a junction with San Leandro Creek West. Once across the bridge, bear right on the Arrowhead Marsh Trail as it passes a large parking area, fishing pier, and picnic area. (Toilets and water are available here.)

Although your attention may be focused on birds, you may also notice large numbers of California ground squirrels, standing at attention by their burrows or scurrying through the grass in the open field, left. A squirrel hole is sometimes taken over by a pair of burrowing owls, so it is worth scanning with binoculars all squirrel colonies you come across. Ahead, past the fishing pier, is a board-walk jutting a few hundred yards into the marsh. This is a great spot to scope the mud flats and pickleweed for ducks and shorebirds, but also look under the boardwalk for Virginia rails—dark brown, robin-sized waders that prowl the overgrown areas of the marsh. In addition to pick-leweed, other common salt-marsh plants found here include cordgrass and saltgrass. Each of these plants is tolerant of salt water to a different degree, and this accounts for its distribution, relative to the high-tide line, in the marsh.

Arrowhead Marsh and the nearby mud flats that are exposed at low tide occupy a large part of San Leandro Bay. With the sun at your back, the boardwalk is a fine vantage point for viewing shorebirds. Because the tide dictates shorebird behavior, you should plan your viewing for a few hours before or after high tide. This will allow you to observe birds as they feed, while they are still close enough to identify. Once the tide goes all the way out, the birds disperse and are hard to see clearly. You may notice broken mussel shells near the end of the boardwalk; these are deposited by gulls, which drop them from the air in an attempt to crack them open.

You may see a white, heron-like bird feeding on fish in the shallows near the walkway, and then do a double-take when you notice one just like it, but almost twice as big. The smaller is called a snowy egret, and the larger is the great egret. Careful study reveals other differences besides size. The snowy has a black bill and golden feet, while the great has a yel-low bill and black feet. Both are graceful fliers, and, with their cousin the great blue heron, add an exotic touch to marshes and wetlands of North America.

Southwest of Arrowhead Marsh are Airport Channel, Doolittle Dr., and the hangars of Oakland International Airport. Being in the midst of urban hustle and bustle gives you an appreciation for this wildlife sanctuary, opened to the public in 1979 as the San Leandro Bay Regional Shoreline, and renamed in 1992 to honor the slain civil-rights leader. Along the southwest edge of Arrowhead Marsh is another good place to look for shorebirds, but you will probably need a spotting scope to identify indi-vidual species. Closer in, birds may be feeding along the near shoreline of Airport Channel.

Besides pickleweed and marsh grasses, you may notice tall, thick-leaved plants with bright yellow flowers, growing along the upper edge of the marsh. This is marsh gum-plant or gumweed, which is named for the sticky resin that oozes from the daisy-like flower buds. These attrac-tive plants bring color to marshes around San Francisco, San Pablo, and Suisun bays from late summer through fall. A dirt road, left, parallels your route from the Arrowhead Marsh parking area to another just off Swan Way, your turn-around point. A grassy field, home for ground squirrels and perhaps a pair of burrowing owls, lies between you and this road.

As you continue southeast on the Arrowhead Marsh Trail, other shore-birds to look for include dunlin, a chunky sandpiper with a long bill curved down at the tip; and black-necked stilt, a black-and-white wader with shocking pink legs. A bit farther along, as you near Swan Way, look for a large black pipe that runs under your path and into Airport Channel. On the mud flats, right, you may find least sandpipers, small brown and white birds with pale legs; on the pipe itself there may be black turn-stones, pecking at barnacles. When you reach the parking area at Swan Way, which has water, a toilet, a picnic table, and a grove of trees planted to honor Dr. King, turn and retrace your steps to the Garretson Point parking area.

◆ Miller/Knox Regional Shoreline ◆

30	Miller/Knox Regional Shoreline
	SCENIC LOOP

Length: 2.25 miles

Time: 1 to 2 hours

Rating: Moderate

Regulations: EBRPD; hikers only.

Highlights: One of the East Bay's more urban regional parks, Miller/Knox demonstrates the value of setting aside land for recreation and preservation. Less than a mile from the parking area, and barely hidden from a heavily industrialized site, is one of the region's most scenic spots, a 322-foot vantage point straddling San Francisco and San Pablo bays, with views extending in all directions. This loop, using the West Ridge, Crest, and Marine View trails and Old Country Road, also lets you enjoy a lovely assortment of trees, shrubs, and wildflowers. This 295-acre regional shoreline was named for two EBRPD supporters in the state legislature, the late Senator George Miller, Jr. and former Assemblyman John T. Knox.

Facilities: Picnic tables, toilet, water (just past the north end of the parking area), phone.

Trailhead: South end of the north parking area, at the entrance from Dornan Dr.

Directions: From Interstate 580 eastbound in Richmond, take the Canal Boulevard/Garrard Boulevard exit, turn right and go 0.1 mile to Cutting Blvd. Turn right, go 0.3 mile to S. Garrard and turn left. Follow S. Garrard, which becomes Dornan Dr. on the south side of a tunnel, 0.7 mile to the first of two park entrances, right.

From Interstate 580 westbound in Richmond, take the Canal Boulevard/Garrard Boulevard exit, turn left and go 0.2 mile to Cutting Blvd., then follow the directions above.

Cross carefully to the east side of busy Dornan Drive and find a dirt turnout just left of EBRPD's Golden State Model Railroad Museum. From here a dirt path heads southeast to a boardwalk that zigzags across an open marshy area and then enters a stand of willow and coast live oak. After the boardwalk ends, the trail, now a single track lined with bush monkeyflower, toyon, and coyote bush, angles steeply uphill via two sets of wooden steps. Just past the first set of steps, you pass a path heading right and uphill, then continue climbing via switchbacks and a second set of steps.

At a **T**-junction marked by a trail post, you turn right on Old Country Road, a single track, and follow it south and then southwest toward West Ridge Point. As you make the turn, you have a beautiful view of the Richmond–San Rafael Bridge and Mt. Tamalpais, which dominates the western skyline. The route continues climbing, now on a moderate grade, past overgrown thickets of blackberry and manroot. In spring, the grassy hillsides here are splattered yellow with California buttercup. A short steep pitch brings another scenic reward, as you get a sweeping view of San Francisco and San Pablo bays, Angel Island, and the hills of Marin County.

Passing a trail post and an unsigned path, left, you continue straight and begin descending to a clearing where California poppies bloom from late winter through spring on an eroded hillside. Tall Monterey pines stand guard on a ridgetop, and the slopes below are graced with toyon,

30. Scenic Loop

View south from the West Ridge Trail near West Ridge Point.

willow, and bush monkeyflower. A cool breeze off the water is welcome here on a warm day. The trail crosses a ditch on two wood planks, continues through the clearing, and then negotiates a steep hillside that drops to your right. Passing a path going right and downhill, and another heading left and uphill, you continue straight to a T-junction, marked by a trail post, with the West Ridge Trail.

Here you turn left, enjoying a fine view of Brooks Island, Richmond Inner Harbor, and, in the distance, the huge cargo cranes at the Port of Oakland. As you walk northeast, past a path going right and downhill, you may notice a large stand of French broom, blooming bright yellow from late winter through spring. There is also crystalline iceplant up here, a low-growing succulent that produces white and pink flowers during spring and summer. The route, a rocky dirt path, climbs in the open on a moderate grade, and as you gain elevation, landmarks such as Emeryville, UC Berkeley, and the Berkeley Hills come into view. If you turn around, you are treated to a grand vista: San Francisco, Alcatraz, Angel Island, and the Bay Bridge. As you climb higher you can look southwest into Raccoon Strait—the body of water between Angel Island and Tiburon—and beyond to the just-visible north tower of the Golden Gate Bridge.

A steep climb brings you, at about the 0.75-mile point, to an exposed hilltop; this vantage point, one of the most impressive in the East Bay, gives you a 360-degree panorama of the Bay Area, making this a must-visit spot for people who enjoy learning the geography of the region in which they live. After descending briefly, you begin to climb again, soon reaching a paved summit with a rest bench and a trail junction. From this lofty perch you can see east to Wildcat Canyon and Tilden regional parks, and southeast toward Sibley Volcanic Regional Preserve, Round Top, and Redwood Regional Park. Here the West Ridge Trail ends, the Crest Trail goes straight, and an unnamed trail goes left over False Gun Vista Point.

Continuing straight and descending gently on the Crest Trail, a paved path, you approach East Vista Point, ahead, with a Chevron refinery left and downhill. Here you may see an American kestrel, a small falcon well-adapted to a variety of habitats, gliding on the wind or hovering aloft, searching for prey. At about the 1-mile point you reach East Vista Point, where a dirt path leads to a viewpoint, right. Now you follow the paved Crest Trail as it swings left and descends steeply northeast, toward the refinery. Pass a trail post with an arrow pointing left, and at the next post, just before the paved path bends right, look left to find a single track trail, the continuation of the Crest Trail. Turn left here and begin a gentle climb, with a steep hillside falling away to your right.

You are now heading southwest; after several hundred yards you cross a wooden plank bridge and then climb steeply via switchbacks through a landslide area shaded by pines and tall toyon bushes. Bearing right at a fork, you cross another plank bridge and descend through a corridor of French broom, some of it more than 6 feet tall. (A third plank bridge, right, leads to a dead-end.) Where the broom gives way, yellow buttercups and white milkmaids get a chance to show their spring blossoms. The route now comes into the open and climbs through an eroded area, crossing two more plank bridges, the second a more elaborate one over a ravine where water has carved the hillside into weird shapes resembling hoodoos. The refinery you saw earlier has been all but forgotten as you walk through this hidden wilderness.

As you approach a steep section of the trail, aiming for a notch in the ridge ahead, you pass a path going right and uphill. From here Mt. Tamalpais is perfectly framed in the notch, and may have a foreground of colorful poppies. At the notch is a four-way junction; from here the Crest Trail climbs steeply right via steps toward Nicholl Knob, an unsigned trail heads left to False Gun Vista Point, and your route, the Marine View Trail, continues straight. Soon, as you begin to cross a steep hillside where poppies cling to rock outcrops, you can see down to Dornan Drive, the parking area, and the trailhead. Once across a plank bridge, you turn left at a junction and descend moderately on a single track, eventually coming to a set of wooden steps. At the bottom of the steps you come to an unsigned fork in the route; here you bear left and follow Old Country Road, a dirt path, across a wooden bridge, and soon reach the junction you passed earlier on your way up from the boardwalk. Turn right here and retrace your steps to the parking area.

◆ Mission Peak Regional Preserve ◆

| **31** | Mission Peak Regional Preserve
MISSION PEAK |

Length: 6.3 miles

Time: 3 to 5 hours

Rating: Difficult

Regulations: EBRPD; no bicycles on the single-track part of the Peak Trail.

Highlights: A steady climb of more than 2000 feet in just over 3 miles, most of it on the Hidden Valley Trail, a well-graded dirt road, brings you to the top of Mission Peak, one of the East Bay's most dramatic summits, offering views of the entire Bay Area. Not a hike for hot weather, try to do this route just after a winter or spring storm, when the air is clear and the hills green. Even on a warm day, however, take extra clothes and a wind shell—this is a mountain environment which can quickly turn hostile.

Facilities: Water, toilet, horse staging.

Trailhead: East side of parking area.

Directions: From Interstate 880 in Fremont, take the Mission Boulevard/Warren Avenue exit and go northeast on Mission Blvd. 1.8 miles to Stanford Ave. Turn right and go 0.6 mile to a parking area at the end of Stanford Ave.

From Interstate 680 in Fremont, take the Mission Boulevard/Warms Springs District exit and follow signs for Mission Blvd. eastbound. Once on Mission Blvd., follow it for 0.6 mile to Stanford Ave. Turn right and go 0.6 mile to a parking area at the end of Stanford Ave.

From the parking area, the Hidden Valley Trail, a dirt road, heads uphill toward Mission Peak. After about 150 feet a dirt path branches left, and here there are gates across both routes. Once through the gates, the road and path run roughly parallel to each other, so you can take either one. If you follow the road, stay left at the first fork, a unsigned junction with the

Peak Meadow Trail. Vehicles transporting hang gliders to their launch site may be on the road for the first few miles, so use caution. The road and the path soon rejoin, about 0.25 mile from the trailhead. Your route passes stands of coast live oak, western sycamore, California buckeye, and blue elderberry, and then comes to Agua Caliente Creek, which drains Hidden Valley. Along the way to Mission Peak's summit, a number of paths—short cuts and cow trails—leave the main route: ignore these and stay on the wide dirt road.

The Ohlone Wilderness Regional Trail, a 28-mile trek through some of the East Bay's most scenic and remote territory, begins at the Stanford

31. Mission Peak

View west from the Hidden Valley Trail on the lower slopes of Mission Peak.

Avenue parking area and follows the Hidden Valley Trail up the west side of Mission Peak, though many people shun this steep climb and instead hike between Sunol and Del Valle regional parks, a trip described in "Ohlone Wilderness Regional Trail." The emblem for the Ohlone Wilderness Regional Trail, which you may see on trail posts here, is a white oak leaf in a red disk. You may also see numbers on some of the trail posts; these refer to numbered junctions on EBRPD's Ohlone Wilderness Regional Trail map.

After about 0.3 mile, Agua Caliente Creek flows under the road through a culvert, and you reach an unsigned junction with a road heading right. Stay left and begin a gentle climb which soon becomes moderate. Right and downhill is the road coming up from the previous junction; it joins your route just past a gate, only to diverge again at the base of a rocky hill, where you stay left. The terrain in the 2,999-acre Mission Peak Regional Preserve is rolling; the hills are green in winter and spring, brown in summer and fall, with tree-filled canyons. Most of the route stays in the open, so as you climb, be sure to stop often and enjoy the view. If you can plan your hike for a clear day in winter or spring, after a storm front has moved through, most of the Bay Area will be revealed, from Mt. Tamalpais to the Santa Cruz Mountains.

Mission Peak (2517') sits atop a long ridge that trends northwest–southeast, towering over the flatlands of Fremont to the west and Sunol Valley to the east. Immediately southeast of Mission Peak is another ridge, running northeast–southwest, crowned by Mt. Allison (2658'). Farther still to the southeast is Monument Peak (2594'), on the border of Santa Clara County's Ed R. Levin Park. Combined, these three peaks make up a massif that from many places around the East Bay appears to rival Mt. Diablo in stature.

You route passes through a wooded area—mainly coast live oak and California bay laurel—near a stream, then bends south through a rocky area and continues to climb. Except from the air, no other vantage point offers such extensive views this close to San Francisco Bay. Turning back toward the peak, which exposes more of its rocky backbone the higher you get, you soon come to a short, steep section and then reach a junction with the Peak Meadow Trail, right. Now the road begins a series of switch-backs that will carry you to the summit; on most of the way you will have the parking area at the end of Stanford Avenue in view, so you can gauge your progress in both distance and elevation. After 2 miles or so, the ter-rain around you becomes more rugged: a steep, grassy field strewn with boulders, and the dramatic rock cliffs of Mission Peak's summit. Lovers of wilderness often travel many hours for scenes such as this, yet you are only about an hour's walk from a trailhead in one of California's busiest urban areas. Ahead you can see the park residence, a collection of several buildings used by EBRPD rangers, and looming above them to the south-east, Mt. Allison, bristling with communication towers.

Just below the cliffs you come to a T-junction; here the A. A. Moore Grove Trail goes right, but your route, now a gravel road, turns left and climbs. Alfred A. Moore, an early California settler and attorney for the railroad, once owned several thousand acres on Mission Peak, including a ranch with exotic animals, which he used as a weekend retreat for fam-ily and friends. This junction is a fine place to rest, with convenient rocks to sit on and thrilling views west to San Francisco Bay. When you are ready to resume your ascent, climb steeply uphill toward the skyline ridge, perhaps in the company of turkey vultures soaring and banking on the wind. Respite arrives just as you crest the ridge in the form of a broad, flat area. Several dirt paths head right, but you continue straight, getting your first view today of Mt. Diablo and Pleasanton Ridge.

At about the 2.5-mile point, you come to a barbed-wire fence with a gate; the Hidden Valley Trail ends at a four-way junction just beyond the gate. Here you turn right and follow the Peak Trail, a dirt road that paral-lels the fence and heads uphill. The Peak Trail, part of the Bay Area Ridge Trail, runs between Ohlone College in Fremont and the summit of Mission Peak. Just as your route veers left away from the fence, you pass a wide path continuing straight; a bit farther, the Peak Trail is joined by a dirt road coming sharply from the right. As you continue to climb east, toward a flat spot on the skyline ridge, you have a chance to appreciate the tenacity of plants growing in this barren and often windy environ-ment. Clumps of blue bush lupine cling to the rocky soil in the company of California buttercup, and a few bay trees grab footholds farther down-hill. Here you may see a common bird of open places, the horned lark.

Hikers ascending Mission Peak via the Hidden Valley Trail.

Slightly larger than a sparrow, this brown and yellow bird is found on fields, ridges, and beaches across North America.

If the winter or spring day you've chosen is especially clear, you may be thrilled, when you crest the ridge, to see a line of snow-capped peaks in the distance—the Sierra Nevada—rising behind Livermore and Altamont Pass. Ahead, to the east, the land drops away to the Alameda Creek drainage, then rises up on the other side to form the highlands of the Sunol/Ohlone Wilderness. Soon you reach a fork in the route: left is the Eagle Trail, the continuation of the Ohlone Wilderness Regional/Bay Area Ridge Trail; right is the continuation of the Peak Trail. Turn right and begin a gentle climb that soon turns steep, bringing you to the end of the road, marked by two garbage cans and a wooden rail to hitch horses to. From here, several dirt paths head southeast, steeply uphill to the summit. As you climb, the waters of San Antonio Reservoir come into view to your left, but San Francisco Bay is hidden by a ridge, right.

The dirt path quickly gives way to dirt and rock, and you top several false summits, staying just left and below the ridgecrest, until San Francisco Bay is back in view. Before reaching the true summit, you come to metal post, anchored in rock, with holes drilled through it and each hole fitted with a pipe, 19 in all. These pipes are keyed to numbered plaques attached to the post. This clever, if low-tech, observation device allows you to identify more than two dozen Bay Area landmarks in a 360-degree circle around Mission Peak. Besides the ones already mentioned, some of the most notable include Mt. Hamilton's Lick Observatory (4209'); Rose Peak (3817') in the Ohlone Wilderness; Flag Hill, behind the visitor center in Sunol Wilderness; Moffett Field in Mountain View; Mt. Tamalpais; San Francisco; and Coyote Hills Regional Park. A few steps bring you at last to the top of Mission Peak, a climb of 2127 feet in a little more than 3 miles, for an average grade of about 7%. Congratulations, and welcome to one of the premier vantage points in the East Bay! When you have finished enjoying this exhilarating and hard-won summit, retrace your steps to the parking area.

Hang gliders and parasails fill the sky above the Hidden Valley Trail on the west side of Mission Peak.

• Morgan Territory Regional Preserve •

<table>
<tr><td>32</td><td>Morgan Territory Regional Preserve
BOB WALKER RIDGE</td></tr>
</table>

Length: 5.9 miles

Time: 3 to 4 hours

Rating: Moderate

Regulations: EBRPD; no bicycles on the single-track part of the Coyote Trail.

Highlights: This is one of the most remote and scenic parks in the East Bay, perched at 2,000 feet on the southeastern edge of Mt. Diablo State Park, within sight of Livermore, Altamont Pass, and the Central Valley. Seclusion and wilderness make hiking here a special experience; this loop, which uses the Coyote, Volvon Loop, and Volvon trails, takes full advantage of these attributes, dropping into a deep canyon, then climbing lofty Bob Walker Ridge. This is a region of extremes: hot in summer, cold in winter, and potentially windy all year.

Facilities: Picnic tables, water, toilet, horse staging.

Trailhead: Northeast edge of parking area.

Directions: From Interstate 580 in Livermore, take the North Livermore exit and go north 4.1 miles on North Livermore Ave. to Morgan Territory Rd., which is just after a sharp bend to the west. Turn right and go 5.5 miles to the Volvon Staging Area, right. (Use caution: after 0.7 mile, Morgan Territory Rd. becomes a one-lane road with turn-outs.)

From Marsh Creek Rd. in Clayton, turn right on Morgan Territory Rd. and go southeast 10.7 miles to the Volvon Staging Area, left.

As soon as you leave the large gravel parking area, which may be windy, you have a choice of two trails, Coyote and Volvon. Left is the Coyote Trail, a single track for hikers only; the Volvon Trail, a dirt road straight ahead, is open to hikers, horses, and bicycles. These trail names are based on Native American history and tradition: Coyote is a mythic personality in Indian legends, and the Volvon were one of the East Bay groups that resisted the Spanish mission system. The preserve itself is named for Jeremiah Morgan, an early settler, gold miner, and rancher. Bob Walker Ridge and the Bob Walker Regional Trail honor a photographer and environmentalist whose efforts on behalf of EBRPD from 1984 until his death in 1993 led to additional land acquisitions in Morgan Territory and Pleasanton Ridge. The Bob Walker Regional Trail, combining parts of the Volvon, Volvon Loop, Eagle, and Highland Ridge trails, connects Morgan

32. Bob Walker Ridge

Territory with Mt. Diablo State Park.

Following the Coyote Trail, you descend through beautiful grassland, with oaks dotting the hillsides and Mt. Diablo visible to the northwest. At a stock pond bear left, passing the Condor Trail, which continues straight through a gate. Your route climbs gently through stands of blue oak and coast live oak as it skirts the right side of the pond, which is shaded by a large valley oak. After passing the pond, the trail, indistinct in places, descends through a narrow, rocky canyon lined with black oak, California bay laurel, and manzanita, here growing tall as a small tree. As beautiful views open up toward Mt. Diablo, resist the temptation

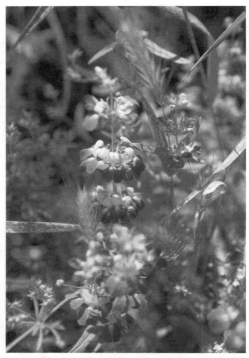

Chinese houses grow on Mt. Diablo.

to look and walk at the same time: the footing gets tricky here.

This is rugged terrain, colorful in fall, with a distinct wilderness feel. Above and right is a high, rocky ridge blanketed with chaparral. As the descent becomes steeper, the trail makes **S**-bends down the hillside. Toyon, coffeeberry, creambush, redberry buckthorn and hop tree are some of the shrubs you may spot along the way. At about the 0.8-mile point, in the canyon bottom, you reach a junction with the Mollok Trail, left. A streambed lined with bigleaf maple and western sycamore is also left, and as you continue straight ahead, the canyon walls relax their grip and the terrain becomes more open and park-like.

Just past the 1-mile point, you come to a fork in the trail; the branches rejoin a short distance ahead at a gate. Passing through the gate, you emerge from forest into grassland and leave the canyon behind. The route, sometimes just a matted path in the grass, stays in the middle of a large valley, and soon reaches another fork. This time, follow the right-hand branch and walk uphill. The weedy plant with blue flowers growing beside the trail is called vinegar weed; rub the leaves and smell your fingers to find out why. Large oaks with clumps of mistletoe grace the hillsides. Ahead is T-junction with a dirt road; here you turn right and climb north on a gentle and then moderate grade through oak savanna. You are now on the continuation of the Coyote Trail, and you will be on dirt roads until you return to the parking area. From his perch on an oak limb, a raucous Steller's jay may announce your arrival; you may also spot a northern flicker, a member of the woodpecker family, here. As you gain elevation via long switchbacks and gradually emerge from the trees, look up to check the sky for hawks.

At about the 2.25-mile point, you pass a trail, right, leading up Bob Walker Ridge to join the Volvon Trail. Continue straight, past a cattle-loading pen on your right, and after a few hundred feet you reach a T-junction; here the Eagle Trail branches left, and your route, the Volvon Loop Trail, goes right. As you continue climbing on a gentle grade, you are rewarded with fine views of Mt. Diablo's North Peak, and, in the distance, Clayton, Pittsburg, Antioch, and the west delta. When you reach the north end of Bob Walker Ridge, the route bends sharply right, presenting a vista that stretches east to the Central Valley and, on a clear day, the Sierra. Now heading southeast, the route stays just below the ridgecrest, right, and passes through lovely stands of blue oak and bay. From here you can see in the distance the windmills near Altamont Pass. At about the 3-mile point, you pass on your left the first of three connections to the Valley View Trail, the first two about 0.1 mile apart, the third about 0.8 mile farther along. Just ahead on the right is a good place for a picnic, with rocks to sit on.

Soon you reach a notch in the ridge, and a trail leading right and downhill to the Coyote Trail. Mt. Diablo looks impressive from here, dominating the northwest skyline. Continuing on the Volvon Trail, you pass the Valley View and Blue Oak trails, left. In the bay trees here you may see flocks of dark-eyed juncos, a western scrub-jay, or perhaps a woodpecker. Tall manzanitas line the left side of the road. At about 4.5 miles, the Hummingbird Trail, a short connector to the Blue Oak Trail, goes straight, but you follow the Volvon Trail as it turns sharply right and passes through an area of chaparral, mostly chamise. Soon you pass two junctions, about 0.2 mile apart, with the Prairie Falcon Trail, right; and just beyond the second of these, a junction with the Condor Trail, also right.

When you reach a junction with the Blue Oak Trail, follow the Volvon Trail as it veers right, and in about 150 feet you come to a T-junction with a dirt-and-gravel road. Turn right here and begin a gentle descent through open grassland, with Mt. Diablo visible on your right. At about the 5.5-mile point you arrive at a fork; stay to the right and follow the gently rolling road until you can see the parking area. As you approach it, another fork presents you with two options: a steep descent, right, or a more circuitous but moderate descent, left. Both arrive at the parking area.

◆ Mt. Diablo State Park ◆

According to a California Department of Parks and Recreation brochure, the history of Mt. Diablo as a state park goes back to 1921, when "a parcel of land on the mountain was designated a state park, and much of the rest of the mountain was declared a game refuge." In 1931, more land was acquired, and the park was formally dedicated and opened to the public. But tourists had been enjoying the mountain since the 1870s, especially the view from its 3,849-foot summit, said to be surpassed in size only by that from the top of Africa's 19,340-foot Mt. Kilimanjaro. Toll roads, opened in 1874, brought visitors via stage from Walnut Creek and Danville to a 16-room hotel, Mountain House, located about three miles from the summit. The hotel, a site of frequent weddings, hosted guests from across the US and as far away as Europe. The hotel and the summit observation platform were destroyed by fires in the 1890s, and the toll roads, closed to public access, did not reopen until 1915.

Prior to its days as the site of a swank resort, Mt. Diablo served as the reference point for surveys of most of California and portions of Nevada and Oregon. In 1851, Leander Ransome designated the summit as the crossing of an east–west *Mt. Diablo baseline* and a north–south *Mt. Diablo meridian*, reference points still used today in official surveys. In fact, the Mt. Diablo baseline passes between the Steam Trains and Vollmer Peak in Tilden Regional Park. According to Dorothy L. Whitnah, writing in *An Outdoor Guide to the San Francisco Bay Area*, the name "Mt. Diablo" may have come from an account of a 1806 battle told to the California state legislature in 1850 by Mariano G. Vallejo, formerly the Mexican governor of Alta California. When Spanish soldiers from the Presidio in San Francisco were fighting Indians in a battle near the mountain, they were scared off by a frightening personage they took to be the Devil, or *el Diablo*, but who perhaps may have been a medicine man in full regalia.

Although it looks like a volcano from afar, most of Mt. Diablo's rock is actually sedimentary, part of an ancient ocean floor that has been tilted and distorted within the last one or two million years by an uplifting core of hard Franciscan rock. Fossil hunters and rock hounds will enjoy areas such as Rock City, where rock formations are exposed and easily studied. Mt. Diablo is a botanist's delight: much of the upper mountain is swathed in chaparral, while lower on its flanks grow pine, oak, and a host of other native trees, shrubs, and wildflowers. Birding is a popular pastime on the mountain, especially in Mitchell Canyon, and the Mt. Diablo bird list, revised in 1987, has 163 species.

Many groups, including the Sierra Club, the Audubon Society, and the California Native Plant Society, schedule hikes and other programs on Mt.

Diablo. A listing of these can be found in *Mount Diablo Review*, published twice yearly by Mount Diablo Interpretive Association (MDIA) and Save Mount Diablo in cooperation with Mt. Diablo State Park. The publication is sent free to MDIA members and is also available at the park's entrance kiosks. (See Appendix C for addresses and phone numbers of these groups and organizations.)

There is a small entrance fee, payable at the North Gate and South Gate entrance kiosks, and a small parking fee at Mitchell Canyon. There are more than 50 picnic sites, each with table and barbecue, along the park's paved roads; there are also three group picnic sites for 25 to 100 people each. Group picnic site reservations and general park information can be obtained by calling Mt. Diablo State Park headquarters.

MT. DIABLO STATE PARK (925) 837-2525

open 8 A.M. to sunset.

VISITOR CENTER, SUMMIT MUSEUM, AND STORE (925) 837-6119

Open Wednesday through Sunday from 10 A.M. to 4 P.M.

CAMPING (800) 444-7275

Camping is available in three campgrounds with a total of 58 sites. These sites can be reserved up to eight weeks in advance for stays from October 1 through May 31.

View east along the Bruce Lee Trail to North Peak, with rising half moon.

33
Mt. Diablo State Park
BACK CANYON

Length: 4.3 miles

Time: 2 to 3 hours

Rating: Moderate

Regulations: Mt. Diablo State Park; no bicycles, no dogs, no smoking.

Highlights: This route, combining parts of the Bruce Lee, Back Creek, and Meridian Point trails, and Back Creek, Meridian Ridge, and Donner Canyon roads, offers a wonderful sample of the joys the north side of Mt. Diablo has to offer. Cool, shady canyons, exposed rocky ridges, chaparral-covered hillsides, and oak woodlands compete for your attention with a terrific assortment of trees, shrubs, wildflowers, and birds. In spring, consider extending your hike to visit a set of hidden waterfalls by following the Middle and Falls trails as described below in "Falls Trail." The Back Canyon Trail and the lower portion of Donner Canyon Road may be very muddy in wet weather. (This is hike 5 on the Mt. Diablo State Park trail map.)

Facilities: None

Trailhead: North side of Regency Dr., about 200 feet from its end.

Directions: From Interstate 680 in Walnut Creek, or Hwy. 24 eastbound (just before the merge with I-680), take the Ygnacio Valley Rd. exit and go northeast 7.6 miles to Clayton Rd. Turn right and at 1.5 miles, pass a junction with Marsh Creek Rd., right. Continue straight, and at 2.5 miles, reach another junction with Marsh Creek Rd., again on your right. Here Clayton Rd. ends and you continue straight, now on Marsh Creek Rd. Go 0.5 mile to a stoplight and turn right onto Regency Dr. Go 0.6 mile on Regency to a dead-end; park along the side of the street.

On the north side of Regency Dr., about 200 feet before it dead-ends, find a paved road, blocked by a gate, heading west. Follow this downhill, reaching in a few hundred feet a junction with the paved Bruce Lee Trail (named to honor a leading equestrian and trail builder, not the martial arts expert), just upstream from the confluence of Donner and Back creeks. Turn left and walk several hundred feet to the Mt. Diablo State Park boundary at Regency Gate. Immediately after entering the park, you come to a trail to Mitchell Canyon Road, leading right and uphill. In front of you are two dirt roads heading straight, parallel to each other, the left-hand one beside Donner Creek. The Bruce Lee Trail continues as the right-hand road, and after following it for about 100 yards you come to a junction marked by a trail post. Here your route, the Bruce Lee Trail, heads uphill to the right, and Donner Canyon Road, which you will use later on the return portion of this loop, goes left.

As the route climbs in the open and you crest a small ridge, take a moment to admire the rugged north side of Mt. Diablo, at 3849 feet the East Bay's tallest mountain. To its left stands North Peak (3557'), admirable in its own right. Below North Peak is Donner Canyon, whose

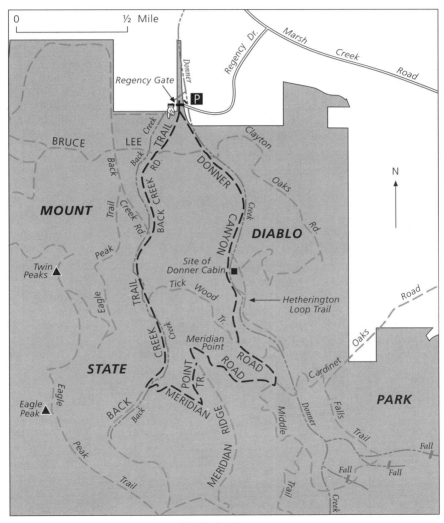

33. Back Canyon

upper reaches provide the source of the waterfalls you may wish to explore as an extension to this loop. Facing south, you have in front of you Meridian Ridge, which divides Donner and Back canyons. To your right, Eagle Peak (2369') and Twin Peaks anchor a high ridge forming the border between Back and Mitchell canyons.

This route offers you ample opportunity to learn to identify some common East Bay trees. Two of our three common deciduous oaks, blue and valley, reside here. Blue oak has light gray bark divided into long strips, and blue-green leaves. Valley oak has checkered, dark gray bark and deeply lobed dark-green leaves. Valley oaks prefer moist soils found in canyon bottoms, and blue oak inhabits rolling foothills at higher elevations. Also here, especially along Donner Creek, is California buckeye, a deciduous tree with long, pointed leaves, arranged mostly in groups of five, like fingers on a hand. In late spring and early summer, buckeyes sprout long, upturned candles of white flowers.

Surrounded by open grassland, you come to an unsigned, four-way intersection. From here the Bruce Lee Trail continues west to Mitchell Canyon, and a road joining sharply from the left heads back to Donner Canyon. Your route, the Back Creek Road, turns left and contours around a ridge before dropping into Back Canyon. As you walk toward the ridge topped by Eagle Peak and Twin Peaks, Back Creek is to your right. Soon the Back Creek Road turns right to cross Back Creek, but your route, the Back Creek Trail, a level dirt road, continues straight. Now enjoying an easy stroll, you have a chance to learn to recognize two more native trees.

The East Bay has three evergreen, or "live," oaks: coast, canyon, and interior. They are very similar, but the coast live oak, growing here beside the road, has spiny leaves that are glossy dark green and curled under at the edges. If you have a hand lens or a magnifying glass, you will see tiny tufts of hair attached to the veins on the underside of the leaf; the other two live oaks are hairless. California bay laurel, related to the Mediterranean bay whose leaves are used in cooking, has long, dark green leaves that are pointed and shiny. If in doubt, rub a leaf and smell the distinctive odor on your fingers. Bay trees produce small clusters of yellow flowers in late winter. Shape, size, and habitat of bay trees varies greatly, from compact, round shrubs on wind-swept ridges to large trees with curved, drooping branches found in cool, dark canyons.

When the road reaches a gate, the Back Creek Trail becomes a single track that climbs gently over rocky terrain, alternating between open and wooded areas and making several crossings of Back Creek. At about the 1-mile point, you pass the unsigned Tick Wood Trail, left. Soon you will see a small canyon branching left from Back Canyon. The next segment of your route, the Meridian Point Trail, climbs this canyon. About 100 yards past where you can see the canyons branching, look for a clearing with an unsigned trail junction. Turn left and descend toward the creek.

Now on the Meridian Point Trail, a single track, you cross Back Creek on rocks and begin to switchback up a steep embankment. The route climbs steeply on the east side of Back Creek, then enters the small canyon you saw earlier. Your efforts are rewarded by fine views north out Back Canyon to the residential developments of Clayton, and, beyond a set of rolling hills, the west delta. Indian paintbrush is plentiful along here, and soon you reach an area where manzanita and other chaparral plants cloak the rocky hillsides.

When the route reaches the head of the side canyon, you cross a small creek bed and turn sharply left to climb the canyon's exposed southwest-facing wall. Here the route is out in the open, hanging onto the edge of the hillside. More great views are in store, including one of Mt. Diablo's main summit ridge. A short while later, at about the 2-mile point, you reach a junction with Meridian Ridge Road. Here you turn left and descend steeply to Meridian Point, where the route bends sharply right. As you make the turn you can see North Peak rising in front of you, with Donner Canyon Road, the final leg of your loop, downhill and left.

You may be able to spot the difference here between two native pines, gray and Coulter. Gray pine, a tree well-adapted to dry conditions, has long gray-green needles in clusters of three, and big, spiny cones that fall to the ground when ripe. A close relative, the Coulter pine, has darker green, bushier needles, stout branches turning up at the ends, and even larger cones. Gray pines often have multiple trunks, but Coulter pines seldom do. Also found here, along with manzanita, are some of the other chaparral plants, including buckbrush, chamise, black sage, and yerba santa.

After descending steeply for about 0.5 mile from Meridian Point, you reach a junction with the Middle Trail heading right and uphill. (If you want to visit Mt. Diablo's hidden waterfalls, active during and after wet weather, turn right and follow the "Falls Trail" route description on pages 194-196.) The gray and twisted limbs of dead manzanita you see here are the result of a 1977 fire that swept across Mt. Diablo. Fire plays a beneficial role in the chaparral plant community, and you will see many young, healthy manzanitas here as well. Just downhill from the Middle Trail junction is the end of Meridian Ridge Road and a junction with Donner Canyon and Cardinet Oaks roads.

At the junction, turn left and walk steeply downhill on Donner Canyon Road through an area of manzanita, chaparral, and blue oak, with Donner Creek on your right. A number of trails will join Donner Canyon Road on the way back to Regency Gate; ignore them. At about the 3-mile point you pass the Hetherington Loop Trail, right, and as the grade changes from steep to moderate, you enter a wonderful area containing most of Mt. Diablo's common trees and shrubs. Soon you pass the Tick Wood Trail, left; then, as the route steepens and you descend through oak woodland, you pass the other end of the Hetherington Loop Trail, right. Also right is a short trail leading to an old homesite called the Donner Cabin; all that remains is a brick fireplace foundation and other stone work.

Large valley oaks, along with California juniper, gray pine, and walnut, enhance this section of the route, a level walk along the west side of Donner Creek. Beautiful blue oaks dot the grassy hillside, left. At about the 4-mile point, you come to a trail to Clayton Oaks Road, right, heading across the creek. Continue straight, and in about 100 yards you reach a trail going left to the Bruce Lee Trail. Again continue straight, and in another 100 yards you reach a fork in the route: from here both paths lead to Regency Gate. If you take the left-hand fork, you soon come to the junction where the Bruce Lee Trail heads toward Back Canyon, the start of this loop. From this junction retrace your steps to Regency Drive.

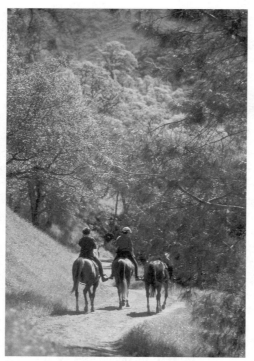

Equestrians on Back Creek Road near its crossing of Back Creek.

34 Mt. Diablo State Park
FALLS TRAIL

Length: 5.85 miles round-trip

Time: 3 to 4 hours

Rating: Moderate

Regulations: Mt. Diablo State Park; no bicycles, no dogs, no smoking.

Highlights: Best in early spring when the creeks are full, this scenic and strenuous route, using the Middle and Falls trails, and Donner Canyon, Meridian Ridge, and Cardinet Oaks roads, gives you views of hidden waterfalls cascading down from Mt. Diablo's North Peak. In addition, the first part of the loop, the Middle Trail, takes you through an area of the mountain burned in 1977, providing a chance to see the regenerative effects of fire on manzanita and other chaparral vegetation. The lower portion of Donner Canyon Road may be muddy during and after wet weather, but that's when the falls are running. (The Middle and Falls trails/Cardinet Oak Road portion of this route can be done as a 2.25-mile extension to the "Back Canyon" route above.)

Facilities: None

Trailhead: North side of Regency Dr., about 200 feet from its end.

Directions: See the directions for "Back Canyon" on p. 188.

This route has the same start and finish as "Back Canyon" above, but where the Bruce Lee Trail climbs right, about 100 yards past Regency Gate, you stay left along the west side of Donner Creek, walking southeast and then south into Donner Canyon. Soon you pass a trail leading to the Bruce Lee Trail, right, and, in another 100 yards or so, a trail heading left across the creek to Clayton Oaks Road. Nearby you may notice a large California ground-squirrel colony with dozens of holes on a southwest-facing hillside across the creek.

Now you enjoy a straight and level walk past stands of valley oak, California juniper, gray pine, California buckeye, and walnut, soon passing Donner Cabin, site of an old homestead, left. Uphill and right, blue oaks and an occasional eucalyptus grace the hillsides. Be alert here for a hummingbird's fast buzz or the western meadowlark's liquid warble.

As the route begins a steep climb through oak savanna, you pass the Hetherington Loop Trail, left, and the Tick Wood Trail, right. The grade eases somewhat, giving you a chance to notice more of the trees and shrubs common to this part of Mt. Diablo State Park, including coast live oak, gray pine, manzanita, coffeeberry, toyon, buckbrush, California sagebrush, chamise, and yerba santa. At about the 1-mile point the road steepens again, and you pass the uphill end of the Hetherington Loop Trail, left. Soon you come to a junction with Meridian Ridge and Cardinet Oaks roads.

Here you turn right and begin walking uphill on Meridian Ridge Road. After about 100 yards, you come to a trail post and a junction with a single-track trail heading left and uphill. This is the Middle Trail, which, as

34. Falls Trail

it climbs toward Prospectors Gap Road, brings you to the Falls Trail. You turn left onto it and begin a gentle uphill climb through chaparral and stands of manzanita—tall, twisted remnants of a 1977 fire and shrubby new growth. The trail, an intimate path very different from the dirt roads that crisscross much of the mountain, alternates between open and wooded areas.

The route next climbs a series of switchbacks and then levels off, giving you fine views southeast to Mt. Diablo's rugged North Peak (3557') and east to Mt. Olympia (2948'). You may hear the sound of running water coming from a tributary of Donner Creek, downhill and left. As the route comes into the open, it swings south toward Mt. Diablo's summit (3849') and crosses a hillside resembling a botanical garden, with manzanita, toyon, California sagebrush, black sage, chamise, buckbrush, and yerba santa.

Now back in the shade, the route meanders on a level grade, then makes a short climb. After crossing a small creek, the route becomes rocky, eroded, and possibly wet in places. As you gain elevation, you begin to have views north to Clayton, the west delta, and the hills of Napa and Solano counties. Continuing to climb on gentle and moderate grades, the trail slices across an open hillside which drops steeply left. Soon you are back in shady, cool thickets of shrubs and small trees.

At about the 2.3-mile point, you reach a junction; here the Middle Trail turns right and climbs, but your route, the Falls Trail, a narrow track overgrown in places, heads straight. Continuing on the Falls Trail, you soon reach an open and very steep hillside above Donner Creek, hidden by trees below. Across Donner Canyon, left, rises the steep, rugged face of North Peak, one of the mountain's most impressive vistas. Please be careful as you gaze skyward; a misstep on these dizzying heights could be fatal. Look here for redberry buckthorn, a shrub with small, holly-like leaves. The route soon drops via switchbacks to the shady banks of Donner Creek, lined with California bay laurel, and then begins a gentle uphill climb on the creek's right-hand bank.

A short distance upstream, Donner Creek bends left around a rocky rib, but your route follows a tributary to the right. (This tributary, not shown on the Mt. Diablo State Park trail map, may be seasonal.) A bit farther

Toyon has clusters of red berries.

upstream, you cross the tributary, veer left, and begin climbing the oppo-site bank, now heading downstream. As you work your way up the rocky rib, you come to a fork in the trail. Continue straight—the right-hand fork rejoins your route in a few hundred feet. Juniper trees thrive here, and may be loaded with gray berries that when crushed smell like gin. Once around the rocky rib, the trail leads upstream through a deep, shady ravine on the right side of Donner Creek. In early spring, look here for milkmaids, a wildflower with four white petals tinged near the base with yellow.

Soon you cross Donner Creek and continue to climb, sometimes steeply, across an open hillside. Mountain mahogany, a tree-like shrub with silver-gray bark and small, serrated leaves, grows here, along with large clumps of California sagebrush. After considerable effort, you are rewarded by a beautiful vista stretching north from Donner Canyon all the way to the hills of Napa and Solano counties. And after reaching a flat area, you see the first waterfall just ahead, a cascade of water tumbling over a large rock cliff. The trail climbs, descends to a seasonal creek, and then climbs again, until you are perched on a cliff above the waterfall. A rough path leads left to the edge of the cliff: use extreme caution!

The view from here includes all of Donner Canyon, Mt. Olympia, Mitchell Canyon Road, and quarry-scarred Mt. Zion (1635'). This is one of the great vistas on Mt. Diablo, but there is more to come. As the route swings east, passing through chaparral, more waterfalls pop into view, spilling across eroded, rocky cliffs, Now directly under North Peak, you step across a seasonal creek and then pass a stream flowing out of Wild Oat Canyon.

Now the trail bends west and then northwest, descending beneath impressive rock cliffs. Ahead a ridge sweeps down from Mt. Olympia to Donner Canyon; your route crosses it and another just beyond. Layers of rock, exposed in places here along the trail, are bent and tilted almost to the vertical, a vivid display of the forces that uplifted Mt. Diablo millions of years ago. Stop from time to time and look downhill to your left: more falls may be visible in the upper reaches of Donner Canyon. In early spring the hillsides here are lush green; within a few months they will turn brown and remain so until the rains arrive in autumn. Lupine in bloom may add dabs of blue to the scene.

The view along the final stretch of the Falls Trail is superb. To the west, Eagle Peak (2369') caps the ridge separating Mitchell and Back canyons. Across Donner Canyon is Meridian Ridge, leading uphill to Bald Ridge and the summit, which is due south. A level walk soon brings you to Cardinet Oaks Road, which you descend via S-bends to Donner Creek. If the creek is overflowing the road, step across on rocks and proceed uphill on a moderate grade, passing another creek flowing under the road through a culvert. At about the 4-mile point, you reach the junction of Cardinet Oaks, Meridian Ridge, and Donner Canyon roads. Retrace your steps from here, descending through Donner Canyon to Regency Drive.

Mt. Diablo State Park
THE GRAND LOOP

Length: 6.5 miles

Time: 3 to 5 hours

Rating: Difficult

Regulations: Mt. Diablo State Park; entrance fee; no bicycles, no dogs, no smoking.

Highlights: A complete circle around Mt. Diablo, the East Bay's tallest peak, plus a trip to the summit, makes this one of the region's premier hikes, and a great way to learn more about the trees, shrubs, and wildflowers that struggle for survival on the rugged mountain's upper reaches. This strenuous route uses Deer Flat, Meridian Ridge, and Prospectors Gap roads, and the North Peak, Summit, and Juniper trails. (This is hike 8 on the Mt. Diablo State Park trail map.)

Facilities: Picnic tables, water, toilet.

Trailhead: North end of Diablo Valley Overlook.

Directions: From Interstate 680 in Danville, take the Diablo Road/Danville exit and follow Diablo Rd. 3 miles east to Mt. Diablo Scenic Blvd. Turn left onto Mt. Diablo Scenic Blvd.—which soon becomes South Gate Rd.—and go 3.7 miles to the South Gate entrance station. Continue on South Gate Rd. another 3.2 miles to Park Headquarters and a junction with North Gate and Summit roads. Turn right onto Summit Rd. and go 2.3 miles to Diablo Valley Overlook, a large parking area at a sharp bend in the road, just above Juniper Campground.

From the north end of the parking area, follow either of two paved roads downhill into the Juniper Campground; from the point where they join, continue walking northwest on a gated dirt road, signed as Mitchell Canyon Road but called Deer Flat Road on the Mt. Diablo State Park trail map. Many of the trees and shrubs growing here are adapted to hot, dry conditions, including gray pine, California juniper, manzanita, and chamise. Other trees which manage somehow to survive here are coast live oak and California bay laurel, normally associated with cooler, wetter terrain. Looking west across Pine Canyon, you have expansive views of the Interstate 680 corridor and the hills of Oakland and Berkeley, with Mt. Tamalpais in distant Marin county visible on a clear day. To the north, the vista extends past Walnut Creek and Concord to Suisun Bay and the west delta.

Soon you pass Burma Road, left; continue straight and then bear right as the road descends via well-graded **S**-bends, giving you a look at Mt. Diablo's 3849-foot summit, today's goal. The variety of trees and shrubs increases dramatically as you near Deer Flat, adding to your list such species as canyon live oak, blue oak, hop tree, toyon, coffeeberry, yerba santa, and redberry buckthorn. Despite all this plant life, the route is open with no shade. When the road levels out in a little valley, you have reached Deer Flat, one of the prettiest spots on Mt. Diablo, especially in fall when bigleaf maple, California wild grape, and poison oak add touches of color to the scene.

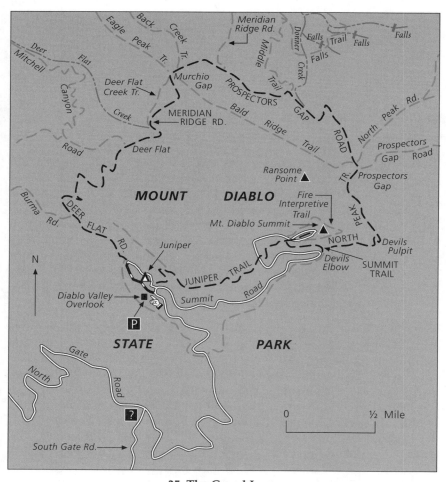

35. The Grand Loop

Soon you come to a junction marking the end of Deer Flat Road. Here, Mitchell Canyon Road goes left, but your route, Meridian Ridge Road, turns right and heads for Murchio Gap. (The distance to Murchio Gap given on the trail post here is wrong: it is 0.75 mile, not 1.75 miles.) Descending on a gentle grade from Deer Flat, the route next turns north and skirts Bald Ridge as it begins to climb. With the grade now steep, you pass Deer Flat Creek Trail, left. A relentless climb in the open helps you win back elevation lost in the descent from Juniper Campground. This is the domain of manzanita, with some species growing as tall as trees and others hugging the ground. Also here are chaparral pea, a thorny, three-leaved shrub that produces magenta flowers in late spring, and toyon, a tree-like shrub with oval leaves that are stiff and serrated.

At about the 2.5-mile point, you reach Murchio Gap, an important junction with many trails. Clockwise from the left as you face north, they are: Deer Flat Creek Trail, Eagle Peak Trail, Back Creek Trail, Meridian Ridge Road, and Bald Ridge Trail. Murchio Gap is home to leather oak, a low-growing shrub with curly, gray-green leaves, confined in the East Bay mostly to Mt. Diablo. As you follow Meridian Ridge Road east, you have a fine view, left, of Clayton, the west delta, and the hills of Napa and Solano counties. Also left is a dark ridge leading northwest to Eagle Peak (2369'); and ahead of you, from left to right, are North Peak (3557'), Prospectors Gap—a notch on the skyline—and Mt. Diablo's summit.

After a gentle descent, you come to a junction; here Meridian Ridge Road turns left, but your route, Prospectors Gap Road goes straight. As you follow Prospectors Gap Road southeast, it holds a level course, postponing the inevitable climb. Where the Middle Trail comes in from the left, near Big Spring, you descend slightly to within earshot of Donner Creek. Here you may see canyon live oak, and on the ground big cones from gray pines. Now comes a steep climb, fortunately in the shade of bay and coast live oak, but soon the shade ends

Hiker rests after climbing steeply to Prospectors Gap.

and the road, now rocky in places, makes a switchback, easing the grade somewhat as you struggle toward Prospectors Gap.

On your left is the steep, rocky face of North Peak. On your right, the top of Mt. Diablo, with its domed summit museum, comes into view. This long, steep climb is a great conditioning hike, but not for the weak-kneed or faint-of-heart. A final pitch brings you, with relief, to Prospectors Gap, at about the 4-mile point. From here, Prospectors Gap Road drops steeply in front of you; North Peak Road heads left to North Peak; and your route, the North Peak Trail, goes uphill and right. (The North Peak Trail is one of the few single tracks on Mt. Diablo open to bicycles.) Views here south and east extend to Curry Canyon, the Black Hills, Morgan Territory, and the Central Valley.

The North Peak Trail, rutted and rocky in places, climbs across an open hillside and soon merges with an unsigned trail, right. Gray pine, interior live oak, canyon live oak, and blue oak dominate here; their shade is welcome on a hot day. A rocky ridge, dropping steeply from Devils Pulpit, just east of the summit, forms the near skyline to the south. As you near this ridge, the terrain becomes more rocky, with a severe drop-off, left, and a steep uphill slope, right. As you come into the open and switchback across the ridge, you are rewarded with a stunning 180-degree view, which takes in the west delta, the Central Valley, Livermore, Pleasanton, the Sunol/Ohlone Wilderness, and Mission Peak.

As the route turns west and you begin walking toward Devils Elbow, a sharp bend in Summit Road, you can see the summit museum and communication towers on Mt. Diablo's summit. Low-growing bay and juniper join pine and oak on a windswept hillside. California fuchsia, a late bloomer, may add a touch of vivid red to the scene. A short climb on loose rock and dirt brings you to Summit Road at Devils Elbow. As you reach the pavement, make a sharp right and begin climbing the Summit Trail, which rises through chaparral to the summit's lower parking area, at about the 5-mile point.

To reach the mountain's 3849-foot summit from the lower parking area, turn right and follow either of two paved roads about 0.2 mile uphill. The summit museum, which has an observation deck on top, was built by the Civilian Conservation Corps from 1938 to 1940, but remained mostly unused until 1993, when the Mount Diablo Interpretive Association opened its visitor center there. The visitor center, where you will find information about the mountain's geology, flora, and fauna, as well as a small book store, rest rooms, telephone, and water, is open Wednesday through Sunday, 10:00 A.M. to 4:00 P.M. Climb to the observation deck for spectacular 360-degree views; it is said that the only vantage place with more land in view on a clear day is the summit of Africa's Mt. Kilimanjaro.

After resting and enjoying the scenery, retrace your steps to the lower parking area, then continue walking west across pavement until you find a trail post marking the Juniper Trail, a single track heading downhill from the edge of the parking area. From here, make a steep, rugged descent past several fenced-in communication towers on loose dirt, rocks, and railroad ties. Soon you reach Summit Road; cross carefully, turn right, and walk uphill a short distance to a trail post, left, marking the continuation of the Juniper Trail.

Now the route loses elevation via a series of switchbacks and passes through an area of pine, oak, bay, and chaparral. You head west and continue to descend along the crest of a broad ridge, with a sea of chaparral on both sides of the trail. As the route flattens out at a saddle, you come to a junction. Here an unsigned trail heads northwest to a high point on Moses Rock Ridge; and a trail post with an arrow pointing left directs you to the continuation of the Juniper Trail, which descends through groves of bay and juniper to the parking area.

36 Mt. Diablo State Park
JUNIPER AND SUMMIT TRAILS

Length: 4.5 miles

Time: 2 to 3 hours

Rating: Moderate

Regulations: Mt. Diablo State Park; entrance fee; no dogs, no smoking, no bicycles.

Highlights: This route to the summit of Mt. Diablo uses the Juniper and Summit trails, and provides unrivaled views on a clear day, when most of the Bay Area, the Central Valley, and the Sierra Nevada appear before you. The mountain's upper reaches contain fine examples of chaparral plants, along with other trees and shrubs adapted to this harsh environment. (This is hike 3 on the Mt. Diablo State Park trail map, but done in reverse, allowing you to reach the summit quickly and avoid the steep descent on the upper leg of the Juniper trail.)

Facilities: Picnic tables, water, toilet.

Trailhead: North end of Diablo Valley Overlook.

Directions: See the directions for "The Grand Loop" on p. 197.

After you've had your fill of the fine views from the overlook—and they just get better as you ascend—walk east past the campground entrance and find a trail post with a sign for the Juniper Trail pointing uphill. The distance given on this sign, 1 mile to the lower summit parking area, somehow has lengthened by the time you get there, where a sign indicates 1.24 miles back to the campground. You will also see a sign for the Juniper Trail, left to Deer Flat Road, this trail being your return route. The trail, a gravelly single track, passes a large grove of California bay laurel and then heads steeply uphill via a series of switchbacks in the shade of bay and gray pine. As you climb, be sure to pause often and admire the view, which extends west across the Interstate 680 corridor and the towns of Walnut Creek, Alamo, Danville, and San Ramon. An explosion of growth in these areas has brought housing developments right up to the state park boundary.

As you climb to the crest of Moses Rock Ridge, you may notice the California juniper trees that give the trail its name. This evergreen, which produces small gray berries that smell like gin when crushed, is able to withstand the hot, dry conditions found here for much of the year. Once atop the ridge, you pass a trail heading left and uphill along the ridge-crest. Your route now swings right and crosses a rocky area that is home to a variety of wildflowers, making it a colorful place to visit in spring. In

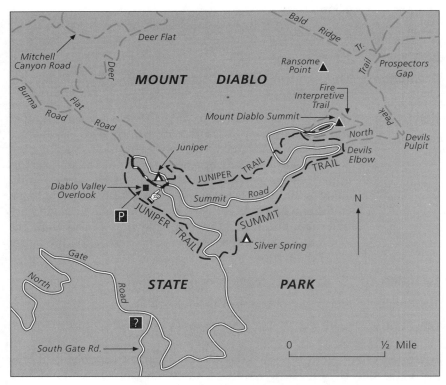

36. Juniper and Summit Trails

places the trail climbs steeply and relentlessly, but each step brings new views: north toward Suisun Bay, the west delta, and the towns of Concord, Pittsburgh, and Clayton; south and southeast across Curry Canyon and the Black Hills.

After about 0.5 mile of steady climbing, the trail levels out, and you can see the communication towers on Mt. Diablo's summit directly ahead. In this area you may hear a California quail giving its distinctive "chi-ca-go" call in a loud voice. The route returns briefly to a wooded area of bay and coast live oak, switchbacking uphill in the shade, before breaking into the open to climb a steep, rocky section beneath the first of several communication towers. The trail skirts to the north side of this tower and then levels out. About 100 feet farther, the trail begins climbing through a narrow corridor of chaparral to Summit Road.

At about the 1-mile point, after an almost continuous climb from the trailhead, you reach Summit Road. Cross carefully, turn right, and walk about 50 feet to find the trail to the lower summit parking area. Now you climb uphill on switchbacks and walk beside a barbed-wire fence surrounding another communication tower. California poppies and lupine dot the exposed rocky hillside with color in spring and summer. Soon, out of breath perhaps, you reach the lower summit parking area. As you continue uphill, you pass the Summit Trail, the return part of today's loop, right. From here the top of Mt. Diablo is just a short climb on a paved road.

The summit stands 3849 feet above sea level and is the highest point in the East Bay. You've climbed 849 feet in 1.5 miles, so take a moment to enjoy your achievement. Here you will find the summit museum, built in the late 1930s by the Civilian Conservation Corps, with an observation deck and visitor center, which is open Wednesday through Sunday, 10:00 A.M. to 4:00 P.M. Rest rooms, water and a telephone are available nearby. From the observation deck, it is said, more land is visible on a clear day than from any other place in the world except the summit of Africa's Mt. Kilimanjaro.

To the northeast is North Peak (3557'), home to more communication towers, and

Bicyclists rest at the Diablo Valley Overlook.

reachable only by foot, horseback or bicycle. Beyond it is the confluence of the Sacramento and San Joaquin rivers—the delta. To the east is the Central Valley, bordered by the Sierra Nevada; and to the west are San Francisco Bay, the Golden Gate and the Pacific Ocean, landmarks unfortunately often lost in fog or haze. Scattered around the mountain are the suburban communities of Concord, Walnut Creek, Clayton, Alamo, Danville, San Ramon, and Pleasanton.

According to an informational placard placed near the summit, Mt. Diablo was a sacred place for Native Americans and a landmark for Spanish explorers and California settlers in the 18th and 19th centuries. In 1851 a survey led by Colonel Leander Ransome designated the summit as the crossing of an east–west *Mt. Diablo baseline* and a north–south *Mt. Diablo meridian* so that the summit served as a reference point for future surveys of California and parts of Oregon and Nevada. In 1982, the National Park Service designated Mt. Diablo a National Natural Landmark.

If you are coming downhill from the summit on the right-hand (one-way downhill) paved road, the Fire Interpretive Trail, a 0.7-mile loop encircling the summit, leads off to your right just before you reach the lower parking lot. This self-guiding nature trail, which is disabled-accessible as far as Ransome Point Overlook, was built following a 1977 fire, using contributions from more than 1100 individuals, groups and businesses. The trail, whose purpose is to show visitors the role fire plays in the chaparral ecosystem, is dedicated to Mary Leolin Bowerman, a pioneer Mount Diablo botanist.

Now that you've had your fill, for the time being, of Mt. Diablo's heights, walk to the east end of the lower parking lot and find the Summit Trail heading south. As you look out over the southern expanse of Mount Diablo State Park, you can see the suburban communities and housing developments pressing up against the mountain's foothills. Your route now winds through an area of gray pines, chaparral, and wonderful wildflowers as it descends to meet Summit Road at Devils Elbow.

At about the 2-mile point, you reach Devils Elbow, a sharp bend where Summit Road turns west to make its final climb to the summit. On your left is a junction with the North Peak Trail to Prospectors Gap, part of the route described in "The Grand Loop." Here you keep walking straight and find the continuation of the Summit Trail as it continues to descend southwest. The descent is steep and rocky over the first few yards, then less so. Summit Road is above and to your right.

At a junction with a dirt road, you turn right and follow it uphill to Summit Road. Once you reach the pavement, leave it again after a few steps, where the trail immediately descends to the left. Watch your footing here on loose gravel. The route passes through an area full of yerba santa, woody shrubs with white trumpet flowers. Now traversing southwest across a shrubby hillside, the trail next passes under an open scree slope before descending gradually into a grove of gray pine and bay. In places vegetation crowds the trail, but there are also openings that afford sweeping vistas to the south. Soon you are hiking in open grassland, with a large water-storage tank downhill to the left.

At about the 3-mile point, you reach the Silver Spring camping area, with toilets, cooking grills, and a bathtub for watering horses. Walk straight ahead, keeping the bathtub on your left and the big pink water-storage tank on your right. Climb a small dirt embankment and follow the trail. Continue to descend on a rocky trail through a large area of chaparral, mostly chamise, in places too high to see over.

Out of the chaparral at last, you reach a paved service road and walk straight ahead to a gate at Summit Road. (A sign here reads SUMMIT to the right; ROCK CITY to the left.) Carefully cross Summit Road and begin descending a substantial dirt road. This is a continuation of the Summit Trail, which eventually leads to Park Headquarters at the junction of North and South Gate roads. As the road turns left and descends (about 150 feet downhill from Summit Road) look for an unsigned trail climbing to your right. This is the Juniper Trail, which leads back to Juniper Campground.

The trail immediately begins to switchback up the side of a small gully, in a corridor of chamise and other chaparral plants. A couple of switchbacks bring you to a large gravelly area. When you reach this point, you walk uphill to the right, toward Summit Road; but before you reach the road, look left for a small trail going west down the side of an

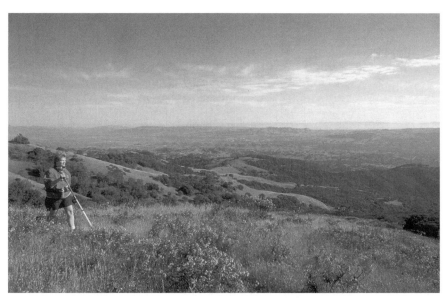

View southwest from the Juniper Trail, just below Diablo Valley Overlook.

embankment. Take it, and still on the Juniper Trail contour north and then northwest across a southwest-facing hillside. On a clear day this vantage point gives you fine views of the Bay Area, including Mount Tamalpais, the Golden Gate Bridge, and the hills of Oakland and Berkeley.

The open, grassy expanse of Mt. Diablo's southwest flank is dotted with groves of blue oak, gray pine, and juniper. On the way back to Juniper Campground, the route dips into several small canyons which may have running water—cool shady areas with stands of bay and coast live oak. When the route breaks into the open again, you climb a narrow track cut into the steep, grassy hillside. Here you may see raptors soaring on thermals rising from Pine Canyon, left. This is a wonderful part of the hike, giving you the feeling of being high on the slopes of a grand mountain—which you are! The route, which has taken you to the top of the East Bay's tallest peak, nears its end as you reach the open area just below Juniper Campground; here you turn right and walk uphill on the paved campground road to the parking area.

37   Mt. Diablo State Park
MITCHELL AND DONNER CANYONS

Length: 8.6 miles

Time: 5 to 7 hours

Rating: Difficult

Regulations: Mt. Diablo State Park; parking fee; no dogs, no smoking.

Highlights: Climbing 1780 feet to Murchio Gap, a high point on Mt. Diablo's north side, this rigorous loop uses Mitchell Canyon, Meridian Ridge, and Donner Canyon roads to let you sample the wonders of our premier East Bay park: great views, spring wildflowers, migrating songbirds, and an abundance of native trees and shrubs. The first part of Mitchell Canyon Road is a self-guiding nature trail, with a descriptive leaflet available at the trailhead. The Mount Diablo Interpretive Association plans to open a visitor center in the Mitchell Canyon parking area in the spring of 1998. (This loop is hike 9 on the Mt. Diablo State Park trail map.)

Facilities: Water, phone, toilets, horse staging.

Trailhead: South side of parking area.

Directions: From Interstate 680 in Walnut Creek, or Hwy. 24 eastbound (just before the merge with I-680), take the Ygnacio Valley

Rd. exit and go northeast 6.9 miles to Pine Hollow Rd. Turn right and go 1.7 miles to Mitchell Canyon Rd. Turn right and go 1.3 miles to the Mt. Diablo State Park entrance. Pay a parking fee at the automated ticket machine, then continue 0.1 mile to a large parking area.

Mitchell Canyon is a great birding area, and if you are here in spring, check the parking area for western bluebirds and other songbirds in the

37. Mitchell and Donner Canyons

trees before starting your hike. Wildflower enthusiasts will want to have guidebooks or note pads handy, as Mitchell Canyon is full of flowers in season. As you stand in the parking area and look south, the hills in front of you are the Twin Peaks (1733', 1507'), with Eagle Peak (2369') in the background. Mt. Diablo's summit (3849') is hidden from view, but a hour or two of hiking, some of it steeply uphill, will reveal the mountain's upper reaches.

Leaving the south side of the parking area, you have a choice of two roads; take the left-hand one, Mitchell Canyon Road. This is a multi-use road, shared by hikers, bicyclists, and equestrians. Continue past a gate and walk uphill on a gentle grade. About 150 feet past the gate, you come to a junction, left, with the Mitchell Rock Trail and a connector to the Bruce Lee Trail. Continuing straight, you pass the park ranger's residence, right, and behind it, heavily quarried Mt. Zion (1635'). Fall brings a spectacle of New England-like color to Mitchell Canyon, thanks to black walnut, bigleaf maple, California wild grape, and poison oak. The woodlands here also contain coast live oak, valley oak, blue oak, gray pine, blue elderberry, and California buckeye.

Look for a large coast live oak on your right; this is the Bicentennial Tree, dedicated in 1987 by the Daughters of the American Revolution. Some of the shrubs here include California sagebrush, bush monkeyflower, coffeeberry, redberry buckthorn, and narrow-leaf bush sunflower. As you begin a moderate climb, Mitchell Creek is on your right, and soon you will spot a marshy area, remnant of a man-made pond, filled with poison hemlock.

Just past the 0.5-mile point, you come to a junction with the Black Point Trail, a dirt road heading right. Continue straight, walking along Mitchell Canyon, with the creek, bordered by willows, now on the left. Also growing here are California bay laurel, toyon, yerba santa, and wild rose. As the canyon walls begin to close in, notice the chaparral growing high on the rocky hillsides. This plant community, composed of hearty, heat-tolerant shrubs such as manzanita, buckbrush, chamise, black sage, and California sagebrush, depends on fire to regenerate itself by recycling nutrients into the soil and cracking the plants' hard seed coats.

Among the profusion of spring wildflowers common in lower Mitchell Canyon are California buttercup, blow wives, blue-eyed grass, blue dicks, Ithuriel's spear, larkspur, California poppy, Chinese houses, clarkia, lupine, and Indian paintbrush. Two exquisite flowers to look for are the multi-hued Mariposa tulip and the lantern-shaped Mt. Diablo globe tulip, a specialty in this state park. In the fall, California fuchsia is one of the last flowers to remain in bloom here.

At the 1-mile point, Red Road starts a climb into White Canyon, right, but your route, Mitchell Canyon Road, holds a level course into the ever-narrowing canyon. Here the creek is on your left, close to the road. On your right is a steep, east-facing hillside of chaparral. Ground cover beside the trail includes blackberry and periwinkle, a non-native plant with dark green leaves and five-petaled, lavender flowers. Two additions to your tree list here include white alder and Fremont cottonwood, species associated with water. If you hear a flock of noisy birds flitting in the trees, they could be bushtits. These tiny gray birds resemble chickadees, but are slightly smaller, with long tails. You may see golden-crowned sparrows on the ground, scraping in the leaf litter for food. And do not be surprised, in the fall, to come upon a tarantula walking slowly along the side of the road. These large, sluggish spiders are generally not poisonous to humans, although they can bite. Unfortunately, they can easily be crushed by a hiking boot, a bicycle tire or a horse's hoof.

Prospectors Gap, a saddle between Mt. Diablo's summit, right, and North Peak (3557'), left, soon comes into view. At about the 2-mile point the route begins to climb, first in shade, then via steep switchbacks in the open. This is a great part of the route for scenery and birds. You have a great view of Mitchell Canyon and its chaparral-clad walls. Look up and

Birders always find something interesting in lower Mitchell Canyon.

you may see turkey vultures or red-tailed hawks gliding overhead; look down and you may spot a secretive hermit thrush.

As you gain elevation, Deer Flat Creek, a tributary of Mitchell Creek, is at the bottom of a canyon, left. Across this canyon is a steep, rocky ridge running between Eagle Peak, an impressive summit in its own right, and Murchio Gap, a place you will visit later today. Ahead of you, unseen, is Deer Flat, gained only by more steep climbing. But the enticement of high ground and the reward of expanding vistas help you overcome the relentless grade. From time to time, take a break from the climb and listen here for the California quail's three-part call: it sounds like "chi-ca-go." As you approach Deer Flat, the grade levels off, and you can see North Peak and its communication towers to the east, just behind Bald Ridge.

At approximately the 3.5-mile point, you reach Deer Flat, a scenic area of gray pine and live oak, with several welcoming picnic benches and a horse watering trough. After stopping to rest and admire the scenery, you resume your walk and soon come to a junction with Deer Flat Road, right, heading toward Juniper Camp; and Meridian Ridge Road going left to Murchio Gap. (The distance to Murchio Gap on the trail post here is wrong: it is 0.75 mile, not 1.75 miles.) Now you turn left and begin a gentle descent through an area, colorful in fall, of manzanita, hop tree, redberry buckthorn, poison oak, narrow-leaf bush sunflower, and wild rose. Be on the lookout here for golden eardrops, a 2- to 6-foot-tall wildflower with fern-like leaves and yellow blossoms that is abundant after fires.

After crossing a small streambed, the route begins to climb, and soon passes the Deer Flat Creek Trail, left. As the route steepens, the air becomes fragrant with the smell of pine, and you begin to glimpse Eagle Peak ahead. Behind you is Mt. Diablo's summit, with its domed summit museum; to your right is the grassy expanse of Bald Ridge. Soon Murchio Gap, at 2320 feet the high point on this route, comes into view. As you near the gap, you pass through a lovely area where Manzanita, toyon, chamise, yerba santa, and chaparral pea thrive on a hot, dry hillside.

At Murchio Gap, at about the 4.25-mile point, you may notice a dense, low-growing shrub with gray-green leaves; this is leather oak, limited in the East Bay to Mt. Diablo and Mines Road. Murchio Gap is an important junction, so take a moment to admire the view and get your bearings. If you stand at the gap and face north, you are ringed by trails. Clockwise from the left these are: Deer Flat Creek Trail, Eagle Peak Trail, Back Creek Trail, Meridian Ridge Road, and Bald Ridge Trail. The top-of-the-world feeling continues as you descend on the Meridian Ridge Road, right, with views north to Clayton, the west delta, and the hills of Napa and Solano counties. Also impressive is North Peak, with its furrowed, rocky ridges and canyons falling steeply from the skyline. We are lucky to have mountain scenery like this, reminiscent of the High Sierra, so close to home.

The descent steepens and covers some rough ground, rocky and rutted. Pay attention to your footing, but also be alert for unusual birds, such as

Townsend's solitaire. This gray bird, slightly smaller than a robin, has a white eye-ring and white on the outside of its tail. Summer residents of the high mountains, solitaires migrate in the fall to lower elevations, where they are often seen feeding on juniper berries. After descending about 0.5 mile from Murchio Gap, you come to a junction with Prospectors Gap Road. Here the route to Mt. Diablo's summit goes straight, but you head left and descend steeply along narrow Meridian Ridge to Meridian Point.

With Eagle Peak now to your left, the route heads north, alternating between steep and not-so-steep pitches on a ridge that is just wide enough for the road. This is an excellent place to study chaparral—it is everywhere you look. Four common chaparral plants seen here belong to the buckthorn (*Rhamnaceae*) family: jimbrush, buckbrush, coffeeberry, and redberry buckthorn. The first two are ceanothuses, or wild lilacs, and the second two belong to the genus *Rhamnus*. Jimbrush is a large shrub with small, dark green leaves having three main veins; it blooms in the spring with pale blue flowers. Buckbrush has small, paddle-shaped leaves, dark green on top, lighter green below; its spring blossoms are white. Coffeeberry has long, slender leaves, with veins that run almost to the leaf's edge, and dark berries. Redberry buckthorn resembles a miniature live oak, with stiff, rounded leaves that are spiny on the edges.

Just before reaching Meridian Point, you pass on your left the Meridian Point Trail, coming from Back Creek. At Meridian Point, your route veers sharply right and descends, steeply at times, toward Donner Canyon.

Hikers heading north on the Mitchell Rock Trail.

Here you have a chance to compare two very similar pines, gray and Coulter: Coulter pines have longer cones, stouter limbs, and denser foliage. Before the junction with Donner Canyon and Cardinet Oaks roads, you pass the Middle Trail, right. (Return to this spot sometime in early spring and follow the "Falls Trail" route description to find Mt. Diablo's hidden waterfalls.)

Just past the 6-mile point, you reach a major intersection; here Cardinet Oaks Road heads right, but your route, Donner Canyon Road, turns left. Now your are on level ground, but soon the route begins to drop again. The variety of trees and shrubs here is stunning—almost everything you've seen so far, together in one area. On your way down Donner Canyon Road you will pass a number of trails: Hetherington Loop (twice), Tick Wood, and a trail to the Donner Cabin homestead site. Ignore them all and continue straight, descending steeply through blue-oak savanna until you are walking on level ground once again, with Donner Creek on your right. Steller's jays and dark-eyed juncos may follow your progress through their neighborhood with interest and an occasional comment.

About 0.5 mile past the trail to Donner Cabin, you pass a trail leading to Clayton Oaks Road, right. Here you continue straight, and almost immediately reach a connector to the Bruce Lee Trail, heading uphill and sharply left. Follow this connector as it climbs west over a grassy hill, passing eucalyptus, black locust, and walnut trees on the way. The scenery is great—Mt. Diablo's summit, North Peak, Eagle Peak, and Twin Peaks are all in view.

Soon an unsigned road, the Bruce Lee Trail, joins from the right, and the Back Creek Road, also unsigned, heads left toward Back Canyon. Continue straight, dropping briefly to cross Back Creek. At the next intersection, a four-way with no signs, again continue straight, with Twin Peaks uphill and left. Your route now maintains a level grade through oak savanna. When you reach another unsigned four-way intersection, you again continue straight. Soon you reach yet another four-way intersection, but this one is marked with a trail post; here the Mitchell Rock Trail goes left and a connector to the Bruce Lee Trail heads right. Ahead is the parking area, which you reach via a long, narrow switchback or a steep, straight descent.

 38

Mt. Diablo State Park
SYCAMORE CREEK

Length:	5 miles
Time:	3 to 4 hours
Rating:	Moderate

Regulations: Mt. Diablo State Park; entrance fee; no dogs, no smoking, no bicycles on the Devils Slide Trail.

Highlights: Most routes on Mt. Diablo involve a good deal of climbing, usually at the start. This loop, which uses the Curry Canyon, Knobcone Point, Black Hawk Ridge, and Sycamore Creek roads, along with the Devils Slide Trail, is different. It starts at mid-mountain, just below 1800 feet, descends into the beautiful canyon that holds Sycamore Creek, explores the Blackhills addition to the park, and climbs almost 1000 feet back up to the parking area. Two rare plants, Mt. Diablo manzanita and Mt. Diablo sunflower, are present, along with a fine array of other trees, shrubs, and wildflowers. This loop, best in spring and fall, may be extremely muddy in wet weather. (This is hike 10 on the of Mt. Diablo State Park trail map, with an additional leg down Sycamore Creek.)

Facilities: None

Trailhead: East side of the parking area.

Directions: From Interstate 680 in Danville, take the Diablo Road/Danville exit and follow Diablo Rd. 3 miles east to

38. Sycamore Creek

Mt. Diablo Scenic Blvd. Turn left onto Mt. Diablo Scenic
Blvd.—which soon becomes South Gate Rd.—and go 3.7
miles to the South Gate entrance station. Continue on
South Gate Road another 1.6 miles to Curry Point Overlook, right, located at a sharp left-hand bend in the road.

From the east side of the exposed and possibly windy parking area, follow a dirt-and-gravel road—signed here as Curry Canyon Road—on a
level grade as it runs slightly south of east along the top of a broad ridge.
Mt. Diablo's summit (3849') rises majestically to your left. This is open
country, and in spring the grassy hillsides are speckled with wildflowers,
including California buttercup, blue-eyed grass, wild pansy, and blue
dicks. After about 100 yards you pass through a cattle gate, and in another 35 yards or so come to a junction. Here Curry Canyon Road heads
downhill and left, while your route, Knobcone Point Road, a dirt road,
continues straight and begins to climb slightly. A deep, forested canyon,
right, holds Sulfur Spring and the headwaters of Sycamore Creek.

Here a few coast live oaks provide the only shade; otherwise this part
of the route is in the open, providing great views east to the Central Valley
and, on a clear day perhaps, beyond to the Sierra. The road, rocky in
places, begins to descend gently, soon passing through a fence and then
entering a wooded area of California bay laurel, coast live oak, and gray
pine. Poison oak is especially rampant here. The deep fold of Curry
Canyon is left, and beyond it in the distance rises North Peak (3557'), Mt.
Diablo's twin summit. As the route begins to bend right, you pass the
Devils Slide Trail, right, which you will use later on your return climb out
of Sycamore Creek canyon.

Passing another fence, the road rises on an easy grade through a mixed
forest, then breaks into the open at a T-junction. Here Knobcone Point
Road turns left, but your route, Black Hawk Ridge Road, turns right. (You
can make an interesting side-trip by turning left here and following
Knobcone Point Road to Knobcone Point, named for a species of closed-
cone pine found here and hardly anywhere else in the East Bay.) If you
look left and uphill at this junction, you may notice a large sunflower-like
blossom on a plant with gray, fuzzy leaves. This is mule's ear (genus
Wyethia), a sunflower relative that grows low to the ground in large
colonies.

Following Black Hawk Ridge Road, through oak and pine, you may
notice Indian warrior poking through the leaf litter and pine needles on
the forest floor. This parasitic plant, related to Indian paintbrush and
owl's clover, is associated with madrone and manzanita, which are
always nearby; it also attracts hummingbirds. You may also notice huge
fallen pine cones, belonging to gray pine, the dominant pine here. Soon
you come to an area of chaparral, where the rare Mt. Diablo manzanita
flourishes in company with more common shrubs such as chamise,

toyon, bush monkeyflower, and silk tassel bush. You may also see here the Mt. Diablo sunflower, another plant confined to Mt. Diablo. This spring bloomer has green, lance shaped leaves and a bright yellow flower held aloft on a single slender stalk.

As the route descends via **S**-bends through rocky terrain, burned in the fall of 1996, you continue to see evidence of plant diversity, with wildflowers such as star lily and Henderson's shooting star, and clematis, a vine that overruns the toyon. In late spring, look for flowering shrubs such as buckbrush and narrow-leaf bush sunflower to brighten this stretch of the route. Losing elevation on a moderate grade, you soon enter a wooded canyon where the sound of frogs may signal the nearby presence of water, and Steller's jays on patrol will proba-

Mule's ear, or mule ears, has big flowers and big leaves

bly give you a noisy welcome. Slightly downstream from the confluence of the east and northeast forks of Sycamore Creek, just shy of the 2-mile point, you come to a junction marked by a trail post. Straight ahead is Black Hawk Ridge Road; to the right is your route, Sycamore Creek Road.

After turning right, you follow the east fork of Sycamore Creek downstream, walking on a dirt road along the creek's right-hand bank. Plants suited to a cooler, wetter environment grow here, including western sycamore, bigleaf maple, white alder, California buckeye, snowberry, creambush, and wild rose. Crossing the creek twice—after the second crossing you pass the Devils Slide Trail, your return route, right—you continue walking downstream, now following the main branch of Sycamore Creek. Soon you pass a clearing where, in spring, blue bush lupine and California buttercup bloom on a steep, open hillside. The landscape becomes more rocky as you continue to descend in the shade of bay and coast live oak.

Now the route emerges into the open, crosses the creek over a large culvert, and soon reaches a gated fence marking the boundary between the state park and the 252-acre Blackhills parcel, which was added to the park—thanks to a compromise negotiated with the parcel's owner by the group Save Mount Diablo—and officially dedicated in April 1997. If the fence is still present and the gate locked, climb over and continue walking in the open, past clumps of California sagebrush and black sage, enjoying a vista that takes in rolling hills studded with oaks, and the Black Hills—

high, rocky cliffs where endangered peregrine falcons were re-introduced from 1989 to 1993.

Large rock outcrops tower close to the road, which is carved out of a hillside that descends to Sycamore Creek, right. Here the creek and road are squeezed between the ends of Fossil and Black Hawk ridges, an area called Devils Slide. Downstream a short distance, several large water tanks may still be present along the creek, near a small dam. (If so, a sign will be there warning you to keep out, as the structures are unsafe.)

About 100 yards past the water tanks, look for an overgrown trail, unsigned, going right at a sharp angle and downhill to the creek. Watch your footing to avoid tripping on a metal pipe that crosses your path, and descend carefully to the creek. Please avoid trampling any of the delicate streamside vegetation. The trail leads upstream to two pools, the second of which is filled by a lovely waterfall that tumbles over slick rock. After enjoying this secluded spot, retrace your steps to the junction of Sycamore Creek Road and the Devils Slide Trail, about the 3.5-mile point.

Turn left onto the Devils Slide Trail, a single track, and continue walking uphill in dense forest, following Sycamore Creek, which is on your right, upstream. About 100 yards past the junction, search the area between the trail and the creek for giant trillium, a large, three-leaved plant with a single maroon, pink, or white flower that appears in spring. Another unusual plant, California barberry, can be found here, along with the more common coffeeberry, creambush, and snowberry; you may also see a delicate white spring wildflower called woodland star. Soon you cross the creek on rocks and continue upstream with the creek now on your left. After a short distance, the route re-crosses the creek and swings right, passing a trail post and a faint path that continues straight.

Now on a moderate grade, you climb to the next creek crossing, just below Sulfur Spring, where the smell of sulfur is noticeable. Turning right and stepping across the creek here, you follow the rocky and eroded trail as it continues uphill, passing a path, left, that continues upstream toward the spring. Another tributary of Sycamore Creek, not on the map, is to your right. The route, mostly shaded, passes stands of bay, buckeye, coast live oak, and toyon, and at about the 4-mile point reaches a fork. Bearing right, you descend to the tributary creek, then cross it and continue walking upstream on a slight uphill grade. The trail may be muddy at the crossing and overgrown farther on with creambush and poison oak.

Soon you merge with a trail, left, coming from the previous fork, then swing sharply left and climb across an open, grassy hillside, with the summit of Mt. Diablo just peeking over a ridge ahead. In spring this beautiful area is full of blue-eyed grass. Climbing a bit farther, you arrive at the junction you passed earlier with Knobcone Point Road; turn left here and retrace your steps to the parking area.

◆ Ohlone Wilderness Regional Trail ◆

<table>
<tr><td>**39**</td><td>Ohlone Wilderness Regional Trail
SUNOL TO DEL VALLE</td></tr>
</table>

Length: 19.4 miles

Time: Three days

Rating: Difficult

Regulations: EBRPD; permit, camping reservations, and sign-in required; no bicycles; no pets in campsites overnight. The Ohlone Wilderness Regional Trail permit, good for one year, is a large map with route description, distances, trail elevations, and regulations. Trail permits are available for a small fee at the entrance kiosks at Sunol Wilderness and Del Valle Regional Park, the visitor center at Coyote Hills Regional Park in Fremont, and the EBRPD reservation office, 2950 Peralta Oaks Ct., Oakland. Permits for overnight parking are available at the entrance kiosks. Reservations for backpacking camps are required; phone EBRPD reservations, (510) 636-1684, 8:30 A.M. to 4 P.M., Monday through Friday.

Highlights: This backpacking trip, the only one of its kind in the East Bay Regional Park system, puts you in the heart of the Ohlone Wilderness, a rugged, remote, and beautiful area. Along the way, you will also pass through Sunol Wilderness and Del Valle Regional Park, and spend two nights (or more if you like) camped in oak woodland, surrounded by wildflowers and birds, perhaps listening to the howl of a coyote or the hoot of an owl. **Boldface numbers** in the route description refer to numbers on the Ohlone Wilderness Regional Trail map. Many of these numbers can be found on trail posts along the trail, but some are missing.

Facilities: Visitor center, picnic tables, water, toilet, phone, and horse staging at Sunol trailhead. Limited water and unimproved campsites along the trail. Picnic tables, water, toilet, phone, and horse staging at Del Valle trailhead.

39a. Sunol to Rose Peak

Trailhead: Information panel and trail register on the south side of
                   Geary Rd., about 100 yards east of the visitor center.

Directions: This is a car shuttle trip, starting at **Sunol Wilderness** and
                   ending at **Del Valle Regional Park**. Drive first to Del Valle
                   Regional Park, leave a car there, then proceed to Sunol
                   Wilderness.

                   To reach **Del Valle Regional Park**: See the directions for
                   "East Shore Trail" on p. 80. At the entrance kiosk go
                   straight. Continue 1.2 miles past the kiosk, crossing a
                   bridge and turning right at a T-junction, until you reach a
                   large parking area at the end of the road, near the Lichen
                   Bark picnic area.

                   To reach **Sunol Wilderness** via Highway 84: Return to cen-
                   tral Livermore and follow 1st St. west 0.6 mile to Holmes
                   St. Bear left onto Holmes St., go 2.1 miles and bear right
                   onto E. Vallecitos Rd. Follow E. Vallecitos and Vallecitos
                   roads 6.6 miles to the Highway 84/Sunol/Dumbarton
                   Bridge exit. Go under Interstate 680, and at a stop sign turn
                   left onto Paloma Rd. Go back under I-680, stay in the left
                   lane, and from the next stop sign continue straight, now on
                   Calaveras Rd. Go 4.2 miles to Geary Rd., turn left, and go
                   1.8 miles to the entrance kiosk. Go 0.1 mile past the kiosk
                   and turn left into a parking area in front of the visitor cen-
                   ter, a green barn.

                   From Interstate 680: See the directions for "Little Yosemite"
                   on p. 260. Park in the parking area in front of the visitor
                   center, a green barn.

After signing the trail register at the trailhead, you walk north about 150
feet, across Geary Rd. and through a small parking area, to a wooden
bridge over Alameda Creek. The entire Ohlone Wilderness Regional Trail
is made up of many trails which, joined together, stretch 28 miles, from
Stanford Avenue at the base of Mission Peak in Fremont, to the Lichen
Bark picnic area on the shore of Lake Del Valle. For the next three days
you will be following the Ohlone Wilderness emblem on trail posts: a
white oak leaf in a red or brown disk.

After crossing Alameda Creek and turning right, you follow the
Canyon View Trail, a wide dirt path lined with white alder, bigleaf maple,
western sycamore, and willow, with the creek on your right. (The first
part of the Canyon View Trail is also part of the Indian Joe Nature Trail, a
self-guiding route with numbered trail posts that correspond to a pamphlet available at the visitor center.) You may also notice here some of the
trees and shrubs that will keep you company for most of the way to Lake

Del Valle, including California bay laurel, California buckeye, coast live oak, California sagebrush, bush monkeyflower, and poison oak. Approximately 100 feet past the bridge, Hayfield Road, **13**, climbs left, and about 30 feet beyond, a path leads to the creek, right. Continuing straight, you soon pass another path, left, and after crossing Indian Joe Creek, you follow the Canyon View Trail over rolling terrain to a Y-junction, **14**, with the Indian Joe Creek Trail.

Here you bear right on the Canyon View Trail and begin a steep climb through mixed oak woodland and grassland colored blue and yellow by Ithuriel's spear and Mariposa tulip. Your chance of seeing a yellow-billed magpie, a large black-and-white member of the crow family, is better on this route than almost anywhere else in the East Bay, and it should be easy to spot other common birds, such as California towhee, American kestrel, turkey vulture, and western meadowlark. At a four-way junction, **15**, you leave the Canyon View Trail, which continues straight, and turn left on the McCorkle Trail. The route, now a dirt road, continues climbing steeply, then gradually levels off to contour around a rocky ridge, and finally switchbacks upward toward a notch in the hills to the northeast.

At about the 1.3-mile point, you reach the notch and a junction with a cut-off to Cerro Este Road, **16**. The large bulk of Mission Peak (2517'), with its companion summits Mt. Allison (2658') and Monument Peak (2594'), appears to the west, while the waters of Calaveras Reservoir shimmer to the south. Bear right, staying on the McCorkle Trail, here a narrow track, and begin descending through an area of chaparral, a striking contrast to the oak woodland and rolling grassland of a few minutes ago. California quail and wrentits may be heard and sometimes seen here, as you climb on a steep, rocky course through a wooded area to a high ridge, where California poppies dot the grassy hillsides with orange.

At a T-junction, **17**, you come to the Cerro Este Road; here your route, still part of the McCorkle Trail, turns left and continues uphill in the open to another T-junction, **18**, where you turn right, staying on the McCorkle Trail, a dirt road here. A nearby cow pond provides habitat for a robin-sized bird called the killdeer, which you may hear giving its alarm call, "kill-dee, kill-dee." This shorebird, a member of the plover family, is at home in many areas besides the shore, and can be found throughout North America. In addition to cows and birds, other wildlife here includes amphibians: watch the ground closely for baby frogs in spring. Now heading east again and descending slightly, you pass large rock outcrops and a barbed-wire fence, where a narrow dirt path heads left and your route bends right.

After ambling a while on level ground, you descend via switchbacks to a small valley, where a wet area may provide a colorful display of spring wildflowers, including lupine, Ithuriel's spear, blow wives, owl's clover, and Mariposa tulip. If the creek that drains this valley is running, you may have to cross it on rocks. At about 3.4 miles, you cross another creek and reach a trail junction, **19**, with Backpack Road. A gate ahead marks the entrance to the Sunol Backpack Area, and a sign board lists camp-sites—Eagles Eyrie, Hawks Nest, Sycamore Camp, Stars Rest—reached by a steep uphill trail. Water and a toilet are available in the backpack area.

If you are spending the night here, Eagles Eyrie is an excellent camp-site, but like all the others it requires advance reservation. To find it, climb about 0.25 mile from the backpack-area entrance and watch for a junction with a signed spur trail veering right. This trail leads to several campsites, including Eagles Eyrie, which is perched at about 1600 feet. The main trail continues straight and is rejoined by the spur trail, in about 0.25 mile, at a gate on the border of San Francisco Water Department land. Eagles Eyrie is a grassy area with a picnic table in the shade of a large blue oak, a mag-net for birds such as woodpeckers, western bluebirds, nuthatches, and hummingbirds. Water is available from a faucet beside the trail, just below the campsite in a muddy area where you may find golden monkeyflower blooming in the spring. Expansive views west from a rock outcrop above the picnic table—a great spot to watch the sunset—reveal much of the ter-rain back to the visitor center.

To rejoin the main route from Eagles Eyrie, walk northeast on an unsigned path across a grassy hillside, past a huge valley oak, joining a trail coming up from the water faucet and a lower campsite. A steep climb brings you to the San Francisco Water Department gate, which has a sign requesting you to stay on the trail while on Department lands. Once

Eagles Eyrie campsite at the Ohlone Backpack Area.

through the gate, now back on the main route, you continue climbing through open grassland, above 2000 feet for the first time on this route, heading generally northeast. Heavily forested Alameda Creek canyon is downhill and right; beautiful oaks grace the hillsides ahead.

Your route dips to cross several small creeks lined with bay and sycamore, then passes through an area of rock outcrops colored by orange lichen. From time to time, dirt paths take off from the main route; ignore them. In open grassland here you may find blue dicks and winecup clarkia, spring bloomers. This part of the route has a supreme feeling of isolation, with no signs of civilization other than jets on approach to San Francisco International Airport. At about the 5-mile point you come to a trail post and an unsigned trail joining from the left; soon you reach a junction, **20**, with unsigned Goat Rock Road, right. Here your route turns left and climbs north toward the skyline ridge. In the distance to the south rise the Santa Cruz Mountains. At the next trail post, **21**, the route bends right, and in 100 yards reaches a fork, where you bear left. After climbing a slight rise, you descend to a four-way junction, **22**, with Billy Goat Road.

After crossing Billy Goat Road, you continue straight on Mid Road and contour southeast, reaching a gully with oak, blue elderberry, and California buckeye—the first shade in miles. Soon you reach a high point with views west, and then come to another gully with a culvert under the road. At about the 7-mile point, there is a T-junction, **23**, with Bluff Road, where your route turns left and climbs steeply. After cresting a small ridge near a cattle pond, you continue across grassy hillsides and through oak woodland to a junction, **24**, with Valpe Ridge Road, left. Here you walk through a cattle gate and turn right, passing another pond, and in about 0.25 mile, **25**, make a sharp left and descend steeply on rocky ground into a small canyon which holds the south fork of Indian Creek.

Now in an oasis of shade and water, you may find an abundance of spring wildflowers in bloom, including fiddleneck, a coiled stem with orange flowers, and Chinese houses, pagoda-like tiers of purple flowers. A steep climb brings you out of the canyon and into a beautiful savanna— a haven for birds—where the grass, brown elsewhere by late spring, stays green in the shade of tall oaks. At a bend in the route, you get your first good look on this route of San Francisco Bay, and at the next bend, just above 3,000 feet, you encounter a stunning vista that sweeps from Mt. Diablo to the Santa Clara Valley and Santa Cruz Mountains. If you like being up high, with unobstructed views, this is the place!

As the route, here called the Buckboard Trail, swings southeast, you have a pleasant walk along a ridgecrest, and soon reach a road, **26**, descending steeply left to Doe Canyon Horse Camp, where a water faucet and toilet await. (Water and a toilet are also available at Maggie's Half Acre campsite, about 0.8 miles ahead.) Now you continue east through oak savanna, home to acorn woodpeckers, toward Rose Peak (3817'), the high point on the Ohlone Wilderness Regional Trail. At a junction with

Portuguese Point Road, **27**, you turn left, pass a small pond on your left, and soon reach a road, **28**, heading left to Maggie's Half Acre. If you are doing this trip in four days instead of three, Maggie's Half Acre makes a good second camp, about 6 miles from the Sunol backpack area.

Continuing east, the route steepens and passes over rocky terrain as you near the summit of Rose Peak, the highest point in Alameda County. About 0.2 mile past the last junction, an unsigned road, steep and rocky, heads left and climbs Rose Peak, while the main route skirts the peak's south side. Having come this far, be sure not to miss the 360-degree views from the summit, and a chance to sign the summit register. After some effort, you arrive, seemingly, on top of the world. Using your map and compass, you can pick out many features of the Bay Area, including Altamont Pass, Mt. Diablo, Pleasanton Ridge, Coyote Hills, Mission Peak, the Santa Cruz Mountains, and Mt. Hamilton. Beyond the Central Valley lies the Sierra Nevada, visible on clear days. You have come nearly 10 miles from the Sunol visitor center; Rose Peak marks the half-way point to Lake Del Valle.

After you have relaxed for a while, continue east and descend steeply to the main road, which you can see below and right. Once back on the main road, you may notice as you continue your descent two trees not seen so far, black oak and gray pine, both found in hotter, drier areas of the East Bay. Canyon live oak is also here, along with blue oak, loaded with mistletoe, and valley oak, making this a good place to compare these species. Just past the 10-mile point, you pass the road, **29**, coming from Maggie's Half Acre, left.

At the next junction, **30**, a road goes straight to the wilderness boundary and Rose Flat, but you turn left and continue downhill, under large black oaks and gray pines—notice the huge pine cones—to the north fork of Indian Creek, losing the most elevation so far, more than 600 feet. The steep, rocky descent brings you to the bottom of a cool, shady canyon, where maple, alder, and bay line the creek, which may be flowing over the road. Climbing back into the open, you have views west to San Francisco Bay and Mission Peak.

As you begin to get a good view southwest across the canyon to Rose Peak, a road joins from the left, **31**, and your route bends sharply right and continues climbing. As you gain a ridgetop, you can look left into Box Canyon, headwaters of La Costa Creek. Descending beside a barbed-wire fence to the head of this canyon, you pass beautiful hillsides of colorful Chinese houses that lie in the shade of gray pines. With La Costa Creek on your left, the route climbs gently past large rock outcrops through a little valley at the head of Box Canyon. A road to the wilderness boundary and Rose Flat joins your route at a T-junction, **32**, where you turn left and begin a gradual descent. From here, the Ohlone Wilderness Regional Trail, generally eastbound since the Sunol visitor center, begins a northward march to Lake Del Valle, about 7 miles away.

If you are taking three days to complete the route, you will spend the second night at Stewart's Camp, on the road to Murietta Falls. When you reach the next junction, **33**, turn left, leaving the Ohlone Wilderness Regional Trail, and descend via a series of gentle switchbacks through an oak-and-pine forest, past stumps of old oaks riddled with woodpecker holes and fine displays of Chinese houses. Stewart's Camp is located just above a pond, where red-winged blackbirds nest in marsh vegetation and the surrounding hillsides are decorated with lupine. Water and a toilet are located near the only marked campsite, a rough area with hardly enough level ground for a small tent.

At just over 3000 feet, a night at Stewart's Camp can be a cold one, and don't be surprised by serenades from owls and coyotes. No need for an alarm clock here, as the chattering of birds at sunrise will get you started early. After passing the pond, you soon come to a junction with a road heading left to the wilderness boundary; your route continues straight and arrives at a small grove of trees. To visit seasonal Murietta Falls, turn left here, before crossing a tributary of La Costa Creek, and follow a narrow path that traverses and then winds behind large rock outcrops. Be careful here as you approach steep terrain. After a short distance the waterfall comes into view, tumbling perhaps 100 feet from a narrow channel in the rocks to a gully below.

The Murietta Falls area is a perfect spot to lounge in the sun, especially if the night has been cold. Once underway again on the main route, you cross the creek and immediately begin to climb north, out of a valley. Yellow Mariposa tulips and goldfinches add touches of color to the scene. At a **T**-junction, turn right and walk along the open crest of a ridge, toward Johnny's Pond—called simply JOHNIES on a sign beside the trail— and your reunion with the Ohlone Wilderness Regional Trail.

Just before reaching the 15-mile point of this route, you rejoin the Ohlone Wilderness Regional Trail at a junction, **35**, and turn left. Much of the land that became the Ohlone Wilderness was at one time owned by a rancher and cowboy named Harry Rowell. Rowell, a British merchant seaman who jumped ship in 1912 when he was 21 years old, settled in Alameda County and had a ranch on Dublin Canyon Road. Rowell died in 1969, but his legacy lives on in the form of the Rowell Ranch Rodeo, which he started in 1920, and Rowell's Saddlery in Castro Valley, founded in 1942. A sign beside the trail reads SCHLEPER, and the map shows Schlieper Rock, named for Fred Schlieper, a silversmith at Rowell's Saddlery in the 1940s. Johnny's Pond, left, was named for John Fernandes, who worked in Rowell's slaughterhouse and was his occasional sparring partner.

After descending slightly, the route climbs to a great vantage point, with views of Mt. Diablo, Morgan Territory Regional Preserve, Livermore, Altamont Pass, and the Central Valley. Shade is at a premium here, offered by a few groves of oak, oases for birds. California quail, western tanager,

39b. Rose Peak to Del Valle

Ithuriel's spear has a bare stem six to 30 inches tall.

and lark sparrow may be found nearby. Even in death, oaks attract birds, providing nesting habitat and food storage for species as varied as woodpeckers and swallows.

At a fork in the route, **36**, bear right past an old pear orchard and begin descending steeply on loose ground. At about the 3000-foot level, the route becomes a narrow trail and begins to drop across a steep, brushy hillside on switchbacks built by the California Conservation Corps. As you enjoy this well-graded descent, you may be treated to a fine display of spring wildflowers, such as Chinese houses, Ithuriel's spear, blue dicks, and globe tulips.

Alternately open and wooded, the trail makes a long, switchbacking traverse across a north-facing hillside, where you may find canyon live oak and black oak; here the trees may be alive with dark-eyed juncos. The sound of rushing water rises from Williams Gulch, a deep canyon ahead. When you reach its shady bottom, after putting your knees and hiking boots to the test, you will have dropped nearly 2000 feet from yesterday's high point, the summit of Rose Peak. Now is the time to relax and enjoy cool, peaceful surroundings. Two creeks—one from the southwest, the other from the southeast—join in Williams Gulch, and the resulting stream flows northwest, eventually reaching San Antonio Creek. Your route crosses their cold, clear waters on rocks, then emerges as a dirt road on an open hillside.

Maples and sycamores growing here indicate a high water table, but as you turn left at a T-junction, **37**, and gain Rocky Ridge, the dryland species—gray pine, black oak, blue oak—again become dominant. California buckeye, with its spring profusion of white, candle-like blooms, is also here. You have just completed the most remote section, from Rose Peak to Williams Gulch, of the Ohlone Wilderness Regional Trail. (When I reached this point, I had not seen any other people for 24 hours, a level of seclusion I have encountered only once before, on the John Muir Trail.)

At a Y-junction, **38**, bear right and descend toward Boyd Camp; there is a toilet here, but water is available only at Stromer Spring, just west of the next junction, **39**, about 0.33 mile farther. (This is the last water until you reach Lake Del Valle.) After getting water, return to the main road, turn northeast and walk steeply downhill through an area of bush monkeyflower, toyon, and coyote bush to the Ohlone Wilderness Regional Trail sign-in board, **40**, and a junction with the Vallecitos Trail, right. To reach the parking area at the Lichen Bark picnic area, continue straight and continue to descend through an area of chaparral, mostly chamise, and wildflowers. Several switchbacks finally bring you to your goal—Lake Del Valle and the parking area.

Briones Reservoir from the Sea View Trail.

• Pleasanton Ridge Regional Park •

| **40** | Pleasanton Ridge Regional Park
PLEASANTON RIDGE |

Length:	12.3 miles
Time:	6 to 8 hours
Rating:	Difficult
Regulations:	EBRPD
Highlights:	The hike along Pleasanton Ridge, combining the Oak Tree, Ridgeline, Bay Leaf, Sinbad Creek, Thermalito, and Olive Grove trails, while one of the longest and most challenging in this guide, is also one of the most rewarding. The views are outstanding, extending from Pleasanton, San Ramon, and Mt. Diablo to Sunol Valley, the Sunol/Ohlone Wilderness, and Mission Peak. The terrain is varied: the route passes through dense woodland, open grassland, and even a restored olive orchard. Bird and plant life flourish in this relatively undeveloped, 3,163-acre park.
Facilities:	Picnic tables, water, toilet, horse staging.
Trailhead:	West side of first parking area.
Directions:	From Interstate 680 in Pleasanton, take the Sunol Boulevard/Castlewood Drive exit and go southwest on Castlewood Dr., staying straight where Pleasanton–Sunol Rd. bends left. After 0.3 mile, you reach Foothill Rd.; turn left and go south 1.6 miles on Foothill Rd. to the Oak Tree Staging Area, right.

After walking a short distance west from the parking area on a dirt road, you come to a cattle gate; once through, bear left at a junction and begin climbing on the Oak Tree Trail, also a dirt road. The grade is moderate at first, and the route passes through alternating areas of open grassland and oak woodland—mostly valley oak and coast live oak—on its way up Pleasanton Ridge. Where there are oaks in the East Bay you are likely to find woodpeckers, two of the most common being acorn woodpecker and northern flicker. Acorn woodpecker is a dark bird, slightly smaller than a

Cr. Tr.

Sinbad

LEAF TR.

BAY

Pond

SINBAD CR. TR.

Pond

PLEASANTON

AUGUSTIN

BERNAL

PARK

Esquestrian
Trail →

RIDGELINE TRAIL

Valley
View Tr.

N

TRAIL

Pond

RIDGE

Sycamore

Grove Tr.

REGIONAL

Kilkare

THERMALITO TRAIL

TREE

OLIVE GROVE TRAIL

RIDGELINE

OAK

TR.

Road

Thermalito Trail

Woodland
Trail

PARK

Ridgeline
Trail

0   ½ Mile

Bernal   Ave.

Foothill

Castlewood
Drive

Pleasanton - Sunol Road

680

Road

Oak
Tree
Staging
Area

40. Pleasanton Ridge

robin, with a black-and-white face, red crown, white rump, and white wing patches. As its name implies, this woodpecker gathers acorns in the winter—it dines on insects in the summer—and often stores them in holes it drills in oak trees. The northern flicker is a larger bird, brown overall, with a white rump, spotted breast, and horizontally striped back. The male of the "red-shafted" form, found west of the Rocky Mountains, sports a red mustache.

Several hundred yards past the trailhead, you come to a bend in the road and a junction with the Woodland Trail, a single track heading left and uphill. (This trail, closed to bicycles, is an alternate way to reach the ridgecrest, and although it switchbacks steeply at first, most of the climbing is in the shade.) Following the Oak Tree Trail as it climbs on a winding, open course, generally northwest, you begin to see the busy Interstate 680 corridor below and right, and in the distance, the twin summits of Mt. Diablo. Joining oaks as one of the earliest trees to leaf out is California buckeye, with its distinctive fan of five bright green leaflets. Buckeyes adapt to hot weather by shedding their leaves early, sometimes in mid-summer. You can identify the leafless tree by its rounded crown and angled branches, which are often colored orange by lichens.

The route continues its gentle and then moderate ascent, crossing a stream that runs under the road through a culvert. Venerable oaks—coast live and valley—give you occasional shade, but most of the time you are in open grassland. As the route turns west, you pass a junction, right, with the Sycamore Grove Trail, and you can see some of the large, light-barked trees that give this trail its name. There is a constant hum here from the freeway, but that will soon diminish, to be replaced by the breezy rustling of oak leaves. The route completes a 180-degree bend and now heads south, passing a junction with a grass-covered road, left, that is closed to bicycles. Toyon, blue elderberry, and poison oak grow here beside the road.

At about the 1.25-mile point you emerge from a wooded area and reach a four-way junction near a barbed-wire fence. The trail merging from your left is the Woodland Trail. Straight ahead, and staying left of the fence, is an unsigned dirt road. Your route, the Oak Tree Trail, turns right and goes through an opening in the fence. About 30 feet beyond the fence is a trail post, and a choice of three dirt paths. The left-hand path is the continuation of the Oak Tree Trail. The right-hand path, a rutted single track, is an unfortunate shortcut that has scarred a grassy hillside. (You will see several PLEASE STAY ON THE TRAIL signs in this area.) The center path, your route, is the Ridgeline Trail.

The view from here is wonderful, taking in Mission Peak to the south, San Antonio Reservoir to the southeast, and behind it, the Sunol/Ohlone Wilderness. Skirting the north side of Mission Peak is Interstate 680, carrying its heavy load of traffic between Fremont and Pleasanton. To the west, heavily forested Sunol Ridge, topped by a single communication tower, rises above Kilkare Canyon and Sinbad Creek, reaching an elevation of just over 2,000 feet. The Ridgeline Trail makes a 180-degree bend to gain the ridgetop, passing an unsigned path, right. Bending left, the route reaches a fork marked by a trail post: the left-hand fork is a short connector to the Olive Grove Trail; the right-hand fork is the Ridgeline Trail, your route.

The large olive grove you see in front of you is one of several planted here between about 1890 and the 1920s. No record exists of who planted the trees, which are currently being restored by the park district and a private concessionaire. About 125 feet past the fork, you pass a junction, right, with a rough dirt road that runs along a barbed-wire fence. The Ridgeline Trail now parallels this fence, heading generally northwest and climbing past the olive grove on a moderate grade. Just beyond the grove is a drinking faucet, a watering trough for animals, and another fork, where you continue straight. The view east from here is unobstructed, and park district rangers sometimes lead twilight hikes along Pleasanton Ridge to watch the rising full moon.

Rising steeply over rocky ground, your route, shared by hikers, bicyclists, equestrians, joggers, and dog walkers, passes more olive trees, their leaves quaking in the breeze. At the end of the olive orchard, the route levels and comes into the open, with views extending north to Mt. Diablo and south to Mission Peak. The northeast face of Pleasanton Ridge drops steeply to Interstate 680, right and now far below. Just shy of the 2-mile point, you pass a junction with the Olive Grove Trail merging sharply from the left. On its way along the ridgetop, the route climbs over several high points, the first of which is just ahead. (You will find a picnic bench atop one of these rounded summits.)

Soon you descend to a flat spot and a four-way junction. Here, on the left, is a short connector to the Thermalito Trail, a route running generally parallel to and southwest of the Ridgeline Trail. The Thermalito Trail takes its name from the Thermal Fruit Company, which was active nearby from 1904 until the 1930s. On the right, an unsigned path climbs to a cattle gate. Your route continues straight, then bends right and climbs steeply to the summit of a grassy hill. Ahead the ridge continues to rise, and on your right is a boundary with the Castlewood Country Club, private property. Twisted and gnarled valley oaks line the route in places; near one particularly large one is a junction, left, with another connector to the Thermalito Trail.

Continuing on the Ridgeline Trail, you climb steeply over several more hills, with steep drops in between. Finally, the route leaves the ridgetop, veering right and downhill through a cattle gate, then descends on a rutted and rocky road via two switchbacks to a forest of California bay laurel, coast live oak, black oak, and bigleaf maple, with toyon, bush monkeyflower, and vine honeysuckle adding variety to the scene, so different from the ridgetop. At the second switchback, you pass a path that heads right to a gate and the country club, a restricted area. The route resumes its northwest course on a level grade, soon entering the City of Pleasanton's Augustin Bernal Park.

Now out of dense forest, you drop to a flat spot, which may be muddy, and a junction with the Thermalito Trail, a dirt road, left. A beautiful clearing here makes a fine rest spot, and a fallen tree limb may provide you with a comfortable seat. There is drinking water and a trough for animals a short distance down the Thermalito Trail. The valley oaks surrounding this clearing are loaded with mistletoe, especially evident when their limbs are bare. (To shorten your hike, take the Thermalito Trail southwest and follow the route description from about the 8.5-mile point for the return portion of this trip.) Leaving the clearing, still on the Ridgeline Trail, you begin a moderate ascent, passing near some stands of blue oak. Flocks of dark-eyed juncos may move from tree to tree just ahead of you, or you may hear the call of a red-tailed hawk and see it circling high above.

Soon the Valley View Trail, a dirt road, appears on your right; it will merge with the Ridgeline Trail at an upcoming junction. Before the junction, a short connector road, right, leads to the Valley View Trail. About 50 feet past the connector road is the single-track Equestrian Trail, left, for horses only. Continuing straight, you pass these junctions and a pond, left. (The drinking fountain here, indicated on the regional park map by a **W**, may not be working.) This portion of the hike is in the open, but

*View southeast along the Ridgeline Trail at about the
2.0-mile point.*

sheltered from the wind, so it may be hot. The route rises to a little saddle and passes a junction, left, with the other end of the Equestrian Trail. Ahead is a gate, the boundary between the city and regional parks.

Once through the gate you arrive at a junction; here a dirt road continues straight, but your route turns right and leads you through a beautiful oak savanna, with a fence marking the park boundary on your right. After a mostly level walk you merge with the road that went straight just after the gate and begin to gain elevation. As the route breaks into the open, you pass a pond, left, which may be full of tadpoles, frogs, or both. A large coast live oak at the water's edge provides shelter for songbirds. There is a junction here with the Sinbad Creek Trail, left, part of your return route. For now continue straight, passing another small pond, and enter a wonderful area of rolling hills punctuated by groves of oak. You may see ground squirrels standing at attention in front of their burrows or scampering across the grass as you approach.

The route soon swings west and reaches a junction. From here a dirt road leads to a gate and the park boundary, right, but your route—shown on the March 1997 revision of the EBRPD map as the Bay Leaf Trail—continues straight, then bends left and begins to descend. There are deep, tree-filled ravines on both sides of you now, as you follow a spur ridge southwest. Soon the route swings sharply right and drops into the right-hand ravine on a moderate grade. Approaching the bottom of the ravine, you enter a shady realm of bay, black oak, and California buckeye, remarkably different from the open ridgetop you traversed earlier.

Now the route bends almost 180-degrees left, crossing two creeks that flow under the road through culverts. The freeway noise which accompanied the start of this hike has been replaced perhaps by a serenade of running water, coming from a creek in a gully to your left. After an open section, where bright sunlight encourages plants such as California sagebrush, coyote bush, and bush monkeyflower to take hold on a rocky hillside, you reach a junction, right, with the single-track Sinbad Creek Trail. (A trail post here shows the Sinbad Creek Trail also continuing downhill.)

Your route follows the road downhill and soon reaches Sinbad Creek, at the bottom of Kilkare Canyon, just before the 6-mile point. Step across the creek on rocks, and at a T-junction with a dirt road, turn left. Walking downstream along the creek and following a level course, you pass large western sycamore trees and groves of bay and coast live oak, interspersed with shrubs such as hillside gooseberry and coyote bush. After about 0.75 mile of pleasant streamside walking, you reach another T-junction, where you turn left, re-cross the creek, and begin climbing steeply on the Sinbad Creek Trail, a dirt road. As the road winds uphill, you may notice some rock layers that appear to have been tilted from horizontal to vertical, an indication of the powerful forces that formed these hills. Two parallel fault systems border Pleasanton Ridge, and violent upheavals during the past two to three million years have twisted and rearranged the marine sediments that underlie this area. Passing a large water tank, the route emerges from dense forest into oak savanna, then swings east and crosses a notch in the ridgeline.

Ahead you can see the frog pond you passed earlier, and the large coast live oak growing at its edge. Passing a dirt road, left, you soon come to a T-junction with the Ridgeline Trail. Turn right and follow the Ridgeline Trail, bearing left at a fork about 250 feet past the end of the pond. You are now retracing your steps to the junction of the Ridgeline and Thermalito trails, at about the 8.5-mile point. When you reach that junction, which is in Augustin Bernal Park, you turn right on the Thermalito Trail, a dirt road, passing a drinking faucet and watering trough, and begin a moderate climb in the shade of valley oaks and coast live oaks. Soon you come to a gate that marks the boundary between the city and regional parks; now the route descends over rocky ground, steeply in places, following a southwest course. After passing a picturesque pond, left, the road rises steeply through a serene forest and then comes into the open.

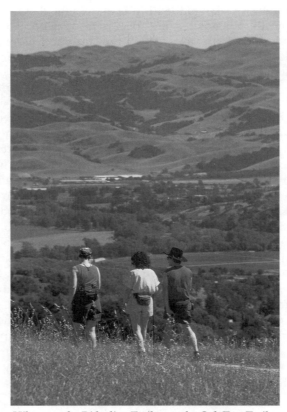

*Hikers on the Ridgeline Trail near the Oak Tree Trail
have a great view south toward Mission Peak.*

The Thermalito Trail runs parallel to the Ridgeline Trail, making many ups and downs along the way. Watch for red-tailed hawks slowly circling overhead and acorn woodpeckers flashing through the trees. Mission Peak is once again in view to the south, across Interstate 680. Passing a connector, left, to the Ridgeline Trail, you continue on a rolling course, alternating between pockets of forest and open areas. Just shy of the 10-mile point, you reach a **T**-junction, where another connector to the Ridgeline Trail heads left, and your route, the Thermalito Trail, bears right.

Out in the open now, the road descends past a stock pond and a ground-squirrel colony to a small ravine, which may hold water during wet weather. Crossing to the other side of the ravine, the route climbs slightly, bringing you to another stock pond, right, and a junction. Leaving the Thermalito Trail as it turns right, you continue straight on a connector to the Olive Grove Trail. Walking east about 100 yards, you come to a junction with the Olive Grove Trail, which heads both left and straight. Continue straight, passing the olive grove on your left as you make a moderate descent on a rutted road. At the next junction, where the Olive Grove Trail swings right, continue straight on a connector to the Ridgeline Trail, which you soon reach. At the junction with the Ridgeline Trail, bear right and retrace your steps to the parking area.

◆ Point Pinole Regional Shoreline ◆

41   Point Pinole Regional Shoreline
BAY VIEW TRAIL

Length: 5.2 miles

Time: 2 to 3 hours

Rating: Easy

Regulations: EBRPD; fees for parking and dogs; dogs not allowed on fishing pier and must be leashed at all times.

Highlights: Point Pinole juts north like a thumb into San Pablo Bay, and the more than 10 miles of easy trails through its marshlands, grassy fields, and groves of eucalyptus offer a sanctuary from the almost continuous industrial and residential development stretching along the East Bay shoreline from San Leandro to the Carquinez Bridge. This loop trip follows The Bay View Trail to the tip of the point, then returns via the Marsh and Cook's Point trails. (A shuttle van from the parking area to a fishing pier at the end of Point Pinole runs daily except Tuesdays and Wednesdays; there is a small fee, but seniors, the disabled, and children under age 6 ride free. The van leaves the parking area at half past every hour beginning at 7:30 A.M. Return trips leave the pier turnaround area at a quarter past every hour. The last trip back to the parking area is a 3 P.M.)

Facilities: Picnic tables, water, toilet, phone, children's play area.

Trailhead: Northwest corner of parking area.

Directions: From Interstate 80 in Pinole, take the Richmond Parkway/Fitzgerald Drive exit and follow Richmond Pkwy. west 1.9 miles to the Giant Hwy. exit. After exiting, go 0.3 mile to a stop sign, turn right, and go another 0.2 mile to Giant Hwy. Turn right and follow Giant Hwy. as it jogs left, crosses railroad tracks, and jogs right for a total of 0.7 mile to the park entrance, left. Go 0.1 mile to the entrance kiosk, then turn left into the parking area.

History buffs will especially enjoy this hike, because Point Pinole was the location of a large explosives manufacturing industry, which, from 1880 to 1960, turned out 2 billion pounds of dynamite. A few remnants, in the form of sunken bunkers and half-buried railroad ties, of this dangerous yet prosperous enterprise are still visible. Before starting out, you might take a moment to visit a commemorative plaque, just west of the entrance kiosk and beyond the parking-area fence, which designates Point Pinole a California Historical Landmark and tells more about the area's unique history.

Leaving the parking area and walking north along the left of two paved roads—the right one is used by a shuttle bus ferrying people to the fishing pier—which soon join, you turn left to cross a bridge over tracks

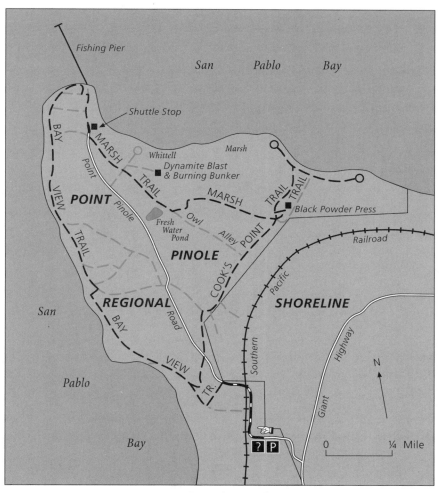

41. Bay View Trail

belonging to the Southern Pacific Railroad. Just past the bridge, turn left and follow the Bay View Trail, here a dirt path, leading downhill through a grove of eucalyptus, Point Pinole's dominant tree, to Parchester Marsh, a large expanse of pickleweed and other marsh plants at the edge of San Pablo Bay. The Bay View Trail is part of the San Francisco Bay Trail, a planned route, about half of which has been completed, which someday will encircle the Bay. As you come out into the open, past large toyon bushes, you can see Mt. Tamalpais and the Marin County shoreline across the bay, and, closer at hand, the industrial areas of Richmond.

Upon reaching the upper edge of the marsh, you come to a T-junction with a broad dirt path; here you turn right and walk past a small sandy beach, then through another fragrant eucalyptus grove. As you pass the Cook's Point Trail (COOKES on the trail post), right, be on the lookout for hummingbirds and, especially in winter, beautiful orange and black monarch butterflies. If the tide has exposed the mud flats to your left, look with binoculars or a spotting scope for feeding shorebirds. Once in a while, a northern harrier will cruise by, causing panic and putting up the birds. Farther out in the bay, you may see rafts of ducks floating on the water.

The route, parallel to the shoreline, is open here, with no shade and no protection from the wind. Just past the 0.5-mile point, a rest bench, left, invites you to sit for a moment and look out over San Pablo Bay. In the East Bay, access by foot to the shoreline is prevented in many places by levees, highways, and industrial development, so it is a pleasure to be able to walk down to the water's edge, which you can do at several points on this loop. Partially exposed railroad ties indicate that this section of the route was probably used to transport explosives. According to the EBRPD brochure, Point Pinole was crisscrossed with "a system of two broad-gauge and extensive narrow-gauge rail lines." Electric and gas-operated locomotives were used to transport dynamite over these rail lines between manufacturing plants, storage areas, and a shipping pier, which was east of the present-day fishing pier.

Just past a beach-access point, you turn right and follow the Bay View Trail as it climbs gently through a grove of eucalyptus, while the path you've been on goes straight, through a fence guarding a restricted area. At a T-junction, your route, now a dirt road, turns left and continues in the shade, soon passing two unsigned roads, less than 0.1 mile apart, on the right. After a brief descent, you reach a four-way junction. The path that went into the restricted area now rejoins your route from the left, and another road goes right. As you continue straight, you pass through an area where EBRPD has used fire to maintain the health of the eucalyptus growing here and remove forest floor debris.

At about the 1.25-mile point, you reach a fork in the road and a cement bunker, another reminder of the area's dynamite days. Take the left-hand fork, and soon you reach a bluff where a rest bench overlooks the bay, and an access path winds down to a gravel beach, perhaps inhabited by a snowy egret. Old wooden pilings, more reminders of Point Pinole's past, jut out of the water close to shore. A lone California buckeye and a hillside of California sagebrush, coyote bush, poison oak, and lupine add variety to the plant life.

Just past the bluff, near a clearing planted with pines, your road is joined by another coming from the right. Now you pass several more rest benches, and soon you can see across Point Pinole—an expanse of meadows and eucalyptus—to the east edge of San Pablo Bay. With the fishing pier in sight, you leave the Bay View Trail as it turns right, and continue straight on a narrow trail along the edge of cliffs overlooking the water. Near the present pier are the remains of a much older shipping wharf used by dynamite manufacturers.

Following the trail around the tip of Point Pinole, you soon join a paved path coming from the fishing pier, and turn south through a picnic area, where water and toilets are available. Just past the shuttle bus turnaround, you leave pavement and bear left on the Marsh Trail, a gravel road; Whittell Marsh, habitat for herons, egrets, and shorebirds, is left. After passing through a four-way junction, you can see another historical

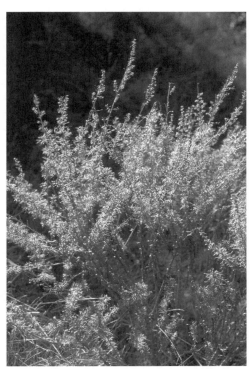

California sagebrush grows throughout the East Bay parklands, including Point Pinole.

remnant, the Dynamite Blast and Burning Bunker, in the marsh. A fresh-water pond bordered by cattails marks an upcoming junction, where the gravel road, now called Owl Alley, continues straight, and your route, the Marsh Trail, a wide dirt path, turns left. (Both lead to the Cook's Point Trail, your return route.)

Turn left and follow the Marsh Trail as it winds past a rest bench along the upland edge of Whittell Marsh, with eucalyptus and acacia bordering your route. In the fall portions of this pickleweed marsh turn brilliant ruby red. Just past the 3-mile point, you come to a rest bench and a junction with the Cook's Point Trail, a dirt road. Just west of the junction is a machine used in making explosives—a black-powder press. From this junction, the Marsh Trail continues 0.25 mile left to the edge of San Pablo Bay, where you have a beautiful view northwest toward the tip of Point Pinole and beyond, to the hills of Marin County. As you approach the shore, turn left at a junction and follow the path to its end near the water. (To explore more of the shoreline, retrace your steps to the previous junction, and then bear left, following signs for the Cook's Point Trail.)

Now retrace your steps to the junction of the Marsh and Cook's Point trails, near the black-powder press, and follow the Cook's Point Trail southwest, through a corridor of eucalyptus. At the junction with Owl Alley, you pass the ranger's residence and continue straight, now on broken pavement, until you reach a fork in the route. Take the right-hand fork and climb slightly on solid pavement, passing a junction, left, with a gravel road. A few feet beyond, you reach another junction; here a paved road goes right and uphill, but your route, now a gravel path, bends left. Ahead you can see a picnic area and children's play equipment. Just past the 4.5-mile point, you cross paved Point Pinole Road, which goes from the parking area to the fishing pier. Continue straight, now on a dirt path in a ravine, and walk downhill toward the water, enjoying a view of Mt. Tamalpais rising in the distance. About 0.25 mile past Point Pinole Road road, you come to a trail post which points you left to the parking area. Ignore this, and continue toward the water, soon joining the Bay View Trail. From here, turn left and retrace your steps to the parking area.

◆ Redwood Regional Park ◆

Redwood Regional Park is a land of ghosts. The stately trees that tower over the park's steep hillsides and shady canyons are second-growth descendants of a vanished race of giants, *Sequoia sempervirens*, or coast redwood, originally found along the coast of Oregon and California. In their prime, if allowed to grow undisturbed for hundreds of years, redwoods become the tallest trees on Earth, reaching skyward more than 300 feet and growing to a diameter of 10 to 15 feet, sometimes larger. Ring counts have found trees more than 2,000 years old, and when a redwood dies or is cut, new trees sprout in a circle around their ancestor. European settlers coming to the West Coast nearly wiped out the redwoods, and today only isolated pockets of virgin forest remain on federal, state, and private lands.

But there are other ghosts here too, shades of rough and rowdy loggers who, in the years from 1840 to 1860, managed to fell nearly every old-growth tree in the East Bay's redwood forest, including two trees so prominent they were used as points of reference by mariners entering the Golden Gate, 16 miles away. At least 10 sawmills operated in the area, including four within or near the park's current boundaries, supplying lumber to fuel the building boom that followed California's gold rush. After the loggers had done their work, an Alameda physician and botanist, Dr. William Gibbons, found 2,000 redwood stumps, some of them 20 feet in diameter, the remains, he wrote, of what "must have constituted the most magnificent forest on the continent." Another visitor to this scene of devastation was John Muir.

This 1,836-acre park has been the hub of much other human activity as well. After the loggers came woodcutters, who removed redwood stumps and even roots for firewood. After the 1906 earthquake, young redwood trees were cut for timber to rebuild San Francisco. Farming and ranching took place here, and as you walk the trails you may see fruit trees, remnants of old orchards. At the end of the Depression, WPA workers built roads, trails, and four stone huts near the banks of Redwood Creek. During World War II the park was used by Naval Air Cadets for survival training and by a grave-registration training battalion as a practice cemetery. The line between Alameda and Contra Costa counties neatly bisects Redwood Park, attesting to the importance each county placed, when they split in 1853, on getting an equal share of the valuable trees.

Although Redwood Regional Park, dedicated in 1939, was officially the fourth member of the East Bay Regional Park District's fledgling system, in some ways it was actually the first. During the difficult negotiations that took place in the mid-1930s to acquire EBMUD's surplus land, the

District's first board president, civic leader and businessman Major Charles Lee Tilden, advanced his own money to buy 60 acres of private land in Redwood Canyon for $35 per acre, a Depression-era bargain price. This helped get the ball rolling for the 1936 purchase of the first three regional parks—Lake Temescal, Roundtop (now Sibley Volcanic Regional Preserve), and Wildcat Canyon, soon renamed Tilden Regional Park.

42 Redwood Regional Park
EAST RIDGE

Length: 6 miles

Time: 3 to 4 hours

Rating: Moderate

Regulations: EBRPD; fees for parking and dogs when entrance kiosk is attended; no bicycles on Stream Trail from Skyline Gate to Trail's End picnic area.

Highlights: This loop, using the East Ridge and Stream trails, pairs a vigorous hike along an exposed ridge with a secluded downhill ramble in the shade of tall redwoods, an unbeatable combination. Views from the East Ridge Trail, especially of the surrounding East Bay parklands, are superb, and the redwood forest along Redwood Creek, though merely a shadow of its former old-growth self, is nevertheless majestic. As an extra bonus, water is available not only at the trailhead, but also at Skyline Gate and various points along the Stream Trail.

Facilities: Picnic tables, water, toilet, phone; horse staging at the Wayside picnic area, about 0.25 mile before the Canyon Meadow Staging Area.

Trailhead: Northwest end of the parking area.

Directions: From Interstate 580 southbound in Oakland, take the 35th Avenue exit, turn left and follow 35th Ave. east into the hills. After 0.8 mile 35th Ave. becomes Redwood Rd., and at 2.4 miles it crosses Skyline Blvd., where you stay in the left lane and go straight. At 4.6 miles from Interstate 580 you reach the park entrance; turn left and go 0.5 mile to the Canyon Meadow Staging Area.

From Interstate 580 northbound in Oakland, take the Warren Freeway/Berkeley/Hwy. 13 exit and go 0.9 mile to the Carson Street/Redwood Road exit. From the stop sign

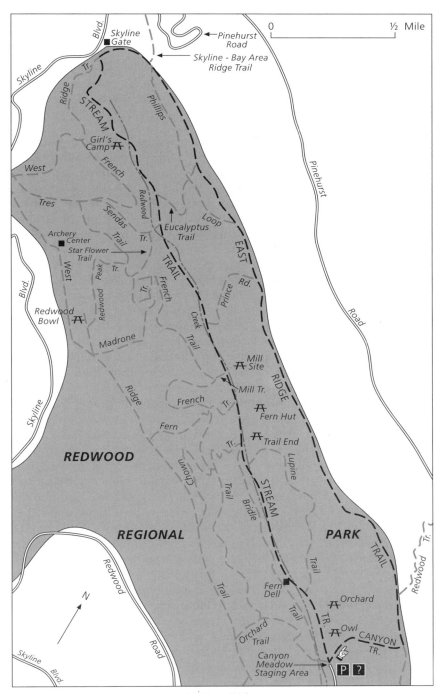

42. East Ridge

at the end of the exit ramp, continue straight, now on Mountain Blvd., 0.2 mile, and bear right onto Redwood Rd. Go 3.2 miles to the park entrance; turn left and go 0.5 mile to the Canyon Meadow Staging Area.

From Hwy. 13 southbound, take the Redwood Road/ Carson Street exit, turn left onto Redwood Rd. and follow the directions above.

Before leaving the Canyon Meadow parking area, take a moment to notice the variety of trees here—coast redwood, California bay laurel, coast live oak, bigleaf maple, willow, black walnut—a preview of what you will see on this wonderful hike. From the parking area, walk northwest, past a gate marked FIRE TRAIL, on a paved path, reaching a junction with the Canyon Trail, a dirt-and-gravel road heading right and uphill. Another fine tree, a large Fremont cottonwood, towers over this junction, where a path also heads left across Redwood Creek to the Bridle and Orchard trails. As you look up to admire the cottonwood, you may see a red-tailed hawk circling overhead or hear one giving its "keeer, keeer" call.

Turning right on the Canyon Trail, a dirt road, you pass picnic tables at the edge of an open field, then merge with another dirt road joining from the right. Soon you are climbing on a moderate grade in the shade of coast live oak, California bay laurel, willow, Monterey pine, and blue elderberry. A few small redwoods, the tree for which this park is named, have taken root under the canopy of bay and oak. You will see their much larger cousins later along the Stream Trail, your return route.

Now in the open, the route bends left just before merging with the East Ridge Trail, a wide dirt road, where you bear left. Western scrub-jays may loudly announce your arrival on the ridgetop, where you have a great view east to Mt. Diablo and west across Redwood Creek to the high ground near Skyline Blvd. Invasive plants such as coyote bush, French broom, and pampas grass have taken hold here, but you will also see oak, bay, madrone, and more small redwoods. The route follows a rolling course along the ridgeline, passing the Redwood Trail, right, and climbs above 1000 feet to a rest bench in the shade of a tall pine. Now you can pick out other prominent East Bay summits, including Round Top, northwest, and Rocky Ridge, east, both topped with communication towers.

Just past the 2-mile point, Prince Road leads left and downhill, but your route stays straight and climbs past a large pine grove, soon reaching a fork with the Phillips Loop, left. Here you bear right, and continue climbing through pines, grateful for shade on a hot day. Dark-eyed juncos and nuthatches thrive in wooded areas, and you may see them here. Now heading through a corridor of pine, eucalyptus, and madrone, the route passes a junction with the Eucalyptus Trail, left, and begins to bend west. Red-tailed hawks and turkey vultures may be seen high above the trees, riding the wind.

With the Skyline Gate parking area in view, you pass the Phillips Loop, left, and the East Bay Skyline/Bay Area Ridge Trail, right, on its way north to the Huckleberry Botanic and Sibley Volcanic regional preserves. Just before reaching the parking area, where water, toilets, a rest bench, and a phone are available, the route becomes paved and leads to a junction with the Stream and West Ridge trails. The West Ridge Trail, straight, is the continuation of the East Bay Skyline/Bay Area Ridge Trail, and is open to bicycles all the way to Canyon Meadow, making a round trip on bicycle possible. The Stream Trail, left, is for hikers and horses only, from Skyline Gate to the Trail's End picnic area.

Turn left and begin a moderate downhill walk on a dirt road, past willow, California hazelnut, and tangles of vine honeysuckle. You soon come to Girls Camp, a grassy meadow with picnic tables shaded by walnut trees. Now on a gentle descent beside Redwood Creek, you pass the Eucalyptus Trail, heading left and uphill. Here, at about the 4-mile point, the vegetation changes dramatically, and you now walk in a shady forest of magnificent redwoods growing straight and tall, towering overhead. (Redwood seedlings are so spindly, that it is hard to imagine them reaching such statuesque proportions.) The creek is in a deep ravine, right, and a moderate descent soon brings you to a rest bench and a junction with the Tres Sendas Trail, right. You route continues straight.

(If you are here in the fall, you may be in for a treat. I did this hike in September, and was puzzled by what appeared to be reddish growths covering the California hazelnut, blackberry vines, and sword ferns beside the Stream Trail. To my amazement, I discovered thousands of breeding ladybugs clustered on the foliage, with others flying through the air and soon covering me as well. I had seen a similar display in Muir Woods, but never with this quantity of bugs.)

With Redwood Creek on your right, continue on the Stream Trail through deep forest, where only ferns, lovers of the dark and damp, grow in soil littered with bay leaves and redwood twigs. Now you cross several bridges, as the creek meanders back and forth under the road, and pass a junction with Prince Road, climbing left, before emerging into an open area surrounded by coast live oak, walnut, and willow. Back in redwoods, you pass the Mill Trail, right, and two stone shelters at the Mill Site picnic area, left across the creek. A unique strain of rainbow trout lives in Redwood Creek, prompting park officials to develop a creek-restoration program to protect spawning areas. Signs here ask you not to climb on creek banks and to keep dogs and horses from doing so.

As you continue your level walk on the road, you pass a wooden bridge leading left across the creek, and the Fern Hut picnic area, right. At about the 5-mile point, the Fern Trail heads right, uphill, and another bridge, left, crosses the creek. Continue straight, and if you look up here, you may notice that the redwoods grow straight and tall, but the bay trees arch over the road. Especially on the steep hillside to your right, the bays start out growing straight, then begin to curve. Because they cannot compete with the redwoods in height, bays choose this devious strategy to seek sunlight.

Soon you reach a junction with the Chown and Bridle trails, right, and a bridge over the creek, left. Continuing straight, you reach pavement at the Trail's End picnic area, and after a short walk, leave the forest near the Fern Dell picnic area, a lovely meadow with white alder, bigleaf maple, box elder, and walnut. A sign, right, points to the camper exit, used by drive-in camping groups, but you follow the paved road as it bends left to cross Redwood Creek, passes through another meadow, then enters redwoods again. When you come out of the trees, you will see ahead the junction with the Canyon Trail; after you reach it, retrace your steps to the parking area.

43 Redwood Regional Park
FRENCH TRAIL

Length:	7.7 miles
Time:	4 to 6 hours
Rating:	Moderate
Regulations:	EBRPD; fees for parking and dogs when entrance kiosk is attended; no bicycles; no horses on park entrance road, on the Stream Trail south of Trail's End picnic area, or in picnic areas except Trail's End.
Highlights:	This loop, combining the Stream, West Ridge, French and Orchard trails, takes you into the heart of this unique regional park, the only one in the East Bay where coast redwoods, heavily logged in the mid-1800s, have been preserved to such an extent. The climb along the Stream Trail to Skyline Gate is easy, steepening only at the very end, and the rolling, meandering return through the redwoods via the French Trail, an alternate segment of the East Bay Skyline/Bay Area Ridge Trail, although strenuous, is not to be missed.
Facilities:	Picnic tables, water, toilet, phone; horse staging at the Wayside picnic area, about 0.25 mile before the Canyon Meadow Staging Area.
Trailhead:	Northwest end of the parking area.
Directions:	See the directions for "East Ridge" on p. 242.

43. French Trail

Walking northwest from the parking area on a paved road, you soon reach a large Fremont cottonwood marking a junction with the Canyon Trail, right, and a trail leading left across Redwood Creek to the Bridle and Orchard trails. Water and toilets are available here, at Skyline Gate, and at various points on the Stream Trail.

Just past this junction, the route enters the shade of a beautiful redwood grove, a taste of things to come, then emerges into the open at the Orchard picnic area, a large grassy meadow, and bends left to cross Redwood Creek. You pass six more picnic areas along the Stream Trail before leaving the pavement at Trail's End. Steller's jays—blue birds with black, crested heads—may give you a raucous welcome as you walk through their forest home, and you may see a black phoebe, also black-headed, a member of the tyrant flycatcher family.

After the pavement ends, you follow the Stream Trail, a dirt road along the banks of Redwood Creek, with steep hillsides rising up on either side. A bridge, right, leads to the Lupine Trail, across the creek. The air here may be fragrant with the smell of California bay laurel, a relative of the Mediterranean tree whose leaves are used in cooking, and at times the only sounds reaching your ears will be bird song and the trickle of water in the creek. Soon you pass a junction, left, with the Chown and Bridle trails. At the Fern Hut picnic area you will pass the Fern Trail, left, and a water fountain presented to the park by the California Federation of Women's Clubs, Alameda District. Just ahead, across the creek, is the Mill Site picnic area. A restoration project to protect a unique species of rainbow trout that inhabits Redwood Creek is in progress here; signs ask you to stay off the creek banks and make sure your dogs and horses do too.

At about the 1.3-mile point, the Mill Trail climbs left, but you continue straight to an open area surrounded by California hazelnut, bay, and willow. Thimbleberry, a shrub with white flowers, red berries, and large, fuzzy leaves—a relative of blackberry and raspberry—grows here, as does a prehistoric-looking plant called horsetail. You may also see periwinkle, a non-native ground cover with dark green leaves and blue, five-petaled flowers, blooming year-round. Overhead, watch for turkey vultures, soaring on uplifted wings. Back in the shade of tall redwoods, the route passes a junction with Prince Road, heading right and steeply uphill, and you continue straight on a carpet of bay leaves and redwood twigs. A steep hillside, left, is covered with similar litter, fertile ground for sword ferns, which thrive in dense forest.

The route crosses Redwood Creek over small bridges in several places; with it now on your left you reach a clearing in a large grove of redwoods and a junction, left, with the Tres Sendas Trail. Here the Stream Trail, your route, bends right and begins a moderate climb, then levels off in an open area lined with French broom and poison oak, where the Eucalyptus Trail branches right, steeply uphill. Eucalyptus, madrone, toyon, coyote bush, and bush monkeyflower are crowded together here, taking advantage of a break in the forest canopy to bask in sunlight.

At about the 2.4-mile point, after crossing the creek, you reach Girls Camp, a lovely picnic area with a stone hut, water, a rest room, and picnic tables shaded by black walnut trees. As the route, still a dirt road, begins to climb again, you pass stands of willow and coast live oak lining the upper reaches of Redwood Creek. Flowering currant and California buttercup bloom here from late winter through spring, and vine honeysuckle and red columbine continue the colorful show into summer. Uphill and right, a large forest of eucalyptus and Monterey pine graces a ridgetop, not far from Skyline Gate, the high point of this route. As you pass a small stream flowing under the road, the grade steepens, and you climb via S-bends to Skyline Gate, where water, toilets, phone, and a rest bench await you.

After stopping to rest for perhaps a few minutes, head south on the West Ridge Trail, a dirt road that is part of the East Bay Skyline/Bay Area

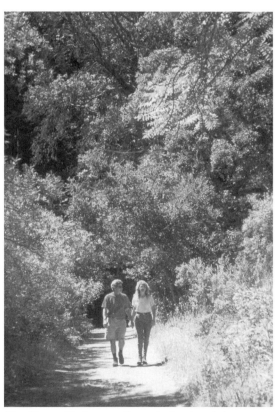

The Stream Trail passes through clearings between groves of coast redwoods.

Ridge Trail. Along this part of the route you may see large thistles with purple flowers and crinkled, white-veined leaves—non-native milk this-tle. The East Bay parks host several varieties of non-native thistles, one of which, cardoon, an invasive relative of the artichoke, is the subject of an eradication program run by the park district. Two birds often heard but not seen, California quail, whose call sounds like "chi-ca-go," and wren-tit, which may remind you of someone trying to start a reluctant car, may let you know of their nearby presence.

At about the 3.3-mile point, where the West Ridge Trail bends sharply right, find the single-track French Trail heading left and downhill through a forest of bay, madrone, California hazelnut, and pine. (The French Trail is an alternate and more scenic leg of the East Bay Skyline/Bay Area Ridge Trail.) Despite the shade, this route, sheltered from any sea breeze, may be hot. The trail switchbacks down to a tributary of Redwood Creek, nestled in the bottom of a heavily wooded canyon, and arrives at a junc-tion, left, with the Tres Sendas Trail, a wide dirt road. Continuing straight—for the next 0.1 mile or so the French and Tres Sendas trails are combined—you begin a moderate climb to the next junction, where the Tres Sendas Trail continues straight, and your route, the French Trail, turns left. The redwoods here, despite being second growth, grow tall, some reaching neck-craning heights.

After crossing the creek on a stone bridge, you climb steeply on a wide dirt path littered with redwood cones and needles. If the air is hazy or foggy, you should be able to see shafts of sunlight filtering through the giant trees. While not a true wilderness, given the area's history as a tim-ber center in the mid-1800s, Redwood Regional Park, especially this sec-tion, has many wilderness attributes, including natural beauty, seclusion, and tranquillity. At the same time, it is one of the East Bay's most accessi-ble and enjoyable parks.

The French Trail is a rolling route, mostly moderate or steep, with occa-sional level areas where you can catch your breath and admire the scenery. After passing an unsigned trail, left, the route narrows and climbs over rocky, rutted ground, past sword fern and huckleberry, to a junction, right, with the Redwood Peak Trail. Continue straight, and make a mod-erate descent past some fire-scarred redwoods to a four-way junction with the Star Flower Trail, which you cross. The French Trail, here a wide dirt road, climbs in shade to the top of a ridge and soon reaches a junction with the Madrone Trail. Turn left and follow the French Trail, now a sin-gle track, as it makes a gradual, then steep descent.

At about the 5.3-mile point, you come to a junction with the Mill Trail, left, heading downhill to the Stream Trail and Mill Site picnic area; here you continue straight on the French Trail. For a short distance, the red-woods are replaced by bay and coast live oak, and there is much more light reaching the ground. But soon the tall trees resume, and where they grow the only other trees usually found are bay and California hazelnut.

As you are about to climb over a rise, you pass on your left the Fern Trail, unsigned; about 20 feet farther are a trail post and the continuation of the Fern Trail, right. Continue straight, passing a break in the redwoods that allows enough light for madrone trees to establish a foothold.

At the next junction, as the Chown Trail heads straight and climbs, bear left; in about 100 yards the continuation of the Chown Trail goes left. Stay to the right, still on a rolling, single-track trail, through forest that alternates between redwood, bay, and, in clearings, madrone. At about the 7.3-mile point, in a grove of madrone, the French Trail ends at a junction with the Orchard Trail, a wide dirt path. (If you are using the French Trail as an alternate East Bay Skyline/Bay Area Ridge Trail route, turn right here, follow the Orchard Trail 0.2 mile uphill on a moderate grade, and join the West Ridge Trail. Then follow the route description in "Skyline Gate to MacDonald Gate" on pages 115-116.) Turn left here and begin descending on a moderate grade, via S-bends, to the Bridle Trail, a dirt road. Turn right, and in about 40 feet turn left onto a narrow trail, signed TO CANYON MEADOW, which crosses Redwood Creek on large rocks. Once across the creek, you arrive at the junction of the Stream and Canyon trails; turn right and retrace your steps to the parking area.

◆ Sibley Volcanic Regional Preserve ◆

 44

Sibley Volcanic Regional Preserve
ROUND TOP LOOP

Length:	1.6 miles
Time:	1 to 2 hours
Rating:	Easy
Regulations:	EBRPD; no bicycles on the Round Top Loop Trail between the quarry pit and the visitor center.
Highlights:	This delightful loop circles Round Top, an extinct volcano and one of the highest peaks in the Oakland and Berkeley hills, and also provides access to a volcanic area that will be of interest to geology buffs. The preserve, named for Robert Sibley, director and president of EBRPD from 1948 to 1958, is one of the oldest East Bay regional parks. Originally called Roundtop, it was dedicated in 1936, just two years after the District was formed. The preserve was enlarged to its present size by additions of old Kaiser Sand and Gravel quarry sites. The Sibley Volcanic Regional Preserve brochure and map, available free at the visitor center, has descriptions that correspond to numbered posts on the self-guiding Volcanic Trail. Boldface numbers in the route description below refer to these markers. Because this is a short and easy hike, you may also have time to visit nearby Huckleberry Botanic Regional Preserve, just 0.4 mile south on Skyline Blvd.
Facilities:	Visitor center with exhibits explaining the area's volcanic past, as well as its plant and wildlife communities; water, toilets.
Trailhead:	Just west of visitor center.
Directions:	From Hwy. 24 just east of the Caldecott Tunnel, take the Fish Ranch Rd. exit and go uphill one mile to Grizzly Peak Blvd. Turn left and go 2.5 miles to Skyline Blvd. Turn left and go 0.1 mile to the preserve entrance, left.

Although the terms "rock solid" and "on firm ground" are common figures of speech, anyone who has spent much time in California knows that the terra here can sometimes be less than firma. As you hike this enjoyable loop around Round Top (1763'), remember that it once was an active volcano—there are three other former volcanoes nearby—and that the surrounding hills were created by unimaginable forces acting along nearby fault lines. The volcanic activity took place approximately 10 million years ago, but occasional moving and shaking, sometimes violent, continues to this day.

The trailhead here serves several trails: the Round Top Loop and Volcanic trails, joined as one at first; and the East Bay Skyline/Bay Area Ridge Trail. As you approach the visitor center from the parking area, you will notice a paved road, right, which goes to the summit of Round Top, and another, left, that goes around the west side of the center. Follow the left-hand road to a junction just past the center and just before a gate across the road. Here a single-track dirt trail heads right and uphill, marked by a trail post reading TO ROUNDTOP LOOP TRAIL, TO VOLCANIC TRAIL, and a sign indicating that this trail, which reaches Redwood Regional Park in 2.9 miles, is part of the East Bay Skyline/Bay Area Ridge Trail.

Bear right and climb through a wooded area with stands of California bay laurel, Monterey pine, and eucalyptus. As you contour along a steep embankment, past coyote bush, toyon, poison oak, and coffeeberry, the paved road to Round Top's antenna-topped summit is right and downhill. Just before coming to a clearing, you pass a junction, left, with a trail that leads back to the visitor center. In another 100 feet or so, you reach a

44. Round Top Loop

View east to Mt. Diablo from the Round Top Trail.

four-way junction, marked by a trail post, where you turn left onto a wide dirt-and-gravel road that heads north and then northeast into the volcanic area. (If you are following the self-guiding Volcanic Trail description, continue straight through the four-way junction on a narrow dirt path for about 25 feet, then turn left and walk uphill on a paved road to an EBMUD water tank; behind the tank is marker **1**. Then retrace your steps to the four-way junction and turn right.)

Ahead are grassy hills, deep valleys, and rolling ridges, a tranquil scene that masks this area's violent volcanic birth. A mostly level walk over rocky ground takes you around the west and north sides of Round Top to a T-junction, where the Volcanic Trail heads left, and the Round Top Loop Trail continues right. (Markers **2** and **3** can be found just before the junction, a short distance right of the trail.) Turning right and walking uphill, still on a dirt road, you soon come to a wonderful viewpoint above a quarry pit, **4**, left, with Mt. Diablo looming on the eastern skyline. Quarry operations here from the 1930s to the 1960s dug into the side of Round Top, exposing the basalt lava interior of the volcano, to the delight of geologists. Because of its bulk and shape, Mt. Diablo could be mistaken for a volcano as well, but it is not, having been formed instead by a mass of rock pushing upward through sedimentary layers.

Just past the viewpoint, the continuation of the Round Top Loop Trail, here a dirt path, leaves the road, heads right and uphill, and makes a rising traverse across the grassy east side of Round Top. As you follow the trail into an area dense with bay, pine, blue elderberry, and coffeeberry, you soon reach the crest of a low ridge, where a side trail, left, offers access to another east-facing viewpoint. Continuing on the main trail, you descend to a cattle gate, and now enjoy the shade of a pine, madrone, and eucalyptus forest, where, on a sunny day, golden light filters through the trees.

The route swings west and comes to an open area, then reaches an unsigned fork where you bear left. (If instead you go right, you reach Round Top Road, the route to the peak's summit.) Soon you pass a grove of oneseed hawthorn, a beautiful tree with smooth gray bark, thorny branches, and deeply lobed leaves. This hawthorn, which flowers white in the spring and produces red berries in the fall, is originally from Europe, North Africa, and western Asia, but was brought to America as a cultivated species.

The trail next passes through a corridor of stately pines, reaching a junction, left, with the East Bay Skyline/Bay Area Ridge Trail, a route to Huckleberry Regional Preserve and Redwood Regional Park. Continue straight, and in about 125 feet, you arrive at Round Top Road. Cross the road and follow the Round Top Loop Trail as it reenters the pines, here joined by madrone, coast live oak, and eucalyptus. Coming to a clearing, you now cross the paved road leading uphill to the EBMUD water tank, and, in about 25 feet, reach the four-way junction with the dirt-and-gravel road to the volcanic area. From this junction, continue straight—staying left at an upcoming fork—and retrace your steps to the parking area.

• Sobrante Ridge Botanic Regional Preserve •

Sobrante Ridge Botanic Regional Preserve
MANZANITA GROVE

Length: 2.4 miles

Time: 1 to 2 hours

Rating: Easy

Regulations: EBRPD

Highlights: There are two places in the East Bay to see rare and endangered pallid manzanita, also called Alameda manzanita: Huckleberry Botanic Regional Preserve, described elsewhere in this book, and here, a 277-acre preserve that was once part of a vast cattle ranch. Your out-and-back route follows the Sobrante Ridge, Manzanita, and Manzanita Loop trails. The Sobrante Ridge Trail, part of the Bay Area Ridge Trail, runs along a horseshoe-shaped ridge, with views of Mt. Diablo, Mt. Tamalpais, and San Pablo Ridge. The best time to hike here is winter, after the first rains, when the manzanitas are in flower.

Facilities: Water, horse staging.

Trailhead: West side of parking area.

Directions: From Interstate 80 in San Pablo, take the San Pablo Dam Rd. exit and follow San Pablo Dam Rd. 3.9 miles north, east, then southeast to Castro Ranch Rd. Turn left and go 1.2 miles to Conestoga Way. After 0.3 mile you reach Carriage Dr. Turn left, go 0.1 mile to Coach Dr. and turn right. After 0.3 mile Coach ends in a cul de sac, where a short driveway leads to the Sobrante Ridge Botanic Regional Preserve parking area.

From the west side of the parking area walk uphill past a gate on a paved road, and after several hundred feet you come to the Sobrante Ridge Trail, a dirt-and-gravel path. Turn left here and climb south toward a large powerline tower. From the suburban scene before you, it is hard to imagine that one of the East Bay's botanical treasures, a grove of rare and endangered pallid, or Alameda, manzanita lies only a few minutes away. The manzanita here owes its existence to two factors—poor, rocky soil and heat-tempering fog—that allow this species, also found in the Huckleberry Botanic Regional Preserve, to survive.

The housing developments nearby lay nestled in valleys, but beyond them rise high ridges—San Pablo, Sobrante, Oursan—in open space protected from development by EBRPD and EBMUD. Reaching the powerline tower, the route bends sharply right and continues its easy climb across a mostly open hillside where, in spring, California poppies dot the green grass with orange. Powerline towers, while an eyesore, provide perches for birds of prey in an otherwise treeless area, so you may see redtailed hawks, red-shouldered hawks, or an American kestrel. As you head north, Mt. Diablo can be seen peeking over a ridge, right, and you have a steep forested canyon on your left.

45. Manzanita Grove

As you come over the crest of a ridge, the view extends northwest, past the refineries that border San Pablo Bay, to the hills of Napa and Sonoma counties and Mt. St. Helena. The route levels and turns left, taking you past stands of California bay laurel and coast live oak, and brushy areas filled with coyote bush and poison oak. The call of a California quail, the buzz of a hummingbird's aerial display, or the medley of a mockingbird may be the only sound breaking the silence here. Where the route makes a left-hand bend, about the 0.6-mile point, you pass the unsigned Morningside Trail, right; now you have a fine view west to Richmond, San Pablo Bay, and Mt. Tamalpais. Heading south, you soon reach a picnic table and a

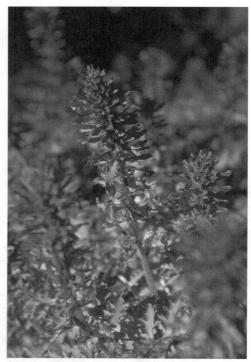

Indian warrior may need a name change.

junction with the Broken Oaks Trail, left. The coast live oaks here are lovely, especially in spring when they flower.

Your route, the Sobrante Ridge Trail, descends through a wooded area decorated with spring wildflowers, then begins climbing to a clearing with another picnic table. Still on the rise, the route soon crests a ridge, turns sharply right, and drops to a junction. Here, at about the 1-mile point, a faint path heads right and uphill, and the Sobrante Ridge Trail turns left, reaching a picnic table in about 100 yards, but your route, now on the Manzanita Trail, a dirt road, continues straight and descends on a gentle grade. Approaching a stand of coast live oaks, the grade steepens and brings you to an unsigned T-junction. Here the Heavenly Ridge Trail goes right, but you turn left and walk in the shade of tall oaks. Now you begin to see pallid manzanita—red-barked shrubs with pointed, gray-green leaves, some tall, others low to the ground. A distinguishing feature of this species is the almost stemless leaves which attach directly to the shrub's branches.

Brittleleaf manzanita, which joins pallid manzanita in Huckleberry Botanic Regional Preserve, is here too. This small shrub has a basal burl—a large knot of wood at or just under ground level—and very stiff leaves with stems. (Manzanitas are hard to identify: they hybridize, and even experts disagree on how to classify certain varieties.) Where there is manzanita you are likely to find Indian warrior, a curious parasitic plant with red and green leaves, related to owl's clover and Indian paintbrush. After a short, level walk you come to a trail post marking the Manzanita Loop Trail, left. Here a sign board describes this portion of the preserve, where the soil is composed mostly of siliceous shale, as an "ecological island," unsuitable for most other plants but perfect for manzanita.

Turning left onto the Manzanita Loop Trail, a single track, you begin walking uphill in a beautiful corridor of manzanitas, some of them holding their limbs high overhead, all with twisted dark-red trunks. Madrone, in the same family (Heather, or *Ericaceae*) as manzanita, is here too. Sharing some of its cousin's characteristics, madrone has reddish bark that turns scaly as the trees mature, larger, finely-toothed leaves, and differently shaped fruit. After passing a clearing with a view of Mt. Tamalpais, the route descends and makes a sharp bend right, now near a housing development that borders the preserve: this juxtaposition of rare and endangered plants with suburban sprawl sends a strong message about the value of habitat preservation. Soon the route bends right and starts uphill, joining a path coming up from the housing development, left. At about the 1.33-mile point, you come back to the start of the Manzanita Loop Trail; from here retrace your steps to the parking area.

◆ Sunol Wilderness ◆

<table>
<tr><td>

46

</td><td>

Sunol Wilderness
LITTLE YOSEMITE

</td></tr>
</table>

Length:	3 miles
Time:	2 to 3 hours
Rating:	Moderate
Regulations:	EBRPD; fees for parking and dogs when entrance kiosk is attended.
Highlights:	This loop is a fine introduction to Sunol Wilderness, one of the gems of the regional park system, and at nearly 7,000 acres one of its largest holdings. A scenic trek along the Canyon View Trail, through oak savanna and grassland, brings you to Little Yosemite, a rocky gorge carved by Alameda Creek. The return portion of the loop, Camp Ohlone Road, takes you beside the tree-lined creek, especially lovely in fall.
Facilities:	Visitor center, picnic tables, water, toilets, phone.
Trailhead:	In front of the visitor center.
Directions:	From Interstate 680 southbound in Scotts Corner, take the Calaveras Road exit, and at a stop sign turn left onto Paloma Rd. Go back under I-680, stay in the left lane, and at the next stop sign continue straight, now on Calaveras Rd. Go 4.2 miles to Geary Rd., turn left, and go 1.8 miles to the entrance kiosk. Go 0.1 mile past the kiosk and turn left into a parking area in front of the visitor center, a green barn. (If this parking area is full, there are two more about 100 yards ahead, on both sides of Geary Road.)
	From Interstate 680 northbound in Scotts Corner, take the Calaveras Road exit, bear right onto Calaveras Rd., then follow directions above.

Leaving the visitor center and main parking area behind, you walk east along a path, paved for the first 150 feet or so, that passes behind two small buildings, the Interpretive Headquarters and the Wilderness Room.

Now continue east for another 200 feet and look left to find a wooden bridge across Alameda Creek. Many of Sunol's trails use this bridge, including the Ohlone Wilderness Regional Trail, a 28-mile route from Mission Peak Regional Preserve to Del Valle Regional Park, 19.4 miles of which are described elsewhere in this book. After crossing Alameda Creek and turning right, you are on the Canyon View Trail, a wide dirt path lined with white alder, bigleaf maple, western sycamore, and willow, with the creek on your right. (The first portion of the Canyon View Trail is also part of the Indian Joe Nature Trail, a self-guiding route with numbered trail posts that correspond to text in a booklet available at the visitor center.)

Other trees and shrubs in this area include California bay laurel, California buckeye, coast live oak, California sagebrush, bush monkeyflower, and poison oak. About 100 feet past the bridge, Hayfield Road climbs left; about 30 feet beyond, a path leads down to the creek, right. Continuing straight, you soon pass another path on your left. After crossing Indian Joe Creek, the trail, now a single track, takes you through several moderate up-and-down sections to a Y-junction with the Indian Joe Creek Trail.

46. Little Yosemite

Hikers heading southeast on the Canyon View Trail.

Where the Indian Joe Creek Trail veers left, continue straight on the Canyon View Trail, a single track, and climb uphill on a moderate, then steep grade through an area shaded by coast live oak, blue oak, and bay. The view, right, takes in the Alameda Creek valley and the highlands of Mission Peak Regional Preserve, crowned by three summits—from north to south, Mission Peak (2517'), Mt. Allison (2658'), and Monument Peak (2594'). After passing through a cattle gate, you come into the open atop a narrow ridge. As the grade eases and you pass through a savanna of blue and valley oak, you may be serenaded by a chorus of bird song. Groves of oaks are like islands in a sea of grass, providing shelter and food for a wide variety of birds, including jays, woodpeckers, yellow-billed magpies, western meadowlarks, brown creepers, and kinglets.

Serpentine and sandstone rock boulders and outcrops, seen here on the ridgetop, are evidence of Sunol's rocky foundation. From this vantage point, the exposed cliffs of Flag Hill, northwest, appear to tower over the visitor center and parking area. At a four-way junction, cross the McCorkle Trail, a dirt road, and continue on the Canyon View Trail,

Alameda Creek makes a nice pool in the rocky jumble of Little Yosemite.

climbing moderately across a steep, grassy hillside. If the deciduous oaks are leafless, you may notice clumps of mistletoe, a parasitic plant, growing in their branches. The sticky seeds of mistletoe, a photosynthesizing plant that has lost its ability to produce roots, are contained in berries eaten by birds. As the bird cleans its beak by wiping it against a tree branch, it "plants" the mistletoe seeds.

The route now traverses along the edge of a steep, south-facing hillside that leads down to Alameda Creek, about 200 feet below. Looking east, you can see the rugged hills that form the heart of the Ohlone Wilderness. After descending to a gully, possibly muddy, and crossing a small wood-plank bridge, you traverse an open expanse of grass dotted with rock outcrops which are tinged orange by lichen. The trail, rocky and eroded in places, rounds the end of a ridge, where a steep drop, right, reveals Camp Ohlone Road, your return route. The canyon below, containing Alameda Creek, is called Little Yosemite, and you may hear the sound of running water as the creek tumbles through its rocky gorge.

In a rocky area shaded by valley oaks, you come to a trail post and a junction with a faint trail, left. Continue straight and descend on a gentle grade, passing an open field with a fenced-off marshy area, left. Birds may be active here, including western scrub-jays and dark-eyed juncos. Crossing a small streambed, you reach, in about 100 feet, a four-way junction with Cerro Este Road. Turn right and follow the dirt-and-gravel road 0.2 mile downhill, via **S**-bends, to a junction with Camp Ohlone Road.

One of the scenic jewels of the regional park system, Little Yosemite features in miniature some of the wonders of its Sierra Nevada namesake, including water rushing through a boulder-strewn gorge, sheer cliffs, forested hillsides, and towering rock formations. A variety of trees and shrubs thrive here, including coast live oak, bay, California sagebrush, toyon, and bush monkeyflower. Stands of western sycamore add color in the fall. Easily accessed on foot, bicycle, or horseback via the Camp Ohlone Road, Little Yosemite is a popular destination for families with children.

After exploring to your heart's content, begin a gentle descent southwest on the Camp Ohlone Road, soon reaching a fenced area, left, and a path heading left toward the creek. Continuing on the road, you make a gentle climb past stands of willow, blue elderberry, and buckeye. Here you may see the bright red flowers of California fuchsia, a late bloomer, on a south-facing hillside. Now descending through an open area, you can see Flag Hill ahead, and when the route forks, stay right, passing a dirt road and a cattle pen, right. A wooden bridge takes you across Alameda Creek, whose banks here are lined with white alder, willow, and sycamore.

Once across the creek, you are on a paved road; about 50 feet past the bridge, a dirt path merges from the left. Continue straight, and after another 200 feet or so, you come to a large parking area. Proceed on the paved road, passing the Leyden Flats picnic area, left, until you reach the visitor center and main parking area.

47   Sunol Wilderness
MAGUIRE PEAKS

Length: 5.9 miles

Time: 3 to 4 hours

Rating: Moderate

Regulations: EBRPD; to park on Welch Creek Rd., you must have either a parking permit, available at the Sunol visitor center on Geary Rd., or a Regional Parks Foundation membership card: leave it on your dashboard. No bicycles or horses on the Upper Peaks Trail. (Horses and bicycles should start at the visitor center and use Hayfield and High Valley roads to reach Welch Creek Rd., then follow the Maguire Peaks Trail.)

Highlights: This circuit of Maguire Peaks, via the Upper Peaks and Maguire Peaks trails and the Maguire Peaks Loop, explores a hidden corner of Sunol Wilderness, divided by Welch Creek Road from the main part of the park. The scenery is beautiful and serene, and the vistas from several vantage points are superb. Literally to top it off, you can make an ascent of Maguire Peaks west summit (1688'), a mountain climb in miniature. (Parts of this route may be extremely muddy during and after wet weather.)

Facilities: None along Welch Creek Rd. Water, toilets, phone, maps, and information are available at the Sunol visitor center.

Trailhead: North side of small parking area.

Directions: From Interstate 680 southbound in Scotts Corner, take the Calaveras Road exit, and at a stop sign turn left onto Paloma Rd. Go back under I-680, stay in the left lane, and at the next stop sign continue straight, now on Calaveras Rd. Go south 3.9 miles to Welch Rd. Turn left and go to the 1.6 mile marker, where two turn-outs have space for about 6 to 8 cars total.

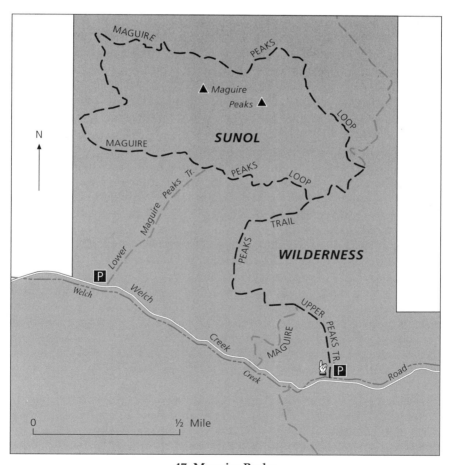

47. Maguire Peaks

From Interstate 680 northbound in Scotts Corner, take the Calaveras Road exit, bear right onto Calaveras Rd., then follow directions above.

To reach the Sunol visitor center: Proceed past Welch Creek Rd. another 0.3 mile, turn left on Geary Rd. and go 1.8 miles to the entrance kiosk. Then continue 0.1 mile to the visitor-center parking area, left.

From the parking area, walk north down a small embankment and cross Welch Creek on rocks, finding a trail post and the Upper Peaks Trail, a single track heading north. This is a lovely wooded area of California bay laurel, California buckeye, coast live oak, bigleaf maple, and western sycamore—remote and secluded. About 50 feet past the trail post you step across a little tributary of Welch Creek, and then follow its left-hand bank upstream on a level grade. At a fork you bear left, away from the tributary, and begin to climb across a steep hillside loaded with poison oak, California sagebrush, and bush monkeyflower, on a generally northwest course.

Having gained elevation, you enter a forest of blue oak, then reach a clearing where you have a beautiful view north to Maguire Peaks, two rocky summits behind a foreground of rolling, grassy hills studded with oaks. The view here also extends west toward San Francisco Bay, although it is often obscured by fog. This 6,858-acre wilderness park is one of the best places in the East Bay to see yellow-billed magpies, large black-and-white birds with long tails, usually found in flocks. Another sociable bird, the band-tailed pigeon, is also here, and the noise of their wings as they take off through the trees is startling. Now you follow an indistinct path, marked by metal trail posts, across grassland, to a T-junction with the Maguire Peaks Trail, a dirt road. A trail post here indicates a right turn for the Maguire Peaks Loop.

Turning right, near the site of an old homestead, you follow the road past pine, eucalyptus, fruit trees, and a large valley oak. After several hundred feet the road bends sharply left and begins to climb on a moderate grade, heading west, giving you views of Mission Peak (2517') and antenna-topped Mt. Allison (2658'). The route here is mostly in the open, with a steep drop-off left. As you turn a corner and head north, you again have a view of Maguire Peaks, both just under 1700 feet high. Now you begin to descend via moderately graded S-bends into a forest of bay, blue oak, and coast live oak, where the silence is broken only by the twittering of birds.

Reaching the bottom of a shady canyon, the route crosses a tributary of Welch Creek flowing through a culvert, and then begins to climb, soon coming to an unsigned junction where you continue straight. Leaving the dense forest behind and entering oak savanna, you arrive at a junction with the Maguire Peaks Loop. Here you continue straight, still on an

Oak trees and cirrus clouds from the Maguire Peaks Trail.

ascending dirt road, and after another 0.25 mile or so reach a junction, marked by a metal trail post with an arrow pointing left. Turn left, with Mt. Diablo just visible over hills to the north, and resume climbing. The route, a dirt road, bends north, skirts the end of a ridge topped by the easternmost of the two Maguire Peaks, left, and reaches level ground in a blue oak savanna. Ahead you can see San Antonio Reservoir, a large body of water about 1.5 miles north of the Sunol Wilderness boundary.

Circling around the north side of Maguire Peaks, you pass a hillside of blue bush lupine and reach an open area where the view extends northwest to Pleasanton and Sunol ridges. Now you have a better view of the Maguire Peaks themselves—the taller is the west peak, (1688'), directly ahead, its grassy summit guarded by a rock rampart. The route climbs on a moderate grade, aiming for a flat spot in a ridge extending northwest from the west peak. Along the way you may see two related shrubs (genus *Rhamnus*), coffeeberry and redberry buckthorn. Coffeeberry, appearing here as a small tree, has dark green elliptical leaves and purple berries. Redberry buckthorn has small, toothed leaves resembling those of holly or coast live oak, and red berries.

Spring wildflowers decorate the open hillsides here, but when the route enters a grove of coast live oak, ferns and moss take over, giving the shaded area a rain-forest feel. Two birds that seek dense cover, spotted towhee and wrentit, may be seen, or more likely heard, here. Now back in the open, the route crosses a rocky ridge, where a flat area with outstanding views of San Francisco Bay, Mt. Diablo, and Mission Peak makes a good rest stop. But to climb the peak, you should continue on the Maguire Peaks Loop, which now turns left and follows the ridgetop toward Maguire Peaks. Just before the route turns right and begins to descend, find an unsigned path going straight and uphill, climbing southeast up a steep hillside of grass and lupine. After you gain the main ridge to the summit, staying well to the right of a severe drop-off, the grade eases. Soon you cross a rocky area, then tackle the final pitch up a grassy slope to the summit. A path leads across the summit, past low-growing coast live oak and blue elderberry, to a 360-degree viewpoint. From here you can see the east summit of Maguire Peaks, the high ground on the other side of Welch Creek Road (which you can explore on the "Vista Grande" hike below), and the waters of Calaveras Reservoir.

Back on the Maguire Peaks Loop, you follow a winding course downhill through a grassy valley, where a kestrel may be hovering overhead, soon reaching level ground. Heading generally west, the route comes to the end of a long ridge, then bends around it to the south, crossing a culvert that drains a marshy area with a stock pond, right. Eventually the route finds a southeast course, and just shy of the 4-mile point, reaches a junction with the Lower Maguire Peaks Trail. (This alternate route leads to a parking area at mile marker 0.72 on Welch Creek Road.) From here the route climbs slightly, passing a number of creeks that flow down from Maguire Peaks, left, and run under the road through culverts. Now in oak woodland, you may hear the sharp cry of a northern flicker or the soothing call of a mourning dove. At about the 4.5-mile point, you come to the junction of the Maguire Peaks Loop and the Maguire Peaks Trail. From here, turn right and retrace your steps to the parking area.

Hikers enjoying a scenic rest stop on the Maguire Peaks Loop.

48 Sunol Wilderness
VISTA GRANDE

Length: 6.1 miles

Time: 3 to 5 hours

Rating: Moderate

Regulations: EBRPD; fees for parking and dogs when entrance kiosk is attended; no bicycles or horses.

Highlights: High vantage points and great views reward hikers who tackle this loop, which uses the Canyon View, Indian Joe Creek, Eagle View, and Flag Hill trails, along with portions of Eagle View, Flag Hill, and Vista Grande roads. Climbing from tree-lined Alameda Creek through oak woodland to the high ground of Vista Grande Road and then Flag Hill, you experience a wide variety of terrain and plant life. Best on a clear, windless day, the route crosses some very steep hillsides, where caution is advised.

Facilities: Visitor center, picnic tables, water, toilets, phone.

Trailhead: In front of visitor center.

Directions: See the directions for "Little Yosemite" on p. 260.

Leaving the visitor center and main parking area behind, you walk east along a path, paved for the first 150 feet or so, that passes behind two small buildings, the Interpretive Headquarters and the Wilderness Room. Now continue east for another 200 feet and look left to find a wooden bridge across Alameda Creek. While crossing the bridge, pause for a moment to enjoy the creek below and the water-loving trees—willow, white alder, western sycamore—that line its banks; once across, turn right and begin walking southeast on the Canyon View Trail, a wide dirt path.

    Many of the trails in this nearly 7,000-acre wilderness park begin here or share this path, including the Canyon View Trail, the self-guiding Indian Joe Nature Trail (booklet available at the visitor center), and the Ohlone Wilderness Regional Trail. About 100 feet upstream from the bridge, you pass Hayfield Road, left, leading uphill to High Valley. In another 30 feet or so, you come to a junction with a path heading down to the creek, right, but you continue straight on a level route beside the creek. After passing a path leading left and uphill to a cattle gate, you cross Indian Joe Creek, and then, at a trail post, turn left and climb uphill on a rocky dirt path, following a narrow ridge that divides Alameda and Indian Joe creeks.

California sagebrush, toyon, snowberry, and bush monkeyflower flourish in this sun-warmed area. As you climb higher, more of Sunol's rolling, oak-dotted hills come into view. At a **Y**-junction, the Canyon View Trail, a segment of the Ohlone Wilderness Trail, veers right, but you take the left-hand fork, the Indian Joe Creek Trail. This single track descends from the ridge toward Indian Joe Creek, left, and wanders for a while in the shade of large coast live oaks. The route follows the creek northeast, passing a junction where the self-guiding nature trail turns left and crosses the creek. Continuing straight, you pass through a cattle gate, cross the creek's shallow water on rocks, then walk upstream in a narrow canyon filled with California sagebrush, bush monkeyflower, toyon, and coffeeberry. In the fall, sycamore and bigleaf maple add gold and orange to this wonderful area, helping it live up to its "wilderness" name.

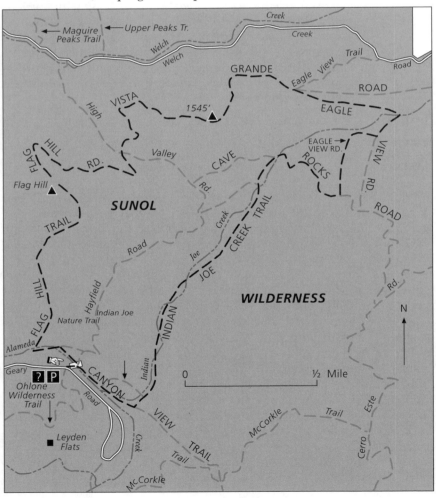

48. Vista Grande

A short, steep section, which soon levels out, brings you to an open hillside, then two more creek crossings. As the canyon that holds Indian Joe Creek steepens, you cross again, and now on its right bank begin a moderate climb, turning temporarily away from the creek. Once on top of a ridge, you have a great view south toward the Alameda Creek canyon and the start of this loop. Valley oaks here are loaded with mistletoe, and you begin to see rock outcrops, colored green and orange by lichen.

At about the 1.5-mile point, an unnamed trail, left, connects to Hayfield Road, and a narrow path, also unnamed, heads right. Your route continues straight to Indian Joe Cave Rocks, a fantastic jumble of cliffs and boulders towering next to Indian Joe Creek. The trail here may be covered with leaf litter, prompting you perhaps to notice a peculiar fact: leaves come in such a wide variety of sizes, but the trees that produce them may be similarly sized. For example, valley oak and western sycamore are both large trees, ranging from 40 to 80 or 100 feet tall. Yet the valley oak's leaf, 2 to 4 inches, is dwarfed by the sycamore's 6- to 9-inch leaf.

From here, switchbacks take you to the top of another ridge, this one more exposed to wind, but with grander views. The Indian Joe Creek Trail ends at the next junction, where you turn right on Cave Rocks Road, a dirt road, and make a moderate uphill climb through an open area heavily used by cows. The view southwest from this wind-swept vantage point takes in the high ground of Mission Peak Regional Preserve, dominated by three summits—from left to right, Monument Peak (2594'), Mt. Allison (2658'), and Mission Peak (2517').

When you reach a trail post and a junction, turn left on Eagle View Road and continue your moderate, sometimes steep climb on a rutted dirt road, with views now west toward San Francisco Bay. Soon Eagle View Road ends at a T-junction with the Eagle View Trail; here you turn left and descend on a single-track trail into a wooded ravine, with the upper reaches of Indian Joe Creek at the bottom. The trail hugs a steep wall of the ravine as it loses elevation, makes a short climb via wooden steps, and then drops and crosses the creek on rocks.

About 100 feet past the crossing, the route turns sharply left and begins a moderate climb out of the ravine, then levels out to cross a very steep hillside loaded with California sagebrush, blue bush lupine, and toyon. California fuchsia, a lover of rocky soil, may be blooming here as late as Thanksgiving. As the route begins to gain elevation again, two bodies of water—Calaveras Reservoir, south, and San Francisco Bay, west—come into view. This is one of the prettiest spots in the East Bay, but please be careful: the dropoff to your left is hazardous. (A warning sign, which you can see only if you are coming from the opposite direction, is just ahead.)

Finally you reach Vista Grande Overlook, a level area and important junction, giving you a place to relax and take in the stunning 360-degree views, which include Pleasanton and Mt. Diablo (north); Apperson Ridge (northeast), site of an environmental battle in the late 1960s and early 1970s over a proposed rock quarry; and Maguire Peaks (northwest), two craggy summits described elsewhere in this guide. Here a stone marker with attached wooden signs has directions and mileages to various points in the wilderness, but you have to walk around to the marker's north side to see them. From this point, the Eagle View Trail, now a dirt road, continues northeast across Vista Grande Road, which runs east–west.

Turn west on the dirt-and-gravel Vista Grande Road and walk downhill, past large valley oaks, on a moderate grade. The route turns south, reaches a narrow saddle, and then climbs to another terrific viewpoint, from where most of the Sunol Wilderness can be seen. A moderate, then steep descent via S-bends, past stands of black oak, coast live oak, almond, and peppertree, brings you to an old homestead in High Valley. This bucolic area, with its large barn, windmill, water tower, and grazing cows, is used by EBRPD as an outdoor campsite. Other trees here include eucalyptus, cottonwood, fig, and walnut.

Just shy of the 4-mile point, you come to a four-way junction with High Valley Road, and another stone marker, right, signed with routes and mileages. From here, High Valley Road heads right to Welch Creek Road and left to the campsite. To find your route, Flag Hill Road, cross High Valley Road just right of a large eucalyptus. Then bear left on a dirt road heading southeast and uphill through a cattle gate. This road, muddy in wet weather, makes an end run around a low, grassy ridge, turning first south, then southwest. As you gain back some of the elevation lost in the descent on Vista Grande Road, you begin to glimpse some of the now-familiar landmarks, such as Mission Peak and Maguire Peaks.

Now on top of a ridge, in the realm of grasses and oaks, you travel south to a junction, left, and a third stone marker. To visit Flag Hill, named for an American flag displayed here by a picnicking family on July 4th, 1903, continue straight. From where the road ends in a few hundred feet at a turn-around, follow a dirt path to the edge of a steep, rocky promontory—use caution! The sweeping view from here takes in Calaveras Reservoir, Alameda Creek canyon, Camp Ohlone Road, Mission Peak Regional Preserve, and Maguire Peaks. After relaxing for a while on the summit of Flag Hill, return to the stone marker and begin a moderate descent southeast on the Flag Hill Trail, a single track, with the visitor center and parking area in sight.

The trail now crosses steep open hillsides and descends through mixed woodland. After passing an eroded area where a sign urges hikers to stay on the trail, you pass through a cattle gate and fence guarding a beautiful grove of trees near the rushing waters of Alameda Creek. The trail continues to wind downhill, past an area of star thistle and beard grass, to a barbed-wire fence with a turnstile that lets you out of this cow-free area. When you reach a T-junction near Alameda Creek, turn left on a wide dirt path and follow it to the bridge, where you cross the creek, and then retrace your steps to the parking area.

◆ Tilden Regional Park ◆

One of EBRPD's original three holdings, this park is named for District founding father and first board president Major Charles Lee Tilden, a prominent civic leader, businessman, law-school graduate, and Spanish-American War veteran. The name was changed from Wildcat Canyon Park on Major Tilden's 79th birthday in 1936. As leader of EBRPD, Tilden had two goals: to acquire parklands before they were lost to development, and to do so without floating bond measures. To this end, he even advanced the District money to pay expenses until tax revenues arrived, and to purchase 60 acres of private land in Redwood Canyon, the nucleus of a

Family enjoying the Little Farm in the Tilden Nature Area.

future Redwood Regional Park. Tilden's 93rd birthday in 1950, like nine previous ones, was celebrated in the park's Brazil Building, a WPA stone building whose interior came from the 1939 World's Fair held on Treasure Island. On that occasion, a bronze bust of Major Tilden was unveiled, commemorating his public service.

The 2,000-acres of rolling hills and forested ravines that became Tilden Regional Park had been used by ranchers and dairy farmers in bygone days. In the Depression, New Deal work projects brought roads, trails, and picnic sites to the new park. An old military tractor was used to construct an 18-hole championship golf course. During World War Two, Tilden Regional Park, like Redwood, was used by the military: the Army ran survival training in the woods for its troops, and the Air Force used a windowless blockhouse in what is now the Tilden Service Yard as the "nerve center" for 15 radar stations. The Army returned the favor by maintaining trails, cutting trees, building bridges, and putting up signs. During the Cold War the Army returned, bringing Nike missiles via Nimitz Way to a site atop San Pablo Ridge.

In addition to its many miles of trails, Tilden Regional Park has other wonderful attractions. One of California's finest native plant gardens, Regional Parks Botanic Garden, is set on a 10-acre site at the junction of Wildcat Canyon Road and South Park Drive. Lake Anza, located in the middle of the park off Central Park Drive, is a man-made impoundment on Wildcat Creek with a public swimming beach and a lovely trail around its perimeter. Scattered throughout the park are several dozen picnic sites, many suitable for large groups and available by reservation.

At the north end of the park, in the Tilden Nature Area, are the Environmental Education Center, Little Farm, and Jewel Lake, reached by a self-guiding nature trail—all great places to take children. The Environmental Education Center has a display of Wildcat Creek ecology plus books, maps, and pamphlets. A separate map is available for the Tilden Nature Area, including the Jewel Lake, Pack Rat, Sylvan, Peak, Pine Tree, Laurel Canyon, and Memory trails. There is also a brochure for the self-guiding Jewel Lake Nature Trail, which may be borrowed or purchased for a small fee.

Bicycles in Tilden are allowed on these trails: Big Springs, Curran, Golf Course, Meadows Canyon, Nimitz, Quarry, Redwood, and Sea View. Bicycles are not allowed on these trails: Arroyo, Grizzly Peak, Lake Anza, Lupine, National, Selby, and Tower.

Bicycles in Tilden are allowed on the East Bay Skyline Trail, except between the Sea View Trail and the Steam Trains overflow parking lot. Bicycles are allowed on the Vollmer Peak Trail, except between the Steam Trains overflow parking lot and the north end of Tilden Corporation Yard. Bicycles are allowed on the Wildcat Gorge Trail from Lone Oak Road to the Curran Trail only during dry weather, and are not allowed on the Wildcat Gorge Trail from the Curran Trail to Anza View Road.

Botanic Garden (510) 841-8732

8:30 A.M. to 5 P.M. daily.

Environmental Education Center (510) 525-2233

10 A.M. to 5 P.M., closed Mondays,
Thanksgiving, Christmas and New Year's Day.

Lake Anza (510) 848-3028

open for swimming May through October.

Picnic reservations (510) 636-1684

Tilden Regional Park
LAKE ANZA

Length: 1.4 miles

Time: 1 hour

Rating: Easy, but involves some scrambling over rocks.

Regulations: EBRPD

Highlights: Crowded with swimmers on warm weekends, Lake Anza can also offer a sample of East Bay solitude, provided you pick a quiet time to explore the Wildcat Gorge Trail, east of the lake. Combined with the Lake Anza Trail, this makes an easy loop, suitable for children beyond the toddler stage.

Facilities: Swimming, bath house, water, toilets, phone.

Trailhead: On the east side of the parking area, facing the lake.

Directions: From Interstate 80 in Berkeley, take the University Avenue exit and go east 2.1 miles to Oxford St. Turn left and go 0.7 mile to Rose St. Turn right and go one block to Spruce St. Turn left and follow Spruce St. 1.8 miles to an intersection with Grizzly Peak Blvd. and Wildcat Canyon Rd. Cross the intersection and immediately turn left from Wildcat Canyon Dr. onto Canon Dr. There is a sign here for NATURE AREA, PONY RIDE, WILDCAT CANYON. Go downhill 0.3 mile to a junction with Central Park Dr., then turn right and go southeast 0.7 mile to Lake Anza Road. Turn left and go 0.3 mile to a large parking area.

From Hwy. 24 just east of the Caldecott Tunnel, take the Fish Ranch Rd. exit and go 1 mile uphill to a junction with Grizzly Peak Blvd. Turn right and go 5.4 miles to the intersection with Wildcat Canyon Rd. and Spruce St. mentioned above. Turn right onto Wildcat Canyon Rd., then immediately left onto Canon Dr. From here follow the directions above.

From the parking area, walk east, downhill on a paved path toward Lake Anza. Where the path branches to the bath house, right, turn left on the Lake Anza Trail, here a paved path that borders the lake, and walk north under coast redwood, white alder, willow, and coast live oak. At the next junction, turn right, cross a bridge over Wildcat Creek, and follow a wide dirt path on top of the dam that forms Lake Anza. The creek, which empties into San Pablo Bay north of the Richmond–San Rafael Bridge, gets its start high on the northwest flank of Vollmer Peak, then flows through Tilden's Botanic Garden into Lake Anza. Once across the dam, you will see two trails, one rising steeply uphill, the other turning right and hugging the lake shore. Your route stays by the water's edge, crosses a narrow, rocky section beneath a steep cliff, left, and then enters a eucalyptus grove from where you can look across the lake to the popular swimming beach.

California bay laurel trees form the next grove, where the route passes up and over the first of several rocky ribs jutting into the lake. Near the southeast corner of the lake, you scramble through a notch in the final rib and step down over some rock ledges near where Wildcat Creek flows into the lake. Crossing a bridge, right, will take you quickly around the lake and back to the parking area, but to explore a bit more, stay on the creek's left side and walk upstream on the narrow and rocky Wildcat

49. Lake Anza

Gorge Trail, a shady route that rises abruptly to avoid rock outcrops and large bay trees, then drops steeply to the creek.

This small canyon, where the sound of running water accompanies your footfalls, is home to shrubs such as thimbleberry, snowberry, and western creek dogwood, and its shaded slopes provide fertile ground for ferns. After crossing the creek on a wooden bridge, the route begins to climb across a steep hillside and head west, past a sign for the Brazil Building, which is left and uphill. Now in the realm of bays, their trunks curved and twisted, you begin a gradual descent and soon come to a level clearing with picnic tables and a trail post. Here, at about the 1-mile point, the Wildcat Gorge Trail ends and you join the Selby Trail, straight, a wide dirt path littered with eucalyptus leaves and strips of bark. (The Selby Trail also climbs left from here to Wildcat Canyon and Shasta roads.)

You now pass through a weedy area, full of coyote bush, California hazelnut, blackberry vines, and even rose bushes. Descending on a moderate grade, you soon you come to a flat spot under a tall Monterey pine, near Lake Anza's beach area, which is just behind a fence. Turn right on a dirt path, then left on the Lake Anza Trail, passing a grove of redwoods; from the bath house, follow the paved path to the parking area.

50 Tilden Regional Park
WILDCAT PEAK

Length:	3.25 miles
Time:	1.5 to 2 hours
Rating:	Moderate
Regulations:	EBRPD; no horses, bicycles, or dogs.
Highlights:	This scenic loop hike takes you from the Tilden Park Environmental Education Center to the summit of Wildcat Peak via the Jewel Lake, Sylvan, Peak and Laurel Canyon trails. Terrific views of the Bay Area and a variety of plants and birds keep this route interesting throughout. This route may be very muddy in wet weather.
Facilities:	Visitor center with displays, books, maps, guided walks; picnic tables, water, toilets, phone.
Trailhead:	Behind the Environmental Education Center, which is a short walk north from the parking area on a paved path.
Directions:	Follow the directions on p. 275 for "Lake Anza," and when you reach the junction of Canon Dr. and Central Park Dr., turn left and go 0.1 mile to a large parking area.

From the back deck of the Environmental Education Center walk north across the lawn and look for a sign that reads JEWEL LAKE NATURE TRAIL and a trail post with the Jewel Lake emblem, a duck with upraised wings. Around you are stands of Monterey pine, coast live oak, eucalyptus, and California bay laurel. After following the Jewel Lake Trail, a single track,

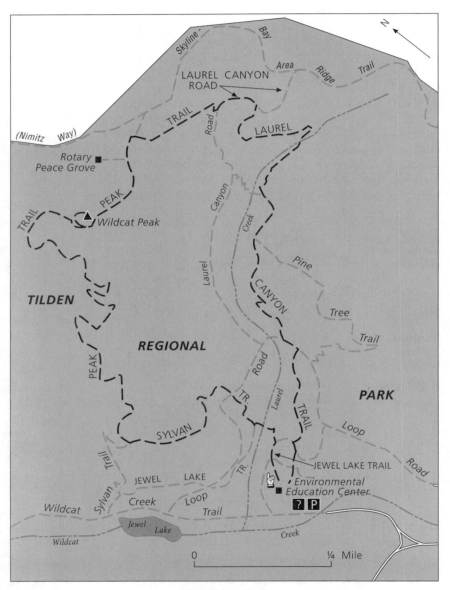

50. Wildcat Peak

for about 100 yards, you come to a dirt road. Cross it and walk ahead about 50 yards on a wide dirt path until you come to a trail post and a trail veering left. This post has the Jewel Lake emblem, and also emblems for other trails in the Nature Area—Sylvan (three trees), Laurel Canyon (a leaf), and Pine (a single conifer). Both the Jewel Lake and Sylvan trails are left; the Laurel Canyon and Pine Tree trails are right.

Turn left and follow the Jewel Lake Trail as it crosses two small streambeds on wooden planks, and then a larger streambed on a wooden bridge. If the trail is muddy, you may see animal tracks here, especially deer. Just after the bridge, you walk up a few wooden steps and reach a junction marked by another trail post. From here the Jewel Lake Trail climbs steeply on more wooden steps to the left, but your route, the Sylvan Trail, heads right. You will also see on the trail post the emblem for the Peak Trail (a rounded hill), which you will reach in a few minutes.

Turn right and follow the Sylvan Trail as it makes an easy uphill climb through groves of eucalyptus, bay, and coast live oak, with underbrush of coyote bush and poison oak. The route begins to switchback uphill, in places climbing steps made of railroad ties. After about 0.3 mile you come to Loop Road. Crossing this dirt road, you find the continuation of the

A family returning from Jewel Lake on the Jewel Lake Trail.

Sylvan Trail heading northwest: a trail post here has emblems for the Sylvan and Peak trails. Follow the trail as it crosses an open hillside, then returns to eucalyptus forest.

This forest is a good place to study eucalyptus, an Australian tree introduced to the Bay Area in the 1850s and planted extensively in the East Bay at the turn of the century as part of an ill-fated timber scheme. Although fast growing, eucalyptus wood is worthless unless seasoned and dried carefully over a long time, thus dashing the hopes of would-be timber barons for a quick profit on their investments. But the trees thrived, despite fires and frost, and are now considered, at best, a mixed blessing.

Blue gum and red gum eucalyptus, the two most common in California, shed strips and flakes of bark to allow for a rapid increase in trunk diameter. Notice the difference between the blue-gray leaves on young eucalyptus and the green leaves on adult trees. Leaves on the young, short trees are broad and flat, perfect for absorbing sunlight in dense shade; but leaves on tall adult trees, exposed to the hot sun, are narrow and hang vertically to minimize evaporation and conserve water. If it's breezy, listen to the rustle of the adult leaves in the wind, and the weird groaning sounds the trees make as they rub against each other.

After about half a mile you reach a junction; here the Sylvan Trail swings left, and your route, the Peak Trail, heads right and uphill. On the Peak Trail you begin to climb through groves of eucalyptus and twisted coast live oaks; in late summer or early fall you may find California fuchsia, a bright red wildflower that attracts hummingbirds, in bloom here beside the trail. Although you are climbing steadily, the grade is easy. The trail narrows as it passes under powerlines, then breaks into an open area where willow, blue elderberry, and coffeeberry grow beside the trail, along with thickets of blackberry, coyote bush, and poison oak. In summer and fall the nearby slopes are decorated with asters, bush monkeyflower, California poppies, and lupine in bloom. You may see red-tailed and red-shouldered hawks overhead or hear their plaintive cries, and western scrub-jays, guardians of the forest, are sure to sound their raucous alarms if they detect your presence.

Each switchback brings better views, rewarding your uphill effort. Northeast is your goal for today, Wildcat Peak. West and southwest, most of the Bay Area is revealed: San Francisco, Oakland, Alcatraz and Angel islands, the Golden Gate, Bay and Richmond–San Rafael bridges, Mount Tamalpais. In places the trail hugs a hillside of steep cliffs, with a steep dropoff to your left. Soon an unsigned trail merges from the left, but you follow the Peak Trail as it bends right and climbs toward Wildcat Peak.

At about the 1.4-mile point you reach a T-junction; here you turn left and climb 0.04 mile to the summit of Wildcat Peak (1250'), where you will find the Rotary Peace Monument, a circular stone wall. To the east are San Pablo and Briones reservoirs, along with the hulking form of Mt. Diablo on the horizon. Southeast is Vollmer Peak, at 1913 feet the high point in

Tilden Regional Park. Northwest are the high hills of San Pablo Ridge in Wildcat Canyon Regional Park, linked to Tilden by several routes, including paved Nimitz Way. Once an access road to a Nike missile site atop San Pablo Ridge, this route is named for Chester W. Nimitz, the admiral who commanded the Pacific Fleet during World War Two. After the war he lived in Berkeley and became a regent of the University of California, taking time to hike and sprinkle wildflower seeds along this road, according to Mimi Stein, author of EBRPD's official history, *A Vision Achieved*.

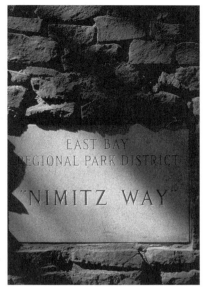

A grove of young giant sequoias, called the Rotary Peace Grove, sits directly below and east of Wildcat Peak's summit, but the metal plaque describing this grove is, for some reason, on the west side of the summit's stone monument. Because these trees are out of their habitat, they will never attain giant status like their cousins in Yosemite and Sequoia parks. More sequoias, along with Monterey pines and eucalyptus, have been planted along Nimitz Way. After spending time on the summit, retrace your steps to the last junction, then continue straight downhill on the Peak Trail, here a dirt road.

Soon you pass the Rotary Peace Grove, left, and reach a junction, just before Nimitz Way, where the Peak Trail turns sharply right and downhill. This junction is marked by a trail post which has the Peak Trail emblem on its downhill side. Here you turn right and follow the single-track Peak Trail as it winds east through stands of eucalyptus, pines, and coyote bush. After a short steep section the route levels off, takes you across an open hillside, and then brings you via a few short switchbacks to Laurel Canyon Road.

Here you turn left and in about 0.1 mile reach the start of the Laurel Canyon Trail, a shady path that descends through a beautiful forested canyon. (The Laurel Canyon Trail may be difficult in wet weather. For an alternate descent, turn right on Laurel Canyon Road, go downhill to Loop Road, and follow the directions given later in this route description.) At the edge of a large pine grove, about the 2-mile point, look for the Laurel Canyon Trail, a single track leading right, downhill. Turn right and walk past large pines and bay trees, where blackberry vines and thimbleberry clog the hillsides, giving color in the fall. The trail hangs on the steep edge of Laurel Canyon: use caution! If you look west across the canyon you can see the summit of Wildcat Peak, where you stood just a few minutes ago.

Stop and listen—you may hear the "dee dee dee" call of a chickadee or the rustling sound that betrays a towhee scraping in the dry leaves.

Soon you come to a small bridge that takes you across Laurel Creek. Ferns are abundant in this cool, shady area, along with blue elderberry and snowberry. You are now on the south side of Laurel Canyon, which drops steeply right, walking west on a level trail. This is one of the prettiest sections of Tilden Park, away from the hustle and bustle of the more popular areas. Here you may find bush monkeyflower, California hazelnut, and beautiful, big, twisted coast live oaks.

Now passing a trail to Laurel Canyon Road, right, you follow the Laurel Canyon Trail as it turns left and continues downhill on a moderate grade. After about 100 yards, the route bends sharply right at a trail post, dips twice to cross tributaries of Laurel Creek, and then emerges from forest into a clearing overgrown with grasses and blackberry vines. Where the Pine Tree Trail heads uphill to the left, you continue straight and descend on an eroded section of trail through a dense stands of bay and coast live oak: here you can enjoy a solitude that belies the park's proximity to a large, metropolitan area. Several downhill switchbacks followed by a climb on wooden steps bring you to another small wooden bridge. On a sunny day, notice the dappled effect the light makes as it filters through the trees. A big pine on your left marks the approaching junction with Loop Road.

At Loop Road, you turn left and walk uphill. After about 100 feet, look for the continuation of the Laurel Canyon Trail, marked by a trail post, heading right and downhill. Here you begin an easy descent through eucalyptus and coast live oak, enjoying the fragrance of the trees and perhaps a serenade from twittering flocks of dark-eyed juncos. In fall, poison oak brightens this area with its yellow and red leaves. Soon you cross a streambed and descend via wooden steps to several small wooden bridges. When you reach a dirt road, turn left and walk uphill, past an unsigned trail heading right. Just ahead is the fence at the corner of Little Farm. When you reach the fence, turn right and go about 0.2 mile downhill to the visitor center.

◆ Upper San Leandro Reservoir ◆

<table>
<tr><td>51</td><td>Upper San Leandro Reservoir
KING CANYON LOOP</td></tr>
</table>

Length: 7 miles

Time: 3 to 4 hours

Rating: Moderate

Regulations: EBMUD; Trail Use Permit required; no bicycles, no dogs, no smoking.

Highlights: This loop, combining the George Wagnon Trail with part of the Rocky Ridge Trail, explores two narrow canyons at the northern end of EBMUD's Upper San Leandro Reservoir. Birders will enjoy the variety of habitats visible from these two trails, from open water to secluded forest, and those out for exercise will profit from many ups and downs. Parts of this route have very steep ground, and parts are extremely muddy in wet weather.

Facilities: Toilet

Trailhead: EBMUD trail register, just southeast of the parking area.

Directions: From Highway 24 in Orinda, take the Orinda/Moraga exit and go southeast on Camino Pablo—which soon becomes Moraga Way—4.6 miles to Canyon Rd. Turn right, and go 1.1 miles to EBMUD's Valle Vista parking area, left.

From the parking area, go through a cattle gate and sign the EBMUD register, then turn left and walk downhill on the Rocky Ridge Trail, a gravel path that crosses an open field of coyote bush and blackberry vines. (Another EBMUD route that starts here, the Redwood Trail, goes right and climbs to the East Ridge Trail in Redwood Regional Park.) Ahead you can see the northernmost finger of Upper San Leandro Reservoir, which you will soon cross. After about 150 feet you reach a dirt road coming from the parking lot; bear right, and when you reach some picnic tables in a grove of Monterey pine and eucalyptus, left, look for a trail post, right, marking the Riche Loop Trail. On your left you will see what appears to be a gravel turn-out, but is actually the continuation of the

Rocky Ridge Trail. Turn left and follow a dirt-and-gravel path through an old orchard, past a fence, and over several small creeks flowing through culverts. When I hiked this route in mid-January, there was a pair of red-shouldered hawks here, perhaps getting ready to nest, calling from the treetops.

The marshy area here provides excellent cover for towhees, both California and spotted, and the tree branches offer lookout posts for western scrub-jays, sentinels of the forest. With Canyon Road just to your left, turn right at a T-junction and cross a bridge spanning a narrow, shallow

51. King Canyon Loop

part of the reservoir, just below the inflow of Moraga Creek. On the other side of the bridge, the Rimer Creek Trail, a path that starts behind a fence, goes left, but your route, the Rocky Ridge Trail, marked by a trail post, veers right. Continue south on the Rocky Ridge Trail, a level dirt road that passes through a wooded area of large coast live oak, pine, and acacia. Large groups of birders may on this route, searching for ducks, songbirds, and raptors. (Large wooden bird houses you may see high on pine trunks are designed for wood ducks.)

Passing a large row of pines, you follow the road as it bends east, away from the reservoir, and, in about 250 feet, come to a cattle gate. Continue straight, past a creek flowing under the road, and in about 150 feet you reach a junction. Here the Rocky Ridge Trail, the return portion of your loop, climbs left, but you follow the former King Canyon Loop Trail, recently renamed to honor George Wagnon, a local horseman who loved to ride EBMUD trails and share them with his friends. Climbing a dirt road through a forest of California bay laurel, coast live oak, and eucalyptus, the route passes over a creek flowing through a culvert, and begins a rolling, zigzag course that traces the wrinkled shape of the hillside above the reservoir.

Where the lush, dense forest gives way to open areas, you may find sun-loving shrubs such as bush monkeyflower, blue bush lupine, California sagebrush, and even an occasional madrone. Back in shade, ferns form the ground cover. Eroded sections of the hillside, left, reveal layers of rock tipped 90 degrees, an indication of the geologic forces at work in the East Bay hills. Powerline towers interfere with the view from time to time, as you look across the reservoir to Anthony Chabot and Redwood regional parks, but provide convenient perches for raptors such as red-tailed hawks.

As you climb to a grassy clearing at about the 2.5-mile point and leave the powerlines to their run across open water, look for an unsigned junction, where you bear left and downhill on a moderate and then steep grade. After reaching the bottom of a gully, where a stream runs under the road through a culvert, you begin an up-and-down course, alternating between open grassland and oak-and-bay forest, and cross several more streams, one of which may have a small waterfall. This is a charming part of the route, with views that take in steep, forested ridges and an expanse of sun-brightened waters. As the road turns northeast around the end of a ridge, you begin to follow an arm of the reservoir filling King Canyon.

The route descends almost to the shore, and here you may see a flock of Canada geese floating on the water, joined perhaps by mallards. Canada geese come in a variety of sizes, the smallest subspecies breeding in western Alaska, and the more familiar form breeding on the Pacific Coast, including the Bay Area. Their V-formation flight and their honking calls are a joy to see and hear. Continuing northeast on an open and mostly level course, you soon reach a marshy area near the inflow of King

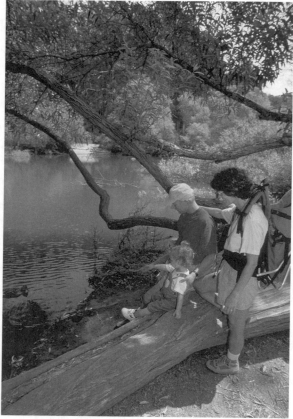

Jewel Lake in Tilden Park is a fine spot for a family outing.

Canyon Creek. A short walk brings you to a large EBMUD trail sign, marking the end of the George Wagnon Trail at its junction with the Rocky Ridge Trail. You have now come a little more than 4 miles from the parking area. On your right is a gate, and beyond it, a dirt-and-gravel road. Your route, the Rocky Ridge Trail, here a single track, stays left of the road, continues straight, and climbs gradually across a grassy hillside.

Now the trail bends left, goes across a streambed lined with bay and California buckeye, and begins to climb on a moderate grade. Turning north, you emerge from dense forest into open grassland, where you have a good view east of the rolling hills that rise up to Rocky Ridge, topped by a single communication tower, on the border of Las Trampas Wilderness. At an unsigned T-junction, turn left on a dirt road and continue moderately uphill, soon reaching a fork where you bear left. Now comes the steepest part of the route, as you climb a rocky dirt road that winds back and forth through an oak-and-bay forest as it gains elevation, giving you a view north to Moraga Valley. At the next junction, marked by a trail post, bear right and go slightly downhill on a dirt road, past a brushy area of coffeeberry, coyote bush, and poison oak.

Passing a gate, right, you follow the road as it swings left and makes a moderate descent, levels out, and then climbs. If the ground is muddy, you may see the tracks of deer or other animals. The route finally reaches a cool, dark forest and tries to hold a contour there before breaking into the open and beginning to descend. The horse pastures and housing subdivisions that greet your eye here are apt symbols of the pressures put on open space by population growth and suburban sprawl. A steep downhill section that soon relents brings you to a junction, right, with the Old Moraga Ranch Trail. Continue straight, with open grassland on your left sweeping down to the reservoir, then veer sharply left and follow the road as it descends moderately to the junction you passed earlier with the George Wagnon Trail. From here, bear right and retrace your steps to the parking area, about 1 mile farther.

52 Upper San Leandro Reservoir
RAMAGE PEAK

Length: 10.6 miles

Time: 6 to 8 hours

Rating: Difficult

Regulations: EBMUD; Trail Use Permit required; no bicycles, no dogs, no smoking.

Highlights: This is one of the most adventurous hikes in the East Bay, combining beautiful scenery, rugged terrain, and a sense of isolation found in few other East Bay parks, most notably the Ohlone Wilderness. Yet the Ramage Peak Trail can be completed in a day, albeit a long one, whereas visiting the Ohlone Wilderness requires backpacking for several days at least. Ramage Peak should be reserved for cool weather: although much of the route stays in the shade, the open stretches can be blisteringly hot. Finally, remember to bring plenty of water and food, and get an early start. (Road names in parentheses in the route description are from the Olmsted & Bros. map, *Trails of the East Bay Hills*, Central Section.)

Facilities: Toilet at the Chabot Staging Area; Las Trampas has picnic tables, toilet, and water (may not be available at certain times of year).

UPPER

Skyway

North

Rock 2

Tower Rd.

UPPER TR.

Bollinger Canyon Rd.

Rocky

Trail

Rocky

Ridge

SOUTH-SKYWAY

Ridge

SAN   LEANDRO

Loop

TRAIL

Two   Dog   Rd.

Ramage Peak

RESERVOIR

Upper
San Leandro
Reservoir

Ridge   Road

Riley

(E.B.M.U.D.)

PEAK

Upper
San
Leandro
Reservoir

Mendonca
Ranch

0   ½ Mile

RAMAGE

Range   Rd.

Rifle   Rd.

San

Flat   Canyon

Leandro

Redwood

Creek

Navy

Dinosaur

N

Road

Ridge

P

Chabot
Staging Area

Rd.

52. Ramage Peak

Trailhead: East corner of parking area.

Directions: This is a car shuttle trip, starting at EBMUD's **Chabot Staging Area** and ending at **Las Trampas Wilderness**. Drive first to Las Trampas Wilderness, leave a car there (with plenty of water, snacks, and a change of footwear), then proceed to Chabot Staging Area.

To reach **Las Trampas Wilderness**: See the directions for "Corduroy Hills," on p. 156.

To reach **Chabot Staging Area**: From the Las Trampas parking area at the end of Bollinger Canyon Rd., return to Crow Canyon Rd., turn right and go 7.5 miles to E. Castro Valley Blvd. Turn right and go 1.1 miles on E. Castro Valley Blvd., which soon becomes Castro Valley Blvd., to Redwood Rd. Turn right and go 3.2 miles north to Chabot Staging Area, right, at a sharp bend in the road.

A journey of 1000 miles starts with the first step, and although your destination is not quite that far away, this hike is a big undertaking, leading you over some of the most remote and rugged terrain in the East Bay. As you take your first steps from the east corner of the parking area, you pass through a gate next to a Bay Area Ridge Trail sign, and turn left onto a dirt-and-gravel road. About 100 feet ahead you come to a toilet, an EBMUD trail sign, and a trail register. After signing in, go through another gate and follow the Ramage Peak Trail, a dirt path, heading northeast and uphill on a gentle grade. The emblem for the Ramage Peak Trail, which you will see on trail posts along the way, is a black arrow on a beige disk. A trail post, right, gives the distance to the Rocky Ridge Loop Trail as 7.4 miles, but this is suspect: the actual distance is almost a mile more. The first 0.9 mile of this hike, which is also part of the Bay Area Ridge Trail, heads northeast and then north past a Christmas-tree farm on a mostly level grade, crosses two streambeds lined with California bay laurel and bigleaf maple, and reaches a junction with a road joining from the left.

The route forks just past the junction. The wide road heading right and uphill is the Chabot-to-Garin Regional Trail (Dinosaur Ridge Road), the continuation of the Bay Area Ridge Trail. Your route, the Ramage Peak Trail, is the path leading straight and slightly downhill, past several watering troughs, left. As you descend, the path crosses a gully, then climbs steeply up an embankment, the air fragrant with the smell of bay leaves. Soon you are out in the open, traversing a grassy hillside under powerlines, then following a gully gently uphill through bay, coast live oak, and blue elderberry.

The route switchbacks and crosses the gully, then climbs in the open, where swallows and red-tailed hawks may circle overhead, to a junction under a powerline tower. Here, at about the 1.5-mile point, a dirt road joins from the right, but you continue straight and slightly downhill, through a forest of oak and bay forest, past a watering trough, to a four-way junction with another dirt road (Navy Flat Canyon Road). Pass through a gate, continue straight, and begin climbing a gravelly dirt path that makes long, steep switchbacks across an open hillside under power-lines. After crossing another dirt road (Rifle Range Road) at the next junction, continue uphill through an area of chaparral, mostly chamise, and then descend over loose ground to a stream bed where coast live oak, bay, and bigleaf maple provide welcome shade.

After crossing the streambed, the route again climbs steeply in the open, levels out in a wooded area, then descends through a sandy, dusty area, where you get your first view of Upper San Leandro Reservoir, left. On a hot day, its water looks inviting. Now the route descends through dense forest, where large ferns thrive in the shade, into a small ravine that holds a tributary of San Leandro Creek. Climbing out of the ravine, you pass a large stand of eucalyptus on your way to a junction with a dirt road, right, closed to hikers and horses. Now descending in the shade on a dirt road, you soon come to a rest bench and a junction with another dirt road joining from the left. Bearing right, you emerge onto a open hillside above Miller Creek, left and downhill. When you reach a wooden fence, turn left and walk downhill, following the route as it passes through an old orchard, site of a ranch owned by J. B. Mendonca, who name first appears on land records in 1915.

After passing through two gates and leaving the ranch area, you begin to climb on well-graded switchbacks, first in forest, then in the open, where California sagebrush, coyote bush, and bush monkeyflower thrive in full sun. At about the 6-mile point, you reach a rest bench and a junction with a dirt road (Riley Ridge Road) joining from the left. You are now climbing above 1,000 feet for the first time on this hike, and your effort is rewarded by terrific views in all directions, especially west to Upper San Leandro Reservoir and Anthony Chabot Regional Park, and northeast to Ramage Peak (1401') and Rocky Ridge, 2000 feet in elevation, capped by a communication tower, guarding Bollinger Canyon.

After dropping from a high point, the route levels off and contours around a hill, then climbs to a junction, left, with a dirt road (Two Dog Road). You are now just west of Ramage Peak, which sits on private land. Veering right, you pass a watering trough and a large water tank, then climb north via a series of switchbacks to a saddle in the ridge running northwest from Ramage Peak. Once over the saddle, you descend a steep and narrow trail, lined with poison oak, that quickly reaches a shady, secluded forest. After crossing a creek, the trail becomes indistinct as it passes north through an abandoned pear orchard, then swings east to switchback up a grassy hillside overgrown with star thistle.

As you near a high point, look for a wooden rail used to tether horses. Here the trail turns north again, and soon merges with a dirt road, right.

Now you are walking on top of the world, or so it seems, with 360-degree views. Ahead is Rocky Ridge, a last obstacle between you and trail's end. At about 8.3 miles the Ramage Peak Trail ends at a junction with the Rocky Ridge Loop Trail; here you turn right, uphill, passing through a gate and climbing steeply on a dirt road. When you soon reach the next gate, do not go through it; instead, turn left, stay on the dirt road (South Skyway), and begin a long, steep climb through chaparral, with a barbed-wire fence—the boundary between EBMUD lands and Las Trampas Wilderness—on you right.

Near the top of Rocky Ridge, the route levels out, giving you a chance to enjoy the scenery and your achievement. Just behind you is Ramage Peak, already shrinking in size; in the distance, southwest, are Upper San Leandro Reservoir and the start of today's hike. Beyond lie San Francisco Bay, the towns of Hayward and Fremont, and the Santa Cruz Mountains. Late in the afternoon, if the moon is near full, look east to see it rise. A final steep push on loose dirt brings you, at about the 9-mile point, to a fence and a gate, where a trail to Rock 2 (2024'), the summit of Rocky Ridge, heads left. Continue straight through the gate and follow the road as it bends northwest, passing another junction, right, with a dirt road coming through a locked gate in a fence.

You are now walking on a level grade (Tower Road), directly toward the communication tower on the summit of Rocky Ridge. Just before the route begins to climb, you reach a gate, right, and a path leading through it to the Upper Trail, in the Las Trampas Wilderness. Once on the Upper Trail, turn left and follow it downhill, across a steep hillside falling away northeast into Bollinger Canyon, to paved Rocky Ridge Road. Turn right and follow the road down to the parking area, where, if it is near dusk, you may hear a great horned owl giving you a well-deserved welcome.

◆ Wildcat Canyon Regional Park ◆

| **53** | Wildcat Canyon Regional Park
SAN PABLO RIDGE |

Length:	7 miles
Time:	3 to 4 hours
Rating:	Moderate
Regulations:	EBRPD; Havey Canyon is closed to bicycles and horses during wet weather.
Highlights:	This loop takes you from the lowlands of Wildcat Creek to the high, open slopes of San Pablo Ridge, using the Wildcat Creek, Havey Canyon, San Pablo Ridge, and Belgum trails, and Nimitz Way. You are rewarded for your efforts by some of the best views in the East Bay, including a 360-degree panorama from an old Nike missile site. Exposed to sun and wind for much of the way, this hike is best done when spring wildflowers bloom or after summer's heat has abated, when the hills are golden brown.
Facilities:	Toilets; at Alvarado Area are picnic tables and water, northwest of parking area.
Trailhead:	East end of parking area.
Directions:	From Interstate 80 eastbound in Richmond, take the Solano Avenue exit, which puts you on Amador St. Go 0.4 mile north to McBryde Ave. Turn right and follow McBryde Ave. 0.2 mile, staying in the left lane as you approach a stop sign. (Use caution at this intersection; traffic from the right does not stop.) Continue straight, now on Park Ave., for 0.1 mile to the Alvarado Staging Area, left.
	From Interstate 80 westbound in San Pablo, take the McBryde Ave. exit, turn left onto McBryde, go over the freeway and follow the directions above from the intersection of McBryde and Amador.

From the east end of the parking area, continue past a gate on pavement, the remnant of Wildcat Canyon Road, closed in the early 1980s by landslides. Renamed the Wildcat Creek Trail, the road, paved here and later dirt, runs southeast to the Environmental Education Center in Tilden Regional Park. Parts of your loop—the Wildcat Creek, Belgum, and San Pablo Ridge trails and Nimitz Way—are used by the East Bay Skyline National Recreation Trail, a 31-mile route that starts here and ends in Anthony Chabot Regional Park.

The grasslands of the Berkeley Hills, which at one time supported large herds of cattle, horses, and sheep, have now been invaded by cardoon, a non-native thistle related to the artichoke. A program is underway by EBRPD to control this pest, which is particularly rampant in this park. Other non-natives flourishing by the side of the road include eucalyptus, cotoneaster, and French broom. Even the tall Monterey pines, planted throughout the East Bay hills, are not true natives, growing in the wild only on California's central coast, around Monterey, Año Nuevo, and Cambria.

As you make a gentle climb past coast live oak and willow, you reach a junction with the Belgum Trail, left, which you will use later to return. Continue straight, alternating on dirt and pavement, parallel to Wildcat Creek, right. The creek gets its start high on Tilden's Vollmer Peak, is interrupted by the impoundment that forms Lake Anza, and empties into San Pablo Bay north of the Richmond–San Rafael Bridge. Other trees and shrubs, objects of interest in an otherwise boring stretch of the route, include California bay laurel, blue elderberry, coffeeberry, toyon, and evergreen huckleberry. Soon the pavement ends and you are walking on a dirt road between the tree-lined creek bed, right, and steep, open hills,

53. San Pablo Ridge

Hikers heading southeast on the Wildcat Creek Trail.

left. At one point the route passes through a tunnel of overhanging coast live oak limbs, offering welcome shade on a hot day.

When the newly formed East Bay Regional Park District in 1935 acquired the southern part of Wildcat Canyon, which soon became Tilden Regional Park, from EBMUD, it left the northern part in the Utility District's hands, and in 1952 ownership of the land passed to private interests; there was even exploratory drilling by Standard Oil in 1966, which fortunately proved fruitless. In 1967 EBRPD bought a nucleus of 400 acres, and in the years that followed further acquisitions expanded the park to its current 2,428-acre size.

At about the 2-mile point, you reach a junction with the Mezue Trail, climbing left. There is a drinking fountain here, and a watering trough for animals. Your route continues straight, but if you want a lovely glimpse of Wildcat Creek, shaded here by bay trees, turn right and walk downhill about 100 yards on a dirt path. Back on the Wildcat Creek Trail, you follow the line of willow, white alder, and western sycamore bordering the creek and soon pass Rifle Range Road, which leads right and crosses the creek on a bridge.

Now the route starts to climb, arriving soon at a junction with the Havey Canyon and Conlon trails. Here your route turns left up Havey Canyon, following a tributary of Wildcat Creek, left, into a shady area lush with bigleaf maple, California buckeye, and California hazelnut. An understory of western creek dogwood, snowberry, vine honeysuckle, blackberry, and ferns gives a wild, almost jungle-like aspect to this dark, wooded canyon. An eroded section of the route, where a culvert tunnels under the trail, is near a stream crossing, and then a cattle gate indicates the canyon is about to give way to open grassland. On a hot day the air here is fragrant with bay and eucalyptus.

As the route abruptly breaks into the open, you see the open slopes of San Pablo Ridge ahead, dotted with coyote bush and stunted coast live oak. As the route, now a dirt road, turns north, powerlines ahead traverse your field of view, but to the west, on a clear day, Mt. Tamalpais is engraved on the unobstructed skyline. Red-tailed hawks, aerial hunters looking for prey in the fields below, cruise overhead, while oblivious cows graze nearby. Passing through another cattle gate, you soon reach a T-junction with paved Nimitz Way, a popular route shared by hikers, horse-back riders, bicyclists, in-line skaters, and joggers.

Now you get your first view of Mt. Diablo, east, and the Santa Cruz Mountains, south. As you wind uphill on a gentle grade toward an unnamed peak, the high points in Tilden Regional Park, topped by Vollmer Peak (1905′), appear to the southeast. San Francisco Bay, shimmering perhaps in late afternoon sunlight, leads your eye south-west to the Golden Gate Bridge. Colorful wildflowers decorate the grassy

View northwest to San Pablo Bay from the upper Conlon Trail.

hillsides here in spring. As you near the summit, just over 1000 feet in elevation, you begin to see north toward San Pablo Bay, the Carquinez Strait, and Mt. St. Helena, a high peak on the border of Lake, Napa, and Sonoma counties. When you reach a junction with a road heading right, uphill, take a few minutes to make the climb to an abandoned Nike missile site, a relic of the Cold War, that is perched above. You will be rewarded with a rest bench, 360-degree views, and a chance to reflect on the fact that, for most people, Nike is a name no longer associated with the fear of nuclear war.

When the paved portion of Nimitz Way ends, continue northwest on a dirt-and-gravel road, with San Pablo Reservoir right and far below. At about the 4.5-mile point, you come to a cattle pen and a choice of three dirt paths. The right-hand path is the continuation of Nimitz Way (called Old Nimitz Way on the EBRPD map), heading downhill. The left-hand path is the Mezue Trail. The middle path, unnamed, just rejoins the Mezue Trail a few hundred feet ahead. Bear left on the Mezue Trail, and after about 100 yards or so, bear right at a fork, where the Mezue Trail heads left and the San Pablo Ridge Trail goes right and uphill.

Now the route climbs up and over a series of high points on San Pablo Ridge, then plunges steeply northwest to a junction with the Belgum Trail, a dirt road. Turning left and leaving the San Pablo Ridge Trail, you climb past an active ground-squirrel colony, whose members may stand up to get a better look at the tired hikers marching past. Soon you pass the Clark-Boas Trail, right, and then an unsigned road cutting sharply left. Now you climb to an unsigned fork, where you bear left, still following the Belgum Trail, a dirt road. The route now makes a well-graded descent, via S-bends, to a forest of coast live oak, bay, and eucalyptus, with a few palm trees thrown in for good measure. A gate ushers you onto a paved section, which you follow downhill to the junction with the Wildcat Creek Trail you passed earlier. Turn right and retrace your steps to the parking area.

Appendix A: Some Other Trails

In addition to the routes described in this guide, there are many other routes in the East Bay worth exploring. Among these are paved, multi-use trails, and short, self-guiding nature trails. Following is a list of some of the trails that I feel are worth including in this guide, but do not require a detailed route description.

Trail Name	Location	Features
Alameda Creek Regional Trail	Coyote Hills Regional Park to Niles Community Park, Fremont.	12-mile linear trail: south side paved for hikers, joggers, bicyclists; north side mostly unpaved for horseback riders.
Contra Costa Canal Regional Trail	Central Contra Costa County, through Pacheco, Pleasant Hill, and Walnut Creek.	14-mile paved pathway for hiking, bicycling, and horseback riding.
Crown Memorial State Beach	South end of Webster Street, Alameda.	Crab Cove visitor center, paved path to marsh overlook and Elsie Roemer Bird Sanctuary; good for children.
Fire Interpretive Trail	Mt. Diablo State Park, just above lower summit parking area on north side of one-way downhill road.	0.7-mile self-guiding loop encircling the summit; numbered markers keyed to brochure available at visitor center.
Garin/Dry Creek Self-Guiding Trail	Dry Creek Pioneer Regional Park.	Short nature walk along Dry Creek; numbered markers keyed to brochure available at visitor center; good for children.
Indian Joe Nature Trail	Sunol Regional Park.	Short nature walk with markers keyed to brochure available at visitor center; good for children.
Iron Horse Regional Trail	Parallel to I-680 through Walnut Creek and San Ramon.	18-mile paved linear trail for hiking, bicycling, and horseback riding.
Jewel Lake Trail	Tilden Nature Area, Tilden	Short nature walk with markers keyed to brochure available at visitor center;

Trail Name	Location	Features
Lafayette/Moraga Regional Trail	Parallel to St. Mary's Road, through Lafayette and Moraga.	7.5-mile paved linear trail for hiking, bicycling, and horseback riding.
Lake Merritt	Off Grand Avenue, Oakland.	3.3-mile paved loop around 150-acre lake; trees and shrubs from many countries; good for children.
Nimitz Way	Tilden Regional Park, Inspiration Point	3.5-mile paved linear trail for hiking, bicycling, and horseback riding.
Pickleweed Trail	Martinez Regional Shoreline	Easy walk through marsh alongside Carquinez Strait; good for children.
Point Isabel Regional Shoreline	West end of Central Avenue, El Cerrito.	Dog walking area and dog-wash concession.
Shore Trail	Lafayette Reservoir, Lafayette.	2.8-mile paved loop around EBMUD's smallest reservoir; good for children.
Volcanic Trail	Sibley Volcanic Regional Preserve	Self-guiding trail with markers keyed to brochure available at visitor center.

Appendix B: Selected Reading Material

BAY AREA

Colbert, Katie, et al., *Parkland Discoveries*. Oakland: East Bay Regional Park District, 1988.

Conradson, Diane R., *Exploring Our Baylands*. 3rd ed. Fremont: San Francisco Bay Wildlife Society, 1996.

East Bay Regional Park District, *Master Plan 1997*. Oakland: EBRPD, 1997.

Knight, Walter, et al., *The Story of Las Trampas*. Oakland: EBRPD, 1973.

Margolin, Malcolm, *The East Bay Out*. Revised ed. Berkeley: Heyday Books, 1988.

Rusmore, Jean, *The Bay Area Ridge Trail*. Berkeley: Wilderness Press, 1995.

Spangle, Frances, and Jean Rusmore, *South Bay Trails*. 2nd ed. Berkeley: Wilderness Press, 1991.

Stein, Mimi, *A Vision Achieved*. Oakland: East Bay Regional Park District, 1984.

Wayburn, Peggy, *Adventuring in the San Francisco Bay Area*. San Francisco: Sierra Club Books, 1987.

Whitnah, Dorothy L., *An Outdoor Guide to the San Francisco Bay Area*. 5th ed. Berkeley: Wilderness Press, 1989.

NATURAL HISTORY

Alt, David D., and Donald W. Hyndman, *Roadside Geology of Northern California*. Missoula: Mountain Press Publishing Co., 1975.

Burt, William H., and Richard P. Grossenheider, *A Field Guide to the Mammals, North America, north of Mexico*. 3rd ed. Boston: Houghton Mifflin Company, 1980.

DeBenedictis, Paul A., et al., *ABA Checklist: Birds of the Continental United States and Canada*. 5th ed. Colorado Springs: American Birding Association, Inc., 1996.

Faber, Phyllis M., and Robert F. Holland, *Common Riparian Plants of California*. Mill Valley: Pickleweed Press, 1988.

Faber, Phyllis M., *Common Wetland Plants of Coastal California*. 2nd ed. Mill Valley: Pickleweed Press, 1996.

Keator, Glenn, *Pacific Coast Berry Finder*. Berkeley: Nature Study Guild, 1978.

Keator, Glenn, *Plants of the East Bay Parks*. Niwot, Colorado: Roberts Rinehart Publishers, Inc., 1994.

Little, Elbert L., *National Audubon Society Field Guide to North American Trees, Western Region*. New York: Alfred A. Knopf, 1994.

National Geographic Society, *Field Guide to the Birds of North America*. 2nd ed. Washington: National Geographic Society, 1987.

Niehaus, Theodore F., and Charles L. Ripper, *A Field Guide to Pacific States Wildflowers*. Boston: Houghton Mifflin Company, 1976.

Peterson, Roger T., *A Field Guide to Western Birds*. 3rd ed. Boston: Houghton Mifflin Company, 1990.

Stebbins, Robert C., *A Field Guide to Western Reptiles and Amphibians*. 2nd ed. Boston: Houghton Mifflin Company, 1985.

Watts, Phoebe, *Redwood Region Flower Finder*. Berkeley: Nature Study Guild, 1979.

Watts, Tom, *Pacific Coast Tree Finder*. Berkeley: Nature Study Guild, 1973.

FIRST AID

Darvill, Fred T. Jr., *Mountaineering Medicine*. 14th ed. Berkeley: Wilderness Press, 1998.

Wilkerson, James A., *Medicine for Mountaineering & Other Wilderness Activities*. 4th ed. Seattle: The Mountaineers, 1992.

Appendix C: Information Sources

GOVERNMENT AGENCIES

AC Transit	(510) 817-1717
Bay Area Rapid Transit (BART)	(510) 817-1717
Don Edwards San Francisco Bay National Wildlife Refuge Box 524 Newark, CA 94560-0524	(510) 792-4275
East Bay Municipal Utility District Trail Use Permit 500 San Pablo Dam Road Orinda, CA 94563	(510) 287-0459
East Bay Regional Park District Reservations 2950 Peralta Oaks Court Box 5381 Oakland, CA 94605-0381	(510) 636-1684
Mt. Diablo State Park 96 Mitchell Canyon Road Clayton, CA 94528	(925) 837-2525

NON-PROFIT AND OTHER ORGANIZATIONS

Bay Area Ridge Trail Council 26 O'Farrell Street, 4th Floor San Francisco, CA 94108	(415) 391-9300
California Native Plant Society Box 5597, Elmwood Station Berkeley, CA 94705	(510) 464-4977
California State Automobile Association 150 Van Ness Avenue San Francisco, CA 94102	(415) 565-2012
Mount Diablo Interpretive Association Box 346 Walnut Creek, CA 94597-0346	(925) 927-7222
Mountain Medicine Institute	(510) 534-6112

National Audubon Society,   (510) 843-2222
Golden Gate Chapter
2530 San Pablo Avenue, Suite G
Berkeley, CA 94702

Regional Parks Foundation, EBRPD   (510) 635-0138, x2203
Box 21074, Crestmont Station
Oakland, CA 94620

San Francisco Bay Wildlife Society   (510) 792-4275
Box 524
Newark, CA 94560-0524

Save Mount Diablo   (925) 947-3535
Box 5376
Walnut Creek, CA 94596

Sierra Club Bookstore   (510) 658-7470
6014 College Avenue
Oakland, CA 94618

Sierra Club   (510) 848-0800
San Francisco Bay Chapter
2530 San Pablo Avenue, Suite I
Berkeley, CA 94702
Other Resources

The Olmsted & Brothers Map Company   (510) 658-6534
Box 5351
Berkeley, CA 94705

Wilderness Press Map Center   (510) 841-6277
2440 Bancroft Way
Berkeley, CA 94704

Index

READ THIS

Hiking entails unavoidable risk that every hiker assumes and must be aware of and respect. The fact that a trail is described in this book is not a representation that it will be safe for you. Trails vary greatly in difficulty and in the degree of conditioning and agility one needs to enjoy them safely. On some hikes, routes may have changed or conditions may have deteriorated since the descriptions were written. Also, trail conditions can change even from day to day, owing to weather and other factors. A trail that is safe on a dry day or for a highly conditioned, agile, properly equipped hiker may be completely unsafe for someone else or unsafe under adverse weather conditions.

You can minimize your risks on the trail by being knowledgeable, prepared and alert. There is not space in this book for a general treatise on safety, but there are a number of good books and public courses on the subject and you should take advantage of them to increase your knowledge. Just as important, you should always be aware of your own limitations and of conditions existing when and where you are hiking. If conditions are dangerous, or if you are not prepared to deal with them safely, choose a different hike! It's better to have wasted a drive than to be the subject of a rescue.

These warnings are not intended to scare you off the trails. Millions of people have safe and enjoyable hikes every year. However, one element of the beauty, freedom and excitement of the outdoors is the presence of risks that do not confront us at home. When you hike you assume those risks. They can be met safely, but only if you exercise your own independent judgment and common sense.